BBC

Speak out

3RD EDITION

B2+

Student's Book and eBook

LISTENING/VIDEO	SPEAKING	WRITING
Listen to a podcast about a friendship app	Describe a friendship	
	Talk about a work or study environment	Write a proposal about transforming a city space
	Ask and answer survey questions **FUTURE SKILLS** Collaboration **MEDIATION SKILLS** simplify a source text	
B B C Street Interviews about comfort food	Have a discussion about comfort food	Write a social media post
Listen to two friends talking about cheating	Discuss cheating **FUTURE SKILLS** Leadership	
	Share ideas about business partnerships	Write an article about rivalry
	Present ideas about productivity incentives **MEDIATION SKILLS** evaluate problems, challenges and proposals	
B B C Programme *Gassed Up*	Have a debate about the pros and cons of competition	Write a reflection
	Describe alternative scenes **FUTURE SKILLS** Communication	Write a review: fiction
Listen to a spoken-word poem	Talk about situations and emotions	
	Discuss methods of persuasion **FUTURE SKILLS** Communication **MEDIATION SKILLS** encourage others to elaborate	
B B C Street Interviews about inspiring people	Describe an inspiring person	Write a biography
	Present a proposal	
Listen to a talk about place branding	Present a rebranding campaign **FUTURE SKILLS** Communication	Write a report: creating a rebranding campaign
	Roleplay a job interview **FUTURE SKILLS** Interviewing **MEDIATION SKILLS** relay information in a professional journal	
B B C BBC Programme *The Truth About ... looking good*	Make a presentation about a new product	Write a product blurb

LISTENING/VIDEO	SPEAKING	WRITING
	Talk about a life-changing decision	Write an informal message
Listen to a radio programme about conservation	Discuss solutions to a conservation problem **FUTURE SKILLS** Teamwork	
	Present a campaign to raise awareness **FUTURE SKILLS** Collaboration **MEDIATION SKILLS** simplify a complicated argument	
BBC Street Interviews about routines	Have a discussion about the pros and cons of routines	Write a blog post
	Have a debate about algorithms **FUTURE SKILLS** Communication	
Listen to two colleagues discussing a mistake	Talk about a mistake	Write an email of complaint
	Roleplay a dispute between a landlord and a tenant **MEDIATION SKILLS** accurately report the outcomes of a meeting	
BBC Programme *W1A*	Discuss solutions to a problem with technology	Write a set of instructions
Listen to part of a talk about how words become more or less popular over time	Present a new English word	Write a comment on a blog post
	Discuss food trends	
	Persuading someone to buy vintage items **FUTURE SKILLS** Leadership **MEDIATION SKILLS** compare, contrast and synthesise information in texts	
BBC Street Interviews about nostalgia and memories	Have a discussion about attitudes to the past and present	Write a blog post
	Have a debate about technology and a dystopian world **FUTURE SKILLS** Self-management	
Listen to a radio discussion about inventions that could change the world	Present predictions about future technologies or inventions **FUTURE SKILLS** Critical thinking	Write an opinion essay
	Discuss ideas about giving money to charity **MEDIATION SKILLS** contribute to collaborative decision-making	
BBC BBC Programme *Doctor Who*	Present a summary of a science-fiction film or series	Write a continuation of a narrative

MEDIATION BANK p144   **AUDIOSCRIPTS** p156   **VIDEOSCRIPTS** p171

GRAMMAR

1A Read what two people say about their hopes and ambitions for this year. Choose the correct options.

At the end of last year, I decided to change my course at university. I ¹**'ve studied / 'd been studying** law for two years, but it became apparent that I was never going to enjoy it. My parents weren't very pleased about it and told me ²**not to give up / don't give up** on law, but my heart just wasn't in it. ³**It was a friend / A friend** who suggested I should do something more creative, so this year I ⁴**'d rather have joined / 'll be joining** the art department to study graphic design. It's a new start, and hopefully I'll find it much more interesting and rewarding.

I've just started a new job, working for a small start-up company. There's only a small team of people, so I know ⁵**it's likely to be / it's due** hard work and I probably ⁶**won't be allowed to / couldn't** take much time off this year, but I think it'll be worth it. I love ⁷**to challenge / being challenged** and I'm determined to work hard. I hope that by next summer, we ⁸**'ll have started / ought to be started** to see some results.

B Look at the correct answers in Ex 1A again. Find examples of:

a a reported order

b the future continuous

c a phrase expressing probability

d the past perfect continuous

e part of a cleft sentence

f the future perfect

g a phrase expressing prohibition

h a passive gerund

C Work in pairs and discuss. What are your hopes and ambitions for this year?

VOCABULARY

2A Complete each pair of sentences with the same word in the box. There are two words you do not need.

> get   let   look   make   mind   run   take   time   top   way

1 a I like to **keep on** _____ of my homework by doing a small amount each day.

b She was shouting **at the** _____ of her voice.

2 a I can't get on with people who _____ **down on** me and don't respect me.

b I've had a difficult few months, but things are beginning to _____ **up** now.

3 a I go to the gym every morning – I don't let anything **get in the** _____ **of** my exercise routine!

b Look at the prices of the meals – **there's no** _____ I can afford to eat here!

4 a I'm really tired, so I need to relax and _____ **it easy** this week.

b I know you're upset, but there's no need to _____ **it out on** me!

5 a Please _____ **me know** if you want to come to the concert with us.

b Jake promised to help, but he _____ **me down** at the last minute.

6 a I **don't** _____ which film we watch – I think they'll both be good.

b I can't **make up my** _____ where to go on holiday this year.

7 a I could see someone in the distance, but I couldn't _____ **out** who it was.

b I don't understand what you're saying – it doesn't _____ **sense**!

8 a It's about _____ Lydia got a proper job!

b If we start early, we should get everything finished **in good** _____ .

B Work in pairs. Look at the phrases and phrasal verbs in bold in Ex 2A. Can you explain the meanings?

FUNCTIONS

3A Put the words in brackets in the correct order to complete the replies. There is one word in each group that you do not need.

1 A: I know you're upset. Do you want to talk about it?
B: No _____ , if that's OK. (rather / I'd / don't / not)

2 A: Oh, this phone is so annoying. The battery only seems to last five minutes!
B: I think you _____ a new one. (do / could / should / with)

3 A: Is the path slippery?
B: Yes, so _____ fall! (don't / wouldn't / you / mind)

4 A: I can't find my bag. I hope I didn't leave it on the bus.
B: _____ phone the bus company to see if anyone's handed it in. (always / you / could / won't)

5 A: There, that's all the clearing up done.
B: Thanks. I _____ help. (really / your / would / appreciate)

6 A: I have to go now, but I hope you feel better soon.
B: Thank you. It _____ you to visit me. (thoughtful / was / for / of)

B Work in pairs. What other phrases with similar meanings could B use to reply in Ex 3A?

connections 1

VLOGS

Q: Which people, places or things are important to you and why?

1 ▶ Watch the video. What interesting people, places or things do the speakers talk about?

2 Which people, places or things in your life are the most special to you? Why?

1A New friends

GRAMMAR | describing past and present habits
VOCABULARY | relationships; phrasal verbs: friendships
PRONUNCIATION | contractions: 'll and 'd

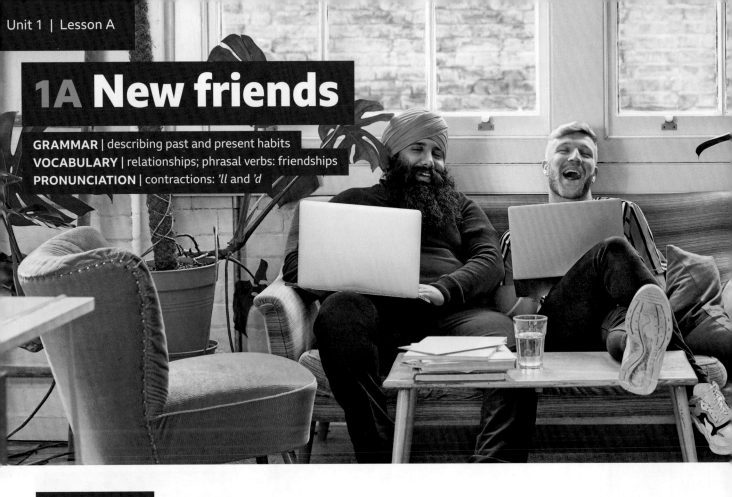

LISTENING

1 **A** Work in groups. How did you meet your closest friend(s)? What's the most common way in your group?

B Read the opinions. Discuss in your groups if you agree or disagree with them. Why/Why not?

C Read the app description and reviews and discuss the questions (1–2) in your groups.

1 What are the advantages of an app like this?
2 Would you ever use an app like this? Why/Why not?

It's easier to make friends when you're a child than when you're an adult.

The friendships you make as children outlast those you make as adults.

It's never a good idea to be friends with people too similar to you.

The friends you've known the longest know you best.

It's easier to make friends online than it is to make friends face-to-face.

Frendz

The app where you'll meet your new best friend.

★★★★★ 1 day ago
AdamB
The app suggested some great people to chat to based on my profile. Good matching!

★★★★★ 3 days ago
ElaineK
I met some amazing people I'd never normally meet. Love it!

★★★ 1 week ago
Pete123
It's not the easiest app to use, but I met a few like-minded people, so worth signing up.

2 A 🔊 **1.01** | Listen to a podcast about apps like the one in Ex 1C. Why did Addy decide to use a friendship app? What was the outcome?

B 🔊 **1.01** | Listen to the podcast again. Choose the correct answers (a, b or c).

1 Addy chose to use a friendship app because
   a he had a colleague who'd recommended it.
   b he wanted to meet people similar to himself.
   c he was unable to find friends at local clubs.

2 Addy believes that the best way to find a match is to look for people
   a from a different culture to you.
   b of a similar character to you.
   c with similar passions to you.

3 Addy liked the first app he used because it allowed him
   a to build connections in his area.
   b to meet up with an old friend.
   c to use his regular social media page.

4 Making friends with other music lovers
   a meant he was more comfortable when attending an event.
   b gave him a chance to discover new music that he liked.
   c allowed him to become part of a band himself.

5 Addy would recommend using friendship apps to people who
   a have found themselves in a similar situation to him.
   b are in a hurry to form new friendships.
   c want to expand their current friendship circle.

3 A 🔊 **1.02** | Read and listen to the extract where Addy is being ironic. Answer the questions (1–2).

1 Does Addy think his colleagues being older and mostly married is just what he wants, or does he mean the opposite?

2 What helps us to understand this?

> My colleagues are nice and all that, but they're at least a decade older than me and most are married – just what you want as a twenty-two-year-old single person!

B 🔊 **1.03** | Listen to six more extracts. What words does Addy use to describe these things? How does he really feel about them?

1 The suitability of the sports app for him.
2 The fact that he and someone he met on an app had a friend in common.
3 The time he spent getting to know a group of people.
4 The way he began his friendship with the first group he met up with.
5 How his new friends felt about him leaving his wallet at home.
6 The fact that he and his friends laugh a lot.

C Work in pairs. Have Addy's experiences changed your mind on the use of friendship apps? Why/Why not?

VOCABULARY

relationships

4 A 🔊 **1.04** | Replace the words in bold in the sentences with the phrases in the box. Listen and check.

> bonded over   click with   confide in
> have a mutual friend   hit it off with
> on the same wavelength   party with
> socialise with

1 Obviously, I wanted people my own age to **spend time with**.
2 You know, people I can hang out with during the day and **eat, dance, etc. with** at night.
3 I mean, I want to hang out with people that are **of a similar opinion to me**, yes, but not exact copies of me!
4 I was able to **like and understand** a few people my age on there.
5 I even discovered one guy and I **have a friend in common**, which was great.
6 And four of us **developed a connection over** our love of a particular band.
7 I know I can **share personal things with** them, too.
8 Try, try and try again and eventually, you'll **immediately like** someone.

B Choose the correct phrases to complete the sentences. Sometimes both are possible.

1 I never **bond over** / **confide in** Nuria because she can't keep a secret.
2 My sister and I **just never hit it off** / **are just not on the same wavelength**.
3 I've got a few friends that I **socialise** / **party** with.
4 My brother-in-law and I **bonded over** / **clicked with** each other as soon as we met.
5 Carl and I **bonded over** / **socialised with** our love for crayons on our first day at kindergarten!
6 I joined a running club so I can get fit and **socialise with** / **party with** people at the same time.
7 Sarka and I **have a mutual friend** / **are on the same wavelength** that we both used to work with.
8 My neighbour João and I **clicked** / **hit it off** as soon as we met and became great friends.

5 A Complete at least five sentences with your own ideas.

1 A person I clicked immediately with was …
2 Someone on a similar wavelength to me is …
3 A mutual friend that … and I have is …
4 One person I hit it off with immediately is …
5 The person I confide in the most is …
6 I enjoy partying with …
7 One friend and I bonded over …
8 The place where I usually socialise with my friends is …

B Share your sentences with a partner. Ask questions to find out more.

C Learn and practise. Go to the Vocabulary Bank.

▶▶ page 134 **VOCABULARY BANK** phrasal verbs: friendships

GRAMMAR

describing past and present habits

6 A 🔊 **1.05 |** Listen to more from the podcast. In what ways are Addy and his new friends like-minded? In what ways are they different?

B Look at the habits in bold from the interview and answer the questions (a–d).

1 She**'s always shouting** even though we're standing right next to her.
2 And she**'ll voice her opinions** very strongly – she's so confident.
3 I **tend to listen** rather than speak.
4 … they **were always trying to make us** go to fast-food places.
5 I **used to sit** and watch them eat …
6 I **kept trying** to get them to order the salad, but they**'d order** extra chips just to annoy me!

a Which sentences (1–6) describe past habits? Which describe present habits?
b Which modal verb is used to describe present habits? And past habits?
c Which tense is used to describe annoying present habits? And annoying past habits?
d What other language is used to describe habits and typical behaviour?

C Learn and practise. Go to the Grammar Bank.

▶▶ page 110 **GRAMMAR BANK**

PRONUNCIATION
contractions: *'ll* and *'d*

7 A 🔊 **1.06 |** Listen to the sentences. Notice the difference in sound between *'ll* and *'d*.

1 She'll voice her opinions very strongly.
2 She'd order extra chips just to annoy me.

B 🔊 **1.07 |** Complete the sentences with *'ll* or *'d*. Listen and repeat the full sentences.

1 We _____ meet up on Fridays and play squash.
2 Jon _____ call me at all hours of the night just for a chat!
3 I _____ message Alex on a Monday and not get a reply until Thursday!
4 They _____ all come round to my house before we went out.
5 Sam _____ spend more time at our flat than his own!
6 She _____ borrow something and forget to give it back.

C Work in pairs. Discuss these habits using *'ll* and *'d*.

1 a good habit you once had in the past
2 a habit you had in the past that you weren't proud of
3 a habit you have now that's rewarding or beneficial
4 a habit you have now that you'd like to stop
5 a healthy habit someone you know has
6 an annoying habit someone you once knew had

D Read the Future Skills box and answer the question.

> **FUTURE SKILLS**
> ### Self-management
>
> When learning a language, a good habit to get into is to pay attention to how different people pronounce words and phrases and how they pronounce them in fast, connected speech. This 'noticing' can help with both listening and speaking.
>
> Think about the English you hear in your life. How and when could you spend time noticing the pronunciation used?

SPEAKING

8 A You are going to describe a friendship. Make notes on these things.

- where and how you met your friend
- your first impressions of each other
- how you bonded
- things you have in common
- ways in which you're different
- things you'd do together in the past
- things you tend to do together in the present
- habits one of you has which annoy the other

B Work in pairs. Describe your friendships to each other. Find similarities and differences.

C Tell another pair about the similarities and differences between your friendships.

1B Places

GRAMMAR | reduced relative clauses
VOCABULARY | transforming places; urban spaces
PRONUNCIATION | the /r/ sound in different accents

READING

1 Work in pairs. Discuss an indoor or outdoor space where you:

- feel comfortable and free from stress.
- can work hard and be productive.
- feel confident and able to express yourself.
- feel sociable and keen to meet new people.

2 A Read the introduction to an article and answer the questions (1–2).

1 How do you think the place you are in affects your personality and the way you behave?

2 What kinds of places do you think the article will go on to discuss?

It depends where you are

It is sometimes assumed that our brain is like a computer, a machine for generating ideas and storing information. However, a big difference between computers and human brains is that the former are not affected by their location. The same computer will function equally well in a bright, well-lit space or in a forgotten corner of an office. Humans, on the other hand, think and behave in very different ways according to the indoor or outdoor surroundings they are in.

B Read the first paragraph of the article and answer the questions (1–2).

1 How does the first paragraph link to the introduction?

2 Choose the better summary (a or b) of the first paragraph.

a People who live close to the coast are healthier than those who live in cities.

b Being close to water seems to improve people's mental health.

1 We are familiar with the idea of green spaces improving our physical and mental health, and it seems that being in 'blue space', i.e. close to water, has similar effects, but with some extra advantages. A study on happiness and natural environments invited 20,000 people to record information on their location and mood at random times of day. The results showed consistently that people experienced a greater feeling of well-being when close to water. Being by the sea seems especially beneficial and visiting the coast for as little as two hours a week can have a positive impact on us. Researchers have speculated that less polluted air and more sunlight are partly responsible for the feelings of well-being, as well as the fact that being close to water encourages us to be more active. Water also seems to have a particular ability to reduce stress and make us feel optimistic. In urban settings, a waterway or even a fountain seems able to help people feel destressed and revived. This could perhaps explain the current trend in some countries to move out of cities to coastal towns.

C Read the rest of the article on page 12 and choose the better summary (a or b) for the remaining two paragraphs.

2 a The way people behave in cities is influenced by the buildings around them.

b The way some cities are built can be confusing for tourists.

3 a People are unable to concentrate on work if their surroundings are too distracting.

b People work best in spaces which reflect their interests and personality.

D Read the whole article again. Are the statements (1–6) True (T) or False (F)?

1 Being close to water is even better for us than being in other natural settings.

2 Water features in urban areas provide very little benefit.

3 People are the least friendly in urban areas with few shops and cafés.

4 Active edges in cities encourage us to think about other people as well as ourselves.

5 More students felt confident in Sapna Cheryan's non-stereotypical classroom.

6 People produced more work in an attractive office than in an office that contained their own possessions.

2 Our physical environment can also affect the way we behave towards each other. It is known anecdotally that people in rural areas seem friendlier than those in cities. But why should this be? And can urban areas be designed to make people less stressed and more approachable? The organisation Happy City Lab studies urban spaces and plans interventions to encourage people to interact more with each other. One study carried out by the lab involves the 'lost tourist' test. Someone pretending to be a tourist stands in a street, looks at their map and appears lost, while observers count the percentage of passers-by who stop to offer help. The findings are fascinating. It seems that streets with lots of blank walls, with no doors or windows and very few shops or cafés, encourage us to feel less safe. We are inclined to walk more quickly and not engage with people around us. If approached, we are more likely to come across as rude and unfriendly. That's because the structures we see have 'inactive edges' – nothing is happening, so there is nothing to interest us or slow us down. On the other hand, streets with cafés, shops and seating areas provide 'active edges' – things are happening, so we slow down and stop focusing just on ourselves and our own goals. We feel safer, so we are more likely to engage with other people and to notice if a tourist needs help. Happy City Lab has found that only two percent of people stopped to help their lost tourist in areas with inactive edges, whereas ten percent of people offered help where there were active edges.

3 Indoor environments can also have a profound effect on us. Sapna Cheryan worked at tech companies in the USA before moving to Stanford University in California. She has researched the influence of the physical environment in attracting a broad range of people to careers in computer science, rather than just those who associate themselves with the stereotypical appeal of science fiction and computer games. In one experiment, Cheryan created a 'stereotypical' computer science classroom, with posters advertising science-fiction films and sci-fi books on the shelves. She then created a second, non-typical classroom, with posters of the natural world and novels on the shelves. She found that a wider range of students introduced to the non-stereotypical classroom were likely to express an interest in the subject and predict that they would do well at it. Cheryan believes that we need to feel that we will 'fit in' in an environment in order to work and perform well. In addition to this, it seems we also perform better if we feel a sense of 'ownership' of a place. Psychologists Craig Knight and Alex Haslam asked volunteers to perform a series of work tasks in different office environments: a bare, minimalist office, an 'enriched' one decorated with plants and posters, an 'empowered' one decorated as they wanted and a 'disempowered' one, in which their own decoration style had been changed. The participants working in the 'empowered' office worked the hardest and completed the most work, suggesting that we work best when we are surrounded by our own 'cues of identity' – things which reflect our personality and interests.

So, it seems that who we are and how we feel and behave is closely linked to the physical space that we inhabit, which should have implications for the way we design work and study spaces, as well as outdoor areas in our towns and cities.

GRAMMAR

reduced relative clauses

3 A Work in pairs. Read the sentences from the article and look at the reduced relative clauses in bold. Rewrite the sentences with full relative clauses.

1 One study **carried out by the lab** involves the 'lost tourist' test.
2 Someone **pretending to be a tourist** stands in a street, looks at their map and appears lost, …
3 … a wider range of students **introduced to the non-stereotypical classroom** were likely to express an interest in the subject …
4 The participants **working in the 'empowered' office** worked the hardest and completed the most work, …

1 One study that/which was carried out by the lab involves the 'lost tourist' test.

B Look at the full relative clauses you wrote in Ex 3A and compare them to the reduced relative clauses in the examples. Answer the questions.

1 Which words have been removed in the reduced relative clauses?
2 Does the meaning of the reduced relative clause change according to the tense (past or present)?

C Learn and practise. Go to the Grammar Bank.

▶▶ page 111 **GRAMMAR BANK**

VOCABULARY

transforming places

4A Read some comments about the article. Are any true for you or a city you know?

TreeHugga   Comment | Share | Like

My city centre is definitely full of inactive edges. They should **demolish** a lot of tower blocks built in the 1970s and **modernise** the centre by adding parks and green spaces.

LondonSal   Comment | Share | Like

People living in cities are well aware of a lot of these problems. I think we need to completely **reconstruct** our urban areas. We should **build in** more green and blue spaces and try to **merge** the city with the country.

Kerem21   Comment | Share | Like

My local authority has spent a lot of money **sprucing up** the city centre by adding flowers and benches, **refurbishing** some of the old buildings and **restoring** an old fountain that had stopped working. It's made a huge difference to the feel of the city.

B Work in pairs. Choose the correct words.

1 When designing an urban space, it's important to **build in** / **demolish** areas where people can socialise.

2 Our office is old-fashioned and needs to be **reconstructed** / **modernised**.

3 A new theatre will be built once the old one has been **refurbished** / **demolished**.

4 We decided to **spruce up** / **reconstruct** the room with a fresh coat of paint.

5 If we **merge** / **build in** the sports fields with the park, we can create a huge green space.

6 It would be good to **demolish** / **restore** the walkway along the river, which was destroyed in the floods.

7 The school was destroyed in a fire, but it was **modernised** / **reconstructed** to the same design.

8 The hotel has been completely **refurbished** / **restored** with brand new furniture and decorations.

C Work in pairs. Think about a town or city you know and discuss the questions.

1 Which old buildings would you like to demolish? Why?

2 Which old buildings need to be modernised?

3 Have any parts of the town/city been spruced up recently?

4 If the central area was being reconstructed, what new features would you build in?

D Learn and practise. Go to the Vocabulary Bank.

▶▶ page 134 **VOCABULARY BANK** urban spaces

PRONUNCIATION
the /r/ sound in different accents

5A 🔊 **1.08** | In some accents of English, people pronounce the /r/ sound in the middle of a word, but in other accents they don't. Listen to two speakers saying the following sentences. Which speaker (A or B) pronounces the /r/ in the middle of the words in bold?

1 This building definitely needs to be **modernised**.

2 It's a great idea to **merge** the city with the countryside more.

3 There's a plan to **refurbish** the old cinema.

B 🔊 **1.08** | Listen to the sentences again, then practise saying them. Do you find it easier to pronounce the /r/ or not?

C Complete the sentences with your own ideas. Then say them to a partner.

1 The best way to refurbish an old building is to …

2 It's important to modernise …

3 In my city, I think they should restore …

SPEAKING

6A Turn to page 143 and look at the photo. Your company or school wants ideas to refurbish this room to create a dedicated work or study area where individuals will be as productive as possible. Answer the questions and plan your ideas.

- How will you refurbish and modernise the room?
- What special features will you build in?
- How will you help as many people as possible to feel that they belong there?

B Complete the sentences with reduced relative clauses, using some of your ideas.

1 … placed in the room might …

2 People using computers could …

3 The desks used by individuals should …

4 People working in groups could …

C Work in groups. Talk about the work or study environment you have designed. Agree on which features make a place easy to work in.

WRITING

a proposal: transforming a city space

7A You are going to write a proposal to transform a city space. Tick the features that are true for a proposal.

A proposal should …

- give information about a problem or issue.
- make some suggestions to improve the situation.
- be organised into paragraphs with headings.
- be written in an informal style.

B Write a proposal. Go to the Writing Bank.

▶▶ page 104 **WRITING BANK** a proposal

1C Things we love

HOW TO ... | talk about hypothetical preferences
VOCABULARY | idiomatic phrases: hobbies and interests
PRONUNCIATION | connected speech: final /r/ sound

VOCABULARY

idiomatic phrases: hobbies and interests

1 A Write a list of five things you enjoy doing. Then compare in groups. How many of your answers were the same?

B Read what four people say about things they enjoy. Which person is most like you?

C Complete the meanings with the correct form of the phrases in bold in Ex 1B.

1 If you _____ something, you want to experience it more and more.
2 If something is _____ , it is very special and you are unlikely to be able to do it again.
3 If you get _____ from something, it gives you a very strong feeling of excitement.
4 If you have _____ , you enjoy yourself a lot.
5 If you _____ by something, you enjoy it a lot.
6 If you _____ , you forget what time it is.
7 If you _____ , you take part in an activity enthusiastically.
8 If you _____ in something, you concentrate on it completely and forget about everything else.

D Work in pairs. Discuss the questions.

1 What activities give you an adrenalin rush? Do you enjoy the feeling?
2 What activities can you lose yourself in? Why?
3 What once-in-a-lifetime experience do you think you would enjoy?
4 Have you ever tried something new and been completely blown away by it?
5 When was the last time you had the time of your life?

 AdrenalinJunkie
56 mins

···

I tried mountain biking for the first time last year and now I **can't get enough of it**. I really **get an adrenalin rush** when I'm at the top of a steep hill and I'm about to set off towards the bottom!

 12   ♡ Like   ♀ Comments   ↗ Share

 EFitzgerald4Ever
52 mins

···

I'm into jazz music. I find I can really **lose myself** in it – I can sit there for hours and completely **lose track of time**. It's so relaxing!

 3   ♡ Like   ♀ Comments   ↗ Share

 SofaSurfer101
28 mins

···

A friend persuaded me to help him with a landscaping project he was working on in his garden. I'd never really been into gardening or doing physical work before, but there was a big group of us and we all **got stuck in** and actually, I **had the time of my life**! It was such fun – and great to see the results when it was all finished.

          ♡ Like   ♀ Comments   ↗ Share

 Paul.Tomas89
4 mins

···

Last year, I won the chance to drive a Formula One car. I must admit I was a bit nervous, but I **was completely blown away by** it. It really **was a once-in-a-lifetime experience**.

 6   ♡ Like   ♀ Comments   ↗ Share

How to ...
talk about hypothetical preferences

2 A Work in pairs. Ask and answer three *Would you rather ... ?* questions from a survey. How many of your answers are the same?

Would you rather ...

1 do a deep-sea dive or do a bungee jump?

2 appear in a reality TV show or act or sing on stage?

3 binge watch a TV show all day or read a book all day?

B 🔊 **1.09** | Listen to two people asking and answering the questions in Ex 2A. Which activity do they agree they would hate?

3 A 🔊 **1.09** | Work in pairs. Choose the correct words to complete the sentences from the conversation. Then listen again and check.

1 I'd **jump / get** at the chance to do it.

2 ... no **time / way** would I ever jump off a cliff or a bridge!

3 ... I'd **run / go** a mile at the thought of deep-sea diving.

4 Given the **event / choice**, I'd choose the bungee jump any day.

5 I'd go **at / for** being in a reality TV show every time.

6 ... you would never **catch / watch** me singing anywhere in public ...

7 Nothing would **get me / make me** get up on a stage and sing!

8 I'd **sooner / prefer** act on stage than ...

9 If it was **for / up to** me, I'd read a book all day.

10 I'd probably give reading a **miss / refuse**.

B Complete the table with the highlighted phrases in Ex 3A.

I'd like to ...	I wouldn't like to ...
I'd jump at the chance to	

C Look at the phrases in Ex 3B again. Which are followed by an *-ing* form?

D Learn and practise. Go to the Grammar Bank.

▶▶ page 112 **GRAMMAR BANK**

PRONUNCIATION
connected speech: final /r/ sound

4 A 🔊 **1.10** | Listen to the sentences. In which words in bold does the speaker pronounce the final /r/ sound?

1 Would you **rather** appear in a reality TV show or sing on stage?

2 I'd **sooner** act on stage.

3 I'd go **for** being in a reality TV show every time!

B Choose the correct alternative to complete the rule.

We always pronounce the final /r/ sound in a word when the following sound is a **vowel / consonant**.

C Complete the sentences with your answers to the questions in Ex 2A. Then practise saying them.

1 I'd rather ...   **2** I'd sooner ...   **3** I'd go for ...

SPEAKING

5 A Work in three groups, A, B and C. Group A: Work in pairs. Complete the survey below with your own *Would you rather ... ?* questions. Group B: Go to page 141 and follow the instructions. Group C: Go to page 143 and follow the instructions.

WOULD YOU RATHER ...

1 fly a plane or parachute out of a plane?

2 be famous for a day or be a millionaire for a day?

3 ....

4 ....

5 ....

6 ....

B Read the Future Skills box and do the task.

> **FUTURE SKILLS**
> **Collaboration**
>
> When we ask someone survey questions, we sometimes have to encourage them to elaborate. We can ask for reasons and we can ask them about their personal experiences, e.g. *Have you tried anything like that before? Wouldn't you be scared?*
>
> Look at your survey questions again. Think of questions to ask to encourage your partner to elaborate.

C Work with a partner from a different group. Take turns to ask and answer your survey questions.

D What is the most surprising thing you learnt about your partner?

> **MEDIATION SKILLS**
> writing for your audience
> simplify a source text
>
> ▶▶ page 144 **MEDIATION BANK**

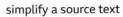

1D BBC Street Interviews
Comfort food

Anugraha

VOCABULARY | the taste and appeal of food
SPEAKING | a discussion about comfort food
WRITING | a social media post

Abiha

PREVIEW

1 A Work in pairs. What do you think 'comfort food' is?

B Read the definition to check your ideas. What are some popular examples of comfort food?

> Comfort food is food that we associate with feeling relaxed and happy. It's the kind of food we eat to gain a sense of comfort. This may be because the high fat and sugar content leads to chemical changes in our brains, or because comfort food reminds us of positive experiences with other people.

Q1: How important is food in your life?

Q2: Describe your comfort foods and why you like them.

VIEW

2 A ▶ Watch the interviews. How important is food to the speakers? What comfort foods do they like? Were you surprised by any of the foods mentioned?

B ▶ Watch the first part of the interviews again. Match the speakers (1–5) with the reasons they give for food being important (a–e).

1 Abiha   a to experience new things
2 Meg   b for the carbohydrates
3 Anugraha   c it is an essential feature of childhood
4 Phoebe   d for physical and mental well-being
5 Shravash   e it's about connecting with people

C ▶ Watch the second part of the interviews again and complete the sentences with the words you hear.

1 My comfort food is cheese – .... cheese, soft cheese, hard cheese – any cheese.
2 … I just really want a brownie – it's sweet and .... and delicious.
3 … it's delicious and it's .... and I can eat it with my hands and it's very .... …
4 … it's made of chickpea and fried doughballs. It's very .... …
5 I'm out of words right now. I cannot describe how .... it is.

VOCABULARY

the taste and appeal of food

3 A Work in pairs. Match the words you wrote in Ex 2C with the meanings 1–6.

1 covered in oil
2 with a strong taste that gives a pleasant burning feeling in your mouth
3 containing a lot of butter, eggs or cream
4 very good, often in an unexpected way
5 made soft by heat
6 makes you feel full

B Which adjective in Ex 3A is formed from a food ingredient?

C Form adjectives from the food items below. What food or dish could each one describe?

> butter   cheese   cream   dough   fruit   juice
> lemon   mint   nut   pepper   salt   sugar

D Work in pairs. Tell each other about the foods you like. Use adjectives from Ex 3A and Ex 3C where possible.

I love crisps, especially when they're really salty.

Meg

Shravash

Phoebe

SPEAKING

a discussion about comfort food

4 A 🔊 **1.11** | Listen to three quotes about comfort food. Which one do you most agree with? Why?

B 🔊 **1.12** | Listen to a conversation about comfort food. What is the main topic being discussed? In what ways do the speakers go off topic?

C 🔊 **1.12** | Listen again and tick the Key phrases you hear.

> **KEY PHRASES**
>
> We've gone off track a bit.
> Getting back to your point/the question, …
> Going back to the point about …
> So, where were we? Oh yes, we were talking about …
> Anyway, back to …

5 A Make notes on your answers to the questions below.

1 Do you think comfort foods are the same around the world? Why/Why not?
2 What do you think is the main reason for comfort food consumption? Why?
3 What do you think are the main effects of comfort food consumption on a society?
4 Do you think there are better alternatives to comfort food when needing comfort? If yes, what? If no, why not?

B Work in small groups. Discuss the questions in Ex 5A and try to agree on the answers. Use the Key phrases to help you if your conversation goes off topic.

C Share what you've agreed with the class or another group. Do they agree with you?

WRITING

a social media post

6 A Work in pairs and discuss the questions.

1 How adventurous are you when it comes to trying new foods?
2 What new food item or dish have you tried recently? Did it meet, exceed or fall short of your expectations? Why?

B Work in pairs. Look at the photo in the social media post. What do you think the food is?

C Read the social media post to check your ideas in Ex 6B.

 Carla.Wong2000 ● ● ●

My first time eating s'mores, the North American snack I've wanted to try for years. Sweet, melted marshmallow on top of chunks of rich, creamy chocolate in between two sweet, crunchy crackers. 😊 Perfect comfort food for a chilly autumn night around a 🔥 IMHO. Great for creating *hygge* – the Danish word for a sense of comfort and cosiness. Just as expected, they're gooey, very messy to eat and extremely sugary. Not sure I'll be sleeping for a while. 😜

#s'mores #comfortfood #campfiretreat
#sugarhigh #dreamcometrue   ♡ 💬 ↗ 🔖

D Choose the correct social media message feature (a or b) in each pair.

1 a first line acts as a photo caption
 b first line gives a detailed description
2 a neutral to formal language
 b informal language
3 a conversational tone
 b polite tone
4 a short, simple sentences
 b long, complex sentences
5 a complete sentences
 b omission of some words, i.e. *It's, I'm*
6 a emojis to only show emotions
 b emojis to show emotions and depict concepts
7 a title and subheadings
 b hashtags and abbreviations

7 A You're going to write a social media post about a new food item or meal that had an impact on you. Find a photo and plan your post.

B Write your post using the features in Ex 6D to help you. When finished, share it with your classmates. Which of your classmates' food items or meals would you like to try? Why?

B B C

17

GRAMMAR

describing past and present habits

1 A Complete the second sentence so it means the same as the first, using the word in brackets. More than one answer might be possible.

1 What silly things do you regularly argue about with your friends? (ARGUING)

What silly things .... about with your friends?

2 What after-school activities did you regularly participate in when you were younger? (USE)

What after-school activities .... when you were younger?

3 What annoying thing do you regularly do by mistake? (KEEP)

What annoying thing .... by mistake?

4 How do you usually start your weekend? (INCLINED)

How .... your weekend?

5 What do you generally not do except during your holidays? (RULE)

..............., what do you generally not do except during your holidays?

B Work in pairs. Take turns to ask and answer the questions in Ex 1A.

reduced relative clauses

2 A Complete the home office tips. Put the words in brackets in the correct present or past participle form.

1 When .... (work) from home, make your space as productive as possible.

2 Consider a standing desk .... (design) to reduce back pain.

3 Alternatively, invest in a chair .... (shape) to suit your body.

4 Use a screen .... (position) at eye level.

5 Daylight bulbs, ... (create) bright, natural light, are good for your mood.

6 A plant .... (act) as both decoration and air purifier keeps you healthy.

B Tell your partner about your home-working space. Does it help your productivity? Why/Why not?

3 A Rewrite each pair of sentences with a participle clause.

1 Active edges are important in city spaces. They are designed to connect people.

Active edges designed to connect people are important in city spaces.

2 Musicians perform in city centres. They can lift people's spirits.

3 Water features are installed in city centres. They can calm people.

4 City areas were unused in the past. They should be turned into green spaces.

5 New cities will be built in the future. They will take mental well-being into account.

B Do you agree with the statements in Ex 3A? Why/Why not? Tell a partner.

VOCABULARY

4 A Choose the correct words to complete the sentences.

1 It's always nice to **bump into / hit it off with** old friends.

2 We should **spruce out / spruce up** a few city areas to improve them.

3 Everyone needs a once-in-a-**life / lifetime** experience.

4 It's best to wait a day before **falling out / making up** with someone we fell out with.

5 Even historical areas should be **merged / modernised** regularly.

6 It's hard to be friends with someone who isn't on the same **idea / wavelength** as us.

B Work in pairs. How much do you agree with the statements in Ex 4A? Give reasons.

5 A Complete the sentences with one word. The first letter is given.

1 When I'm really into an activity, I lose **t**............... of time.

2 I'd like to **r**............... my home so that it looks really modern.

3 I love cheese. I can't get **e**............... of it!

4 I **h**............... it off with most people I meet.

5 I live in a nice, quiet **s**............... street on the edge of the city.

6 I love performing on stage. I get an adrenalin **r**............... whenever I do it.

B Work in pairs. Are the statements in Ex 5A true or false for you? Why?

6 A Complete the text with one word in each gap.

What's your relationship with your phone?

How would you describe your relationship with your mobile device? Did you [1] .... to each other as soon as you met? Or was it a while before you bonded [2] .... each other? Do you [3] .... around together all the time? Or rely on each other only in times of need? Do you lose [4] .... in your phone, spending hours on apps [5] .... especially to pull you in? Or are you able to drag yourself away and focus on other things?

Thinking of our phone as a friend can help us to see if our relationship with it is healthy or not. If you [6] .... a tendency to look at your screen when people are speaking, you may want to rethink your friendship. If you [7] .... always wondering what you're missing out on when your phone is turned off, you may need to embrace the joy of missing out. And those of us [8] .... more time with our phone than with our friends and family? We definitely need to reconsider our priorities.

B Work in pairs. How would you describe your relationship with your mobile device?

competition 2

B B C

VLOGS

Q: In what ways are you competitive?

1 ▶ Watch the video. What are some of the different ways of competing that the people mention?

2 In what ways are you a competitive person?

Global Scale of English **LEARNING OBJECTIVES**

2A LISTENING | Understand a conversation about cheating: idioms: winning and losing

Pronunciation: emphasis in cleft sentences

Discuss cheating: cleft sentences

2B READING | Read an interview about cooperation in industry: industry competition

Pronunciation: phrasal stress

Speculate about products and services: ellipsis and substitution

Write an article about rivalry

2C HOW TO ... | compare and evaluate ideas: business; work benefits

Pronunciation: intonation when comparing

2D BBC PROGRAMME | Understand a TV programme about a driving challenge

Have a debate about competing: competing

Write a reflection

2A Getting away with it

GRAMMAR | cleft sentences
VOCABULARY | idioms: winning and losing
PRONUNCIATION | emphasis in cleft sentences

VOCABULARY

idioms: winning and losing

1 A Work in pairs. Think of some of the different ways that people can cheat in sports or games. What do you think about people who do these things?

B Read the online post and comments. Which opinions do you agree with? Discuss with a partner.

 @Melvin1980

I watched the football last night and was absolutely disgusted by the behaviour of some players. Denby was definitely **faking** his injury, but he managed to get O'Hara sent off. It spoiled the game for me and it definitely affected the result. It was **disgraceful**! Why can't these top players just **play fair** and play by the rules?

💬 3   🔁 00   ♡ 9   ✉

 @Glan96
People will always cheat if they think they can **get away with it** – it's just human nature. If you're a competitive person, you'll do anything to **come out on top**.

💬 00   🔁 00   ♡ 7   ✉

 @Manor123
Confession time: I'm a really competitive person and even when I play games against my young nephews, I can't bear to **let** them **win**. I know it's **not the done thing**, but I just hate losing!

💬 1   🔁 1   ♡ 00   ✉

 @Fowleys89
I can't understand how these players can be pleased with themselves when they've won by unfair means. They just want to **win at all costs** – how **can** they **hold their heads up** and not be ashamed of themselves when they've **conned** other people?

💬 1   🔁 00   ♡ 10   ✉

2 A Complete the meanings (1–10) with the correct form of the idioms in bold in the post and comments.

1 If you ...., you do anything in order to win.

2 If you .... someone, you deceive and mislead them.

3 If you ...., you allow them to win.

4 If you do something bad and .... it, you are not punished for it.

5 If you ...., you feel proud of something that you have done or achieved.

6 If something is ...., it is inappropriate and frowned on by others.

7 If you ...., you follow the rules in a game.

8 If you .... in a game, you win.

9 If something is ...., it is shockingly unacceptable.

10 If you .... something, you pretend it happens in order to mislead someone.

B Work in pairs. Think of a time when:

1 you let someone win.

2 you came out on top in a game or competition.

3 you felt you could hold your head up because you had behaved well.

4 you were tempted not to play fair.

C Learn and practise. Go to the Vocabulary Bank.

▶▶ page 135 **VOCABULARY BANK** winning and losing

LISTENING

3 A 🔊 **2.01 | Listen to two friends talking about cheating. Number the topics (a–d) from 1–4 in the order they discuss them.**

a how people feel when they cheat

b a family member who cheated

c how people respond to seeing others cheating

d the relationship between winning and cheating

B 🔊 **2.01 | Listen again. Are the statements True (T) or False (F)?**

1 Rona knocked another runner over deliberately in her race.

2 Jake forced Rona to admit what she had done.

3 Jake finds it difficult to understand why his sister cheated.

4 People who win by cheating often feel proud of what they have done.

5 Cheaters feel a greater sense of satisfaction when they can see that their opponent is upset.

6 People who win regularly are less likely to cheat.

7 In team sports, players are more likely to break the rules if they see members of their own team cheating.

8 If they see members of the opposite team cheating, they are likely to copy their behaviour.

C Work in pairs. Discuss the questions.

1 Which of the statements 4–8 in Ex 3B do you find the most surprising? Why?

2 Have you ever experienced the 'cheater's high', or can you imagine experiencing it?

3 Do you find it more difficult to lose at things you are good at?

4 Do you ever avoid competing because you fear losing or failing in some way?

GRAMMAR

cleft sentences

4 A 🔊 **2.02 | Complete the sentences from the conversation with the verbs in the box. Listen and check.**

did   do   don't   feel

1 What Rona .... was bump into her, to make her fall over.

2 What I .... understand is why adults cheat.

3 What they .... is that they're smarter than everyone else.

4 What I'll .... is send you the link now.

B Work in pairs. The sentences in Ex 4A are called cleft sentences. Rewrite them as normal sentences.

1 Rona bumped into her, to make her fall over.

C Tick the sentences (1–5) that are true for cleft sentences.

1 We use cleft sentences to emphasise particular information in a sentence.

2 We can start cleft sentences with *What*.

3 The subject of the cleft sentence is different to the subject of the normal sentence.

4 We sometimes add the auxiliary *do* in the cleft structure.

5 We add the correct form of the verb *be* at the end of the cleft structure.

D Choose the correct words to complete the cleft sentences about the conversation in Ex 3A.

1 What Jake **did was tell / told** his mum what Rona had done.

2 What Rona's mum **made / did was make** Rona tell her teachers.

3 What cheater's **experience is / do experience** called 'cheater's high'.

4 What Jake **does want / wants to do is** listen to the podcast himself.

E Learn and practise. Go to the Grammar Bank.

▶▶ **page 113 GRAMMAR BANK**

PRONUNCIATION
emphasis in cleft sentences

5 A 🔊 **2.02 |** Listen to the sentences in Ex 4A again and pay attention to the words in bold. What is different about them? Why do you think this is?

1 What Rona **did** was bump into her, to make her fall over.

2 What I **don't** understand is why adults cheat.

3 What they **feel** is that they're smarter than everyone else.

4 What I'll **do** is send you the link now.

B Think about an example of cheating that you know about. Complete the sentences (1–3). Then say them to a partner, paying attention to where you place the emphasis.

1 What the person did was …

2 What happened was …

3 What I felt about it was …

SPEAKING

6 A Read the Confessions quiz *'Have you ever … ? Would you ever … ?'* and answer the questions for yourself.

B Compare your answers with a partner and give examples of similar situations you have been in.

7 A Read the Future Skills box and do the task.

FUTURE SKILLS
Leadership

In group discussions, some people can be more reluctant speakers than others. When you discuss ideas in a group, it is a good idea to encourage all group members to join in the discussion.

Make a list of things you can do to encourage reluctant speakers to join in.
Make eye contact with them during the discussion.
Ask for their opinion.

B Work in groups. Discuss the situations in Ex 6A. As a group, try to agree on the questions below.

1 Which of the examples of cheating is the most serious? Why?

2 Which examples do you think people are most likely to get away with?

3 What kind of punishment do you think would be most appropriate for each example?

C Compare your ideas with the class. How similar or different are the ideas in your group?

Have you ever … ?
Would you ever … ?

It's confession time! People cheat in all kinds of ways and in all kinds of situations. Answer the questions honestly to find out how much of a cheat you really are!

1 You're in a quiz team with some friends. Your team is in second place at the moment and it's the final round. Would you use your phone to make sure you get the final questions right?

  a Yes. Everyone cheats in quizzes if they can.

  b I might look up one or two answers, but not all of them.

  c No. Where's the pleasure in winning if you haven't played fair?

2 You have an important exam and you've run out of time to revise. You really need to do well and make the grade. Would you secretly take notes into the exam with you?

  a Yes, I've done this.

  b I've been tempted, but I've never actually done it.

  c No, it's wrong. If I haven't done enough work, I deserve to fail.

3 You're writing your CV for a job you really want. The advert asks for experience you don't have. Would you add false information?

  a Of course! Everyone does it, don't they?

  b I might exaggerate the facts a little, but I wouldn't add anything completely false.

  c No. Honesty is the best policy, and it would be so embarrassing to be caught out!

4 You're keen to impress your new manager. A more junior member of your team has produced a piece of work that you know will impress. Would you take credit for it?

  a Definitely. This junior staff member reports to you, so their work is your work!

  b I might allow the boss to think the work is mine, but without me having to lie about it.

  c I'd hate it if someone did that to me, so I'd never do it.

5 You witnessed a street robbery where members of the public chased and caught the thief. The story would be so much better if you had actually been involved. Would you alter the facts to exaggerate your role in the events to impress your friends?

  a If I'm honest, I probably would. It would be impossible to resist!

  b I might hint I was more involved, without saying so directly.

  c No. There's no point trying to impress people with things that aren't true.

6 You've been invited to a day out to celebrate a friend's birthday, but you're meant to be working that day. Would you call in sick to get the day off?

  a With no hesitation. I know loads of people who do it.

  b Yes, probably, if I really wanted to go to the celebration, but I'd try to catch up the hours at work later.

  c No. I'd ask for a day's holiday, but if that wasn't possible, I'd miss the celebration.

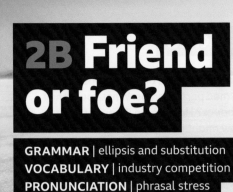

2B Friend or foe?

GRAMMAR | ellipsis and substitution
VOCABULARY | industry competition
PRONUNCIATION | phrasal stress

VOCABULARY

industry competition

1 Work in pairs and discuss the questions.

1 What famous business rivals can you think of? What industries are they in?

2 Is it better for business rivals to compete or collaborate with each other? Why?

3 Is this true of all industries? Why/Why not?

2 A Read the forum comments. Does each person agree or disagree that rivals should collaborate with each other?

@kimmy | 58 mins   comment | share

Collaboration between competitors is best avoided. If it's not done openly, it could be considered illegal.

@markL | 52 mins   comment | share

Competition between **bitter rivals** is what brings results. When these competitors try to **outdo** each other, they do better.

@riverrun | 47 mins   comment | share

If companies **formed an alliance** with each other instead of trying to **gain a competitive edge** all the time, they might be able to solve world issues.

@alesha77 | 21 mins   comment | share

When companies **forge partnerships** with other companies, together, they can **push beyond their limits**. This moves the industry forward and benefits everyone.

@pareshR | 03 mins   comment | share

I prefer to see **adversaries** fighting to be at the top of the industry. They're more likely to **fulfil their potential** that way. Surely **cooperation** stops companies from putting in the effort to come out on top.

B Match the words and phrases in bold in Ex 2A with the categories (1–5). There are two words/phrases for each category. What exactly do you think the words mean?

1 companies competing in the same industry

2 build a relationship with others

3 be better than others

4 working together to achieve something

5 reach or go beyond their capability

C Complete the descriptions with the words and phrases from Ex 2A. More than one answer might be possible.

1 Sony and Microsoft are often considered to be [1]............... in the gaming industry, with both companies trying to [2]............... each other to sell the most consoles and [3]............... over the other. But in 2019, they announced there would be a degree of [4]............... between the two companies as they prepare for a future of cloud-based gaming.

2 Fiat Chrysler and Google [5]............... in 2016 to develop self-driving cars. This [6]............... is benefiting both companies and helping them both to [7]............... and better [8]............... .

PRONUNCIATION
phrasal stress

3 A 🔊 **2.03** | Listen to the pronunciation of the verb phrases (1–5). Which syllable has the main stress? Is it part of the verb or the noun?

1 form an alliance

2 gain a competitive edge

3 forge partnerships

4 push beyond their limits

5 fulfil their potential

B 🔊 **2.03** | Listen and repeat the phrases in Ex 3A. Copy the stress in the phrases.

C Work in pairs. How do you think the two business relationships in Ex 2C benefit the companies and their customers? Use words and phrases in Ex 2A with appropriate stress.

READING

4A Read the interview with Theo Norton, an expert in industry competition. What is 'coopetition'? Why does he support it?

B Read the interview again and answer the questions.

1 How does cooperation help organisations to launch a new product?
2 Why do companies tend to avoid cooperating with rivals?
3 What must companies do to ensure the success of an alliance?
4 Why are scientists often secretive about their work?
5 Why might rivals have to work together in the future?
6 What points in the interview do these companies and projects exemplify?

> Ericsson   Uber   Toyota   Hulu
> The Human Genome Project   Timberland

C What do the idiomatic phrases in bold in the interview mean? Answer the questions (1–5) and share your ideas with a partner.

1 Do any parts of the phrase have a literal meaning?
2 Does the idiom create an image in your mind?
3 Does the context suggest the idiom has a positive, negative or neutral meaning?
4 Is there a definition or synonym before or after it in the text?
5 Do the words near the idiom give any further clues?

D Work in groups. Has the interview changed your view from Ex 1 about business rivals cooperating vs competing? Why/Why not?

GRAMMAR

ellipsis and substitution

5A Look at the highlighted words and phrases (1–8) in the interview. Match them with their explanations (a–h).

a 'do so' substitutes 'gain knowledge and skills'.
b 'That's' is omitted.
c 'do' substitutes 'collaborate'.
d 'That's a' is omitted.
e 'That' is omitted.
f 'so' substitutes 'we see more cooperation in the future'.
g 'a mix of cooperation and competition' is omitted.
h 'they can' is omitted.

B Work in pairs. Discuss the questions.

1 Why do you think the speakers omitted some words?
2 Why do you think the speakers chose to substitute some words?

C Take turns to ask and answer the questions with a partner. Complete the answers with your own ideas.

1 Shouldn't all rivals try to collaborate with each other?
   Easy to say. I think ....
2 Should rivals be forced to collaborate on projects?
   Some people think .... , but I don't. I think ....

D Learn and practise. Go to the Grammar Bank.

▶▶ page 114 **GRAMMAR BANK**

SPEAKING

6A Imagine that the organisations in 1–6 formed partnerships. What could they produce? How would it benefit them? How might it negatively affect them? Make notes.

1 an AI company and a fast-food company
2 a music company and a disaster charity
3 an electric car company and an extreme sports company
4 an energy drinks company and a trainer manufacturer
5 a medical equipment company and a car manufacturer
6 a game app company and a charity supporting people with disabilities

B Work in small groups. Share your ideas. Which partnership do you think would achieve the following? Why?

- the most fun product or service
- the most creative product or service
- the most useful product or service for people
- the most environmentally friendly product or service
- the most beneficial product or service for the world

C Share your conclusions with the class.

WRITING

an article: rivalry

7A Work in pairs. Which do you think is better between siblings: competition or cooperation? Why?

B Read the heading for an article about rivalry in business. Do you think the writer's view of sibling rivalry in business will be positive or negative? What reasons might they give?

Sibling rivalry can boost an industry

C Write an article about rivalry. Go to the Writing Bank.

▶▶ page 104 **WRITING BANK**

The need for 'coopetition'

Chandra Adler interviews industry expert Theo Norton about the need for more cooperation alongside competition between rivals in industry.

Cooperation among organisations in the same industry isn't uncommon, but it's something you think we need to see more of. Why?

Because, quite simply, there are so many advantages to it. It might seem like it should be the last thing organisations do in a **cut-throat** industry – give away their secrets to rivals and possibly help them gain a competitive advantage – but in fact it can make both organisations stronger, it can benefit us, the consumer, and it has the potential to change the world.

Wow, [1]bold statement! OK, let's start with the organisations themselves. How exactly can cooperation benefit them?

It saves costs. **Getting a new project off the ground** is hugely expensive because of the research and development costs, and it can be a lengthy process. By sharing the load, it's financially beneficial and results are faster. Telecommunication companies like Ericsson and Deutsche Telekom have been working together for years for this reason.

Other benefits of cooperation include the ability to innovate together by sharing skills and knowledge, and then using the knowledge and skills they gain from each other for their individual long-term benefit – if they're clever about it and make a concerted effort to [2]do so, of course. Cooperation can also allow organisations to grow their markets and [3]get access to consumers they don't currently have access to. Uber customers can play their Spotify playlists for a more comfortable ride, for example. Toyota worked with General Motors to better understand the U.S. market.

But surely, forming an alliance with a rival is a risky business. It makes them stronger and more able to compete against you.

Well, it's why a lot of businesses avoid it, but if the alliance is conducted in the right way, they can reap the benefits without suffering from the potential disadvantages. Businesses need to set very clear goals for the partnership, and let all employees know what they can and can't share so that everyone **is on the same page**. And they need to have active plans to observe and learn from their partner. In the end, what we want to see most is 'coopetition'.

Is that a mix of cooperation and competition?

[4]It is. We don't want businesses to stop being competitive. The desire to **be ahead of the pack** pushes companies to do better, but cooperation brings so many benefits that for me, it's **a no-brainer**. Companies need to practise coopetition – a perfect mixture of the two approaches.

How does coopetition benefit consumers?

They reap the rewards of innovation that come about because businesses are trying to outdo each other, and because businesses share resources and create things not possible otherwise. Hulu, the TV streaming channel, was created by three companies to show their programmes, but eventually it began to make its own shows to the benefit of viewers.

You made the rather bold claim earlier that cooperation could change the world. What do you mean by that?

There are some industries where, if organisations collaborated much more than they [5]do now, they'd have the potential to truly solve some of the world's biggest issues. Science is the one that immediately comes to mind. Research companies compete with each other for funding, which means research tends to be kept secret until results are published. But if organisations were more open about the work they were doing, they'd be able to collaborate more often which would mean better and faster results. The Human Genome Project is one example. Thousands of scientists from different organisations around the world openly worked together to map the human genome and, as a result, our knowledge of the human body moved on significantly.

[6]Definitely sounds like something we should see more of in science and tech. Do you think we'll see more cooperation in the future?

[7]Hard to say, but I hope [8]so. One thought is that for companies to become carbon zero by the deadlines their governments have set, they're going to have to work together. It requires transforming whole supply chains, which is not easy for one business or organisation to do on its own. We're already seeing collaborations to benefit the environment, such as Timberland working with tyre company Omni United to use old tyre rubber in new shoes. In the future, we could see bitter rivals working together to achieve their carbon-zero goal. And won't the world be better for it? It's not just meeting these targets though. Think of all the other things that could be achieved if organisations worked together for the sake of problem-solving and not making a profit.

2C In the workplace

HOW TO ... | compare and evaluate ideas
VOCABULARY | business; work benefits
PRONUNCIATION | intonation when comparing

VOCABULARY

business

1 Work in pairs. Is it better to encourage competition or collaboration between employees? Why?

2 A Read the first part of an article. What did Dan Price decide to do and why?

B Work in pairs. What do you think happened to the company after the minimum salary scheme was introduced? Why?

C Go to page 141 and check your ideas. Do you think more companies should introduce this scheme? Why/Why not?

3 A Match the words in the box with the meanings (1–8). Use their contexts in the article in Ex 2A to help you.

> bankruptcy   competitiveness   cutback   efficiency
> initiative   productivity   profitability   turnover

1 doing something well without spending too much time/ money/energy
2 the rate at which goods/services are produced/provided in relation to the time/money/energy spent producing them
3 the state of being unable to pay back what you owe
4 the value of goods/services a company sells
5 an important new plan
6 the ability to compete with others
7 the ability to make a profit
8 a reduction in something, e.g. numbers of employees or amount of money spent

B Work in pairs and answer the questions.

1 In what ways do companies increase the efficiency and productivity of their staff?
2 What kind of workplace initiative would encourage you to work harder?
3 Do you think that a high turnover and profitability should always be the main priority for a company CEO?
4 When cutbacks are needed in a company, do you think the CEO should be the first person to take a pay cut?

C Learn and practise. Go to the Vocabulary Bank.

▶▶ page 135 **VOCABULARY BANK** work benefits

Fair pay and the CEO

In 2011, card payment company founder Dan Price was out walking with a friend when she told him how much she was struggling to pay the bills. The friend, who'd served in the military for eleven years, was having to work fifty hours and two jobs to afford a recent rent increase, despite earning a decent salary in her main job.

An employee had earlier accused Price of exploiting employees with average wages in an expensive city. Price, who'd thought he was protecting his company with **cutbacks** in a difficult economy, began to question his policy on salaries. He eventually introduced a minimum salary scheme, selecting a minimum salary that economists had said could provide a happy standard of living. To be able to afford the huge increase in salary for many of his staff, he had to put himself on the minimum wage, taking an annual pay cut of $1 million.

The **initiative** immediately received attention around the world, from curious university researchers, CEOs and employees wanting to work at the company. However, not everyone saw the move as positive. Two senior staff members were unhappy that junior members would get a sudden huge pay increase, even though their own salary was unchanged. They resigned. Some commenters refused to believe that the company could thrive with such a salary scheme, instead suggesting that employees would lose their motivation to work hard and **productivity** would fall. The company would therefore lose its **efficiency** and its **competitiveness** in the market. They thought this would result in a fall in sales and **turnover**, which would impact the company's **profitability**, and eventually result in **bankruptcy**.

How to ...
compare and evaluate ideas

4A Work in pairs and discuss the questions.

1 How many days' paid holiday do people usually get in your country? Does this increase if you stay longer with the company?

2 What do you think should happen if people don't take all their holiday in a year?

3 Would you prefer a company you work for to offer an extra week's holiday per year or a financial incentive such as an end-of-year bonus?

B 🔊 **2.04 |** Listen to two colleagues discussing question 3 in Ex 4A. What is each person's preference and why?

5A 🔊 **2.05 |** Listen and complete the sentences with a word you hear.

1 A twenty percent pay rise this year and an .... **high** pay rise next year?

2 Extra money's .... **for** someone like me who's paying high rent in the city.

3 It'd probably be worth .... **more than** extra holiday leave.

4 ... but extra time off is just **as** ....

5 Time to unwind is every .... **as** important **as** extra cash ...

6 That's .... **near as** appealing as the other two options.

7 They're .... **more** motivating!

8 It wouldn't be very .... **in** inspiring us to work harder either.

B Which phrases in bold in Ex 5A compare (C) and which evaluate (E)?

C Learn and practise. Go to the Grammar Bank.

▶▶ page 115 **GRAMMAR BANK**

PRONUNCIATION
intonation when comparing

6A 🔊 **2.06 |** Listen and underline the word in each sentence that the speaker stresses the most.

1 It's way better to pay everyone a fair salary than not.

2 A month's holiday is equally as appealing as a month's salary.

3 Working from home is infinitely better than working in an office.

4 The scheme is nowhere near as good as I thought it would be.

B Make statements from the prompts which best represent your viewpoint.

1 paying a different salary to all staff / paying the same salary to all staff – way better

   Paying the same salary to all staff is way better than paying a different one.

2 allowing staff to work flexible hours / requiring staff to work at an office – significantly more productive

3 wearing casual clothes on Fridays / working from home on Fridays – nowhere near as appealing

4 receiving emails from your boss at the weekend / having to work late on a Friday – miles worse than

C Work in pairs. Take turns to say your statements from Ex 6B with the correct stress. Do you and your partner agree? Why/Why not?

SPEAKING

7A A CEO is thinking of offering a new incentive to increase productivity. Work alone and select the five incentives you think would be the most effective and consider why.

Potential perks

1 free healthy lunches for all staff

2 health insurance for all family members

3 gym membership

4 funds for social events outside the workplace

5 free yoga lessons at the start and end of each day

6 maternity/paternity leave that is longer than legally required

7 a mentor programme to support junior staff

8 tuition assistance

B Work in groups. Compare and evaluate the incentives in Ex 7A. Agree on the top five and then rank them 1–5.

C Present your ideas to the class. Can you all agree on the best option?

MEDIATION SKILLS
evaluating

evaluate problems, challenges and proposals

▶▶ page 146 **MEDIATION BANK**

2D B B C Entertainment
Challenge

VOCABULARY | competing
SPEAKING | a debate
WRITING | a reflection

PREVIEW

1 A Work in pairs and discuss the questions.

1 When was the last time you challenged yourself?

2 What did you do? Why?

3 What happened?

B Read the programme information. What is the challenge? Who undertakes it?

Gassed Up

With the help of expert driver Becky Evans and petrolhead Ryan Taylor, rapper Mist goes head-to-head with actor Ryan Thomas in a driving challenge in his hometown of Birmingham.

VIEW

2 A ▶ Watch the BBC video clip. What is the driving challenge called? Who wins?

B ▶ Watch the video again and answer the questions.

1 When did Ryan Thomas become interested in cars?

2 What does gymkhana involve?

3 What prompts Ryan to select his car?

4 What helped Ryan to prepare in a day?

5 How will the winner of the race be determined?

6 How did both Ryan and Mist feel about the race results?

B B C

VOCABULARY

competing

3 A Work in pairs. Look at the words and phrases in bold in the extracts from the video (1–8). For each word or phrase, decide if:

a you know the meaning.

b you can guess the meaning.

1 … the mental challenge of **knowing** the unmarked course **inside and out**.

2 You've got **a lot to take in** in one day …

3 Head-to-head racing … three **rounds**.

4 **Best of three** wins.

5 The nerves are **kicking in** now.

6 They were **neck and neck** after two laps.

7 … so it all **came down to** that one last run.

8 I love Mist. He **took it** [the win] really well.

B Work with another pair. Share your ideas from Ex 3A. Use a dictionary to check the meaning of any items you don't know.

C Complete the questions with the correct form of words from Ex 3A.

1 If you lose, do you .... it well or badly?

2 What place do you know .... and out?

3 What game do you know where the winner is decided in the .... of three rounds?

4 How long before a competition do your nerves usually .... in?

5 When was the last time you had a lot of information to .... in. Why?

6 What does winning .... down to? Is it skill, or luck?

D Work in pairs. Take turns to ask and answer the questions in Ex 3C.

SPEAKING

a debate

4 A Work in pairs. How competitive do you think people are in the contexts in the box? Why? Is competition a good or bad thing?

> car ownership   the gym   home and garden
> school   technological devices   the workplace

B 🔊 **2.07** | Listen to two opinions (A and B) and decide which you most agree with.

C 🔊 **2.07** | Listen again. Number the Key phrases in the order you hear them (1–5).

> **KEY PHRASES**
>
> If you … , you end up …
> … is more about … than …
> It's problematic because …
> The result is that …
> … (just) leads to …

5 A Work in groups of four and divide into pairs. Pair A: Prepare to argue for opinion A in Ex 4B. Pair B: Prepare to argue for opinion B. Think about the consequences of competing with others and competing with yourself. Form an argument and a counterargument.

B Work in your groups. Debate the opinions in Ex 4B. Use the Key phrases to help you.

C In your group, decide which arguments presented were the strongest. What's your real view of the opinions in Ex 4B?

WRITING

a reflection

6 A Work in pairs and discuss the questions.

1 How often do you reflect on something you have done?

2 What kind of things do you tend to reflect on? Why?

3 Why do you think it might be useful to reflect after a challenging task?

4 Can you think of any professional or educational situations where reflections might be used?

B Write a reflection. Go to the Writing Bank.

⏩ page 105 **WRITING BANK**

GRAMMAR

cleft sentences

1 A Complete the second sentence as a cleft sentence.

1 Some footballers pretend they have been fouled to get an opponent sent off.

What .... they have been fouled to get an opponent sent off.

2 It annoys me when players complain to the referee to waste time.

What .... players complain to the referee to waste time.

3 One tennis champion asked for a bathroom break when her opponent was close to winning the match.

What .... a bathroom break when her opponent was close to winning the match.

4 Some rugby players will inflict quite serious injuries on each other because they are so desperate to win.

What .... quite serious injuries on each other because they are so desperate to win.

5 I've seen cyclists deliberately bumping into their opponents to knock them off their bikes.

What .... into their opponents to knock them off their bikes.

6 One professional basketball player untied an opponent's shoelaces to slow him down!

What .... an opponent's shoelaces to slow him down!

B Work in pairs. Which actions in Ex 1A do you consider to be cheating? How should the players be punished?

ellipsis and substitution

2 Cross out the words that you can omit from each sentence.

1 Are you ready to leave?

2 I'll talk to Jon and I'll let you know what he says.

3 I went to the gym yesterday, but Sara didn't go to the gym yesterday.

4 She applied for the job and she got it.

5 I'd met Abi before, but Al hadn't met her before.

3 A Choose the correct words to replace the words in bold.

1 I'd been writing novels for years, but I only got **a novel** published when I collaborated with another writer. (one / it / a one)

2 I never enjoyed working on group projects at university, but I had to **work on a group project** once and we got a really bad mark! (do / do so / do one)

3 Most people I know love playing team sports and I **love playing team sports**, too. (do so / love / do)

4 When I was asked to work with a colleague on a project, I was worried she would steal all my best ideas and guess what? She **stole all my best ideas**! (did / stole it / did steal)

5 My boss says I'll have to work in a new team next year, but I hope **I won't have to work in a new team**. (don't / not / I'll not)

B Work in pairs. Talk about a good or bad experience you have had of cooperating with others.

VOCABULARY

4 A Choose the correct words to complete the sentences.

1 I know it's not the done **behaviour / attitude / thing** to be too competitive in games with friends, but I can't help myself!

2 I would always **play / get / make** fair, even if I really wanted to win something.

3 My best friend and I get on really well, but we are **large / bitter / strong** rivals when we play tennis!

4 I'm not very competitive. If someone tries to **overdo / outdo / redo** me at something, I just let them.

5 I think there should be more government **initiatives / productivity / efficiency** to get young people competing in sports.

6 I think gym membership is one of the best job **schemes / programmes / perks** you can get!

B Do you agree with the statements in Ex 4A? Why/Why not? Tell a partner.

5 A Choose the correct options (A–C) to complete the text.

Competing for the countryside

The Peak District, in the north of England, was first designated as a national park in 1951, making it the first national park in the UK. Millions of visitors have enjoyed its beautiful scenery over the years and they continue to [1] .... now. What most visitors are attracted to [2] .... the mountains and open countryside, far from urban areas, and many hotels and campsites thrive on this kind of tourism. However, there are competing views on how far the area should be developed. Owners of some local businesses would like to attract more visitors, to increase their [3] .... This might involve companies providing more popular attractions such as theme parks, to [4] .... a competitive edge over their rivals. On the other hand, environmentalists argue that such attractions are completely out of place in this rural area. They believe that developers should not be allowed to get [5] .... with spoiling the natural beauty and peace, but instead the focus should be on [6] .... to improve the environment. The arguments continue, with few signs of [7] .... between the different groups. It is unclear which side is going to [8] .... on top.

1 A do one	**B** do so	**C** do
2 A is	**B** was	**C** were
3 A cutbacks	**B** profitability	**C** bankruptcy
4 A gain	**B** make	**C** produce
5 A over	**B** away	**C** out
6 A competitiveness	**B** efficiency	**C** initiatives
7 A rivalry	**B** cooperation	**C** alliance
8 A come out	**B** come away	**C** come up

B 🔊 **R2.01 | Listen and check.**

C Work in pairs. Are there any areas in your country where there are competing groups or interests?

inspiration 3

B B C

VLOGS

Q: How do you express creativity in your life?

1 ▶ Watch the video. What creative activities are mentioned? Why do the people enjoy them?

2 What creative activities do you enjoy?

Global Scale of English **LEARNING OBJECTIVES**

3A **READING** | Read different texts about fanfiction: opinions and reactions

Pronunciation: *as* in connected speech

Describe a scene in a book, film, game, TV show or play: *as if/ as though*

Write a review of a scene in a book, film, game, TV show or play

3B **LISTENING** | Understand a spoken-word poem: idiomatic phrases: emotions

Pronunciation: /t/ sound in the middle of words

Describe situations where you felt different emotions: *no matter*

3C **HOW TO ...** | engage with other people's views: persuading and motivating

Pronunciation: intonation: responding tactfully

3D **BBC STREET INTERVIEWS** | Understand people talking about role models

Talk about an inspiring person: describing inspiring people

Write a biography

3A Fanfiction

GRAMMAR | *as if/as though*
VOCABULARY | opinions and reactions
PRONUNCIATION | *as* in connected speech

READING

1 A Work in pairs. Read the description of a BBC Radio programme. Have you ever read or written any fanfiction? What fictional worlds do you think fans write about in particular?

The Why Factor: Fanfiction **B** **B** **C**

Fanfiction is the name given to new stories written by fans of existing fictional worlds. The fans use those fictional worlds as the setting for their own stories and share them online – but why? And why do people read them?

B 🔊 **3.01** | Do you think fanfiction is a new or old concept? Listen to part of the programme and check your ideas.

2 A Match the text genres (1–6) with their typical features (a–f). Think of two more genres and their features.

1 fiction
2 social media post
3 review
4 research report
5 how-to guide
6 humorous article

a personal opinions with examples, conclusion and recommendation, neutral language
b short, maybe incomplete, sentences; informal language, abbreviations, emojis, hashtags
c descriptive language and imagery, past or present tense, direct speech
d short paragraphs, irony, imagery, neutral and sometimes informal language
e facts and figures, tables and graphs, conclusion, formal language
f a series of steps, imperative verbs, explanations of technical terms

B Read the extracts from different text types (A–F). What genre from Ex 2A is each one?

C Work in pairs. Share your ideas and justify your choices in Ex 2B.

A One popular fanfiction website has more than twelve million users with stories published in upwards of forty languages. There are almost half a million fanfiction stories about *Naruto*, a Japanese comic series, and significantly more about a certain boy wizard. A second site has over ninety million users who read and review the stories published in a total of fifty languages. Ninety percent of these are under forty years of age. The site hosts over 665 million stories and an annual competition where almost 300,000 writers from over thirty-five countries compete to win a writing award. These statistics suggest that fanfiction is popular in many regions around the world, with millennials and Generation Z at the forefront.

B Well, that was several hours of my life I'll never get back. All that time spent investing in a character only for him to die at the end. It's **tragic** that the author be allowed to do that. Yes, it's an alternative universe story, but still. Killing off the hero and letting the bad guy get away with it? That's too dark and **disturbing** for me. I know – Steve wouldn't have got to say those beautiful and **profound** last words with a happy ending. (I cried buckets btw.) Just not sure that's enough to justify the final scene for me. #gutted

C His heart was attempting to leap out of his chest, but his eyes were unflinching as he took in the sight before him. Second chances didn't come often like this and he wasn't going to throw it away like an old sweet wrapper. He reached above his glasses and touched his face. The pain that would once have struck him had now been replaced by the absolute certainty he and his friends would prevail.

D It's always **entertaining** to explore the back story of a minor character in a beloved universe, so I was excited to walk in the shoes of this young courageous character who had enthralled us all in the original stories. The author paints a vivid and **convincing** image of life as an adolescent female ruler of adult men, on an island constantly at threat from outsiders. She comes across as a realistic character who is both strong and weak, fierce and sympathetic, and very much a product of her harsh environment. New character Lord Mercer, however, is **unconvincing**. While his actions often made me laugh as the author intended, the two-dimensional nature of his character is limiting and **frustrating**. More aspects to his characterisation would have allowed for a more **fulfilling** story.

E Once you've done thorough research on the fictional universe you're going to write about, decide what type of fanfiction you're going to write. There are various genres to choose from. Alternative Universe (AU) allows you to write about a character in a new setting or create a 'what if?' type scenario, based on what if events in the original story had been different. Fix-it-Fic allows you to 'fix' things in the original story that you were unhappy with, while a Crossover allows you to have characters from two different universes in the same story. Self-insert puts you in the story alongside original characters, and DarkFic takes a light-hearted story, or one meant for children, and adds a darker spin to it. Read examples of each genre before you start to get a deeper understanding of how it works and select the one that you feel will motivate you the most. Note down possible ideas that you have.

F Mention that you're into fanfiction and you can guarantee someone will roll their eyes. While I'm **eager** to promote it, others just don't see it as proper literature. Yet, my **pathetic** attempts aside, there are some brilliantly creative stories out there. It's **encouraging** then, that the value of this genre is starting to be recognised. For one, it inspires people to create and write, as writing about a world you love is less **overwhelming** than writing about a whole new world.

It also helps people to find a voice. In my case, people like me don't tend to play the hero in books, films or games, but fanfiction gives me an opportunity to change that. I've had the joy of getting hundreds of comments criticising my stories over the years. OK, maybe not joy, but I've developed an ability to take and use feedback. Something that's stuck with me.

3 **A** Read the extracts again. In which one (A–F) does the author:
1 regret the time spent doing an activity?
2 suggest researching different types of fanfiction stories?
3 believe that fanfiction allows people to express themselves?
4 admit that something positive came out of a negative?
5 give an example of one literary world that people write about?
6 describe the confidence someone has that a future action will happen?
7 describe an individual affected by the place where they live?
8 prefer more complex people to appear in stories?

B Work in pairs and discuss the questions.
1 Why do you think fanfiction is such a popular phenomenon? What might writers need to be careful of?
2 If you read or wrote a piece of fanfiction, which existing fictional world would it be set in? Why?

VOCABULARY

opinions and reactions

4 **A** Look at the adjectives in bold in the extracts in Ex 2B. Which of them tell us that the author's opinion or reaction is positive (+)? Which of them tell us it is negative (-)?

B Replace the words in bold with an adjective from Ex 4A. Which statements do you agree with? Why?
1 I'm **keen** to create my own fanfiction story or fan film.
2 It's **rubbish** that there are so few characters I can relate to in stories. It's **annoying** there aren't more.
3 Long films or books are **far too much** for me. I prefer short stories or videos.
4 I prefer **deep** stories that make me think rather than stories which are just **amusing**.
5 It's **terrible** when a main character in a story dies, but it should happen more often.
6 Heroes and villains need to be **believable** for a story to be enjoyable. Most are **not believable**.
7 I don't like horror stories. They're too **upsetting**.
8 It's **promising** that young people are into fanfiction. Everyone needs a **satisfying** pastime.

C Choose three positive and three negative adjectives from Ex 4A. For each adjective, think of something you've seen, read or experienced that you could describe in this way.

frustrating – a badly made film adaptation of my favourite book

D Work in pairs. Take turns to describe your ideas in Ex 4C without using the adjective. Guess the adjectives that describe them.
A: A film based on one of my favourite books was badly made.
B: Did you find that frustrating?

GRAMMAR

as if/as though

5 A 🔊 **3.02** | Listen to an extract from a story. Do you recognise it? How is it different to the original?

B 🔊 **3.02** | Listen again and complete the sentences with the words you hear.

1 To anyone else, she looked as if she _____ , but inside there was a big ball of terror.
2 The creature acted as though the disguise _____ convincing.
3 'Well, Grandma, you look as if _____ today.'
4 It was as if a thousand cats _____ the room all at once.
5 … a look of pain on its face as though it _____ physically hurt.
6 It was as if she never _____ to let her grandmother go.

C Look at your answers to Ex 5B and answer the questions (1–3).

1 Is the purpose of *as if* and *as though* to express ability, comparison, preference or regret?
2 What verbs come before *as if* and *as though*?
3 Look at the verbs that follow *as if/as though*. What tense are they in?

D Learn and practise. Go to the Grammar Bank.

▶▶ page 116 **GRAMMAR BANK**

PRONUNCIATION
as in connected speech

6 A 🔊 **3.03** | Listen to the sentences. How is *as* pronounced? Is it stressed or unstressed?

B 🔊 **3.04** | Listen and complete the sentences. Then listen and repeat.

1 It's _____ the author's never read the original book.
2 It seemed _____ the ending had improved.
3 You look _____ you've seen a ghost.
4 I felt _____ you were angry with me.

C Think of books, films or video games you've enjoyed recently where something looked or seemed as if it was something different. Tell a partner about these. Pay attention to your pronunciation of *as*.

At first, it seemed as if the main character was a criminal, but she turned out to be an undercover police officer.

SPEAKING

7 A Work in pairs. Think of a scene from a book, film, game, TV show or play that you're both familiar with. Discuss changes to the scene that you would have enjoyed reading or seeing.

B With your partner, decide what changes you will make. Think about:

• which characters are in the scene and how you'll describe them.
• where the characters are and how you'll describe the place.
• what action happens and how you'll describe it.
• how the characters look, seem, feel, act or react and how you'll describe these things.
• what happens differently from the original.

C Read the Future Skills box and discuss the question in pairs. Think about how you'll describe your scene to create an engaging story. Practise together.

FUTURE SKILLS
Communication

We tell stories in many parts of our lives, for example to share experiences with friends, to entertain work colleagues or to attract clients and customers to our business.

Think about good storytellers. What do they do to engage the listener and make the story entertaining? Think about the language they use, their intonation and the way they engage with their audience.

D Work with a new partner. Take turns to describe your alternative scenes. Do you think they are better than the original scenes? Give reasons.

WRITING

a review: fiction

8 A Work in pairs and answer the questions.

1 What influences your choice in the books that you read?
2 What influences your choice in the films that you watch?
3 Do you ever read reviews of books or films to make your choices? Why/Why not?

B What information do you expect to find in a review? Make notes on your ideas. Then discuss your ideas with a partner.

C Write a review. Go to the Writing Bank.

▶▶ page 105 **WRITING BANK**

3B Street chatter

GRAMMAR | *no matter*
VOCABULARY | idiomatic phrases: emotions
PRONUNCIATION | /t/ sound in the middle of words

VOCABULARY

idiomatic phrases: emotions

1 A Work in pairs and discuss the questions.

1 Why do you think some people might listen in on other people's conversations in public places?

2 Have you ever done this? Why/Why not?

B Read a description of a BBC Radio programme. Where might a poet get their inspiration from?

Finding poetry in city chatter **B B C**

In this programme, we talk to poet Imtiaz Dharker to find out about the kinds of places a poet might find their inspiration.

C **3.05** | Listen to an extract from the programme and answer the questions.

1 How does Imtiaz Dharker get inspiration for her poems?

2 What does she pay attention to?

D **3.06** | Listen to the poem at the end again. Answer the questions.

1 What did the woman on the bus say about cooking with anger?

2 What did the woman on the bus do when she cooked? What was the outcome?

3 What do you think the meaning of the poem is?

2 A **3.07** | Listen to and read the extracts from conversations overheard on the street. Who or what do you think each person might be talking about?

B Work in pairs. Share your ideas. When they differ, which do you think is most likely to be true and why?

¹It doesn't matter what I do or say, nothing is good enough for him. It **drives me up the wall**.

²I always **have butterflies in my stomach**, but doing it last week, they felt like ducks flapping around. No idea why. Maybe it was something I ate!

³He couldn't find it anywhere. We were all **tearing our hair out**. Then he realised it was in his pocket. I mean, why didn't he check there first?!

⁴There he was, covered in mud, looking at me with wide eyes. I nearly **killed myself laughing**.

⁵I knew she'd **lost her temper**, but I didn't know it was because of jam. Who gets angry over jam?! She does, apparently.

⁶I shouldn't have done it. I **was on edge** for the rest of the night and couldn't sleep at all.

⁷I believed it and thought I was doing a good thing by spreading the word. Now I could **kick myself**.

⁸It**'s a real pain** that it stops you getting a good night's sleep. Maybe one of you can sleep outside?

3 A Match the phrases from the extracts in Ex 2A (1–8) with the emotions they convey (a–e).

1 drive someone up the wall
2 have butterflies in your stomach
3 tear your hair out
4 kill yourself laughing
5 lose your temper
6 be on edge
7 kick yourself
8 be a real pain

a annoyance
b anger
c nervousness
d desperation
e amusement

B Complete the questions with one word. Use Ex 3A to check your ideas.

1 When was the last time you .... yourself for doing something silly?
2 What little things drive you up the .... ?
3 When was the last time you got angry and lost your .... ?
4 What kinds of things cause you to get .... in your stomach?
5 When was the last time you nearly .... yourself laughing?
6 What chores would you describe as a real .... ?
7 What things make you nervous and on .... ?
8 What is something that has made you want to tear your .... out?

C Read the Future Skills box and discuss the questions. Then take turns to ask and answer the questions in Ex 3B.

FUTURE SKILLS
Self-management

Idiomatic phrases can be difficult to remember because the individual words don't usually tell us the overall meaning. Creating a visual image of the expression can be useful, e.g. an image of someone driving themselves up a wall of a building in a car while looking furious. What visual image could you create in your mind of the other phrases in Ex 3A? What else can help you to remember phrases like these?

D Learn and practise. Go to the Vocabulary Bank.

▶▶ page 136 **VOCABULARY BANK**
idiomatic phrases: emotions

LISTENING

4 A 🔊 **3.08** | A spoken-word poem is a poem that's designed to be performed rather than read. Listen to one such poem and tick the features (1–6) you notice.

1 rhyming words
2 all lines with the same number of syllables
3 expressions of emotion
4 emphasised/stressed words
5 background music
6 repetition

B What title might you choose for the poem in Ex 4A? Why?

C 🔊 **3.08** | Listen to the poem again. Choose the correct words.

1 The poet's choice of words causes ....
   a arguments   b sadness
2 The poet suggests the voice he hears is ....
   a critical   b supportive
3 The poet says the voice causes him to ....
   a worry   b feel excited
4 The poet says the voice causes him to be .... himself.
   a unkind to   b unsure of
5 The poet reveals that the voice is owned by ....
   a a friend   b himself
6 The poet says the voice doesn't give him any ....
   a advice   b peace
7 The poet .... the voice affect him.
   a lets   b doesn't let

D Work in pairs and discuss the questions.

1 What do you think is the overall message of the poem? What emotions does it describe?
2 Is this something you can relate to? Why/Why not?
3 Which of the extracts in Ex 2A could this poem be based on?

GRAMMAR

no matter

5 A 🔊 **3.09** | Complete the lines from the poem in Ex 4A with one word. Listen and check.

1 No matter .... I say, it's never right.

2 No matter .... I meet, there's always fright ...

3 'Cos no matter .... I feel, you always try your best ...

4 No matter .... I choose, all you want to do is shout ...

5 But no matter .... your voice belongs to me ...

B Look at lines 1–5 in Ex 5A and answer the questions.

1 In lines 1–4, does *no matter* mean something is true or not true whatever the situation?
2 In line 5, does *no matter* mean it's important or not important?
3 What kind of words follow *no matter*?
4 Are these words usually followed by an infinitive, verb + *-ing* or a clause?

C Match the sentence beginnings (1–5) with the endings (a–e). What do you notice about the position of *no matter* in a sentence?

1 No matter how often
2 I can't rest now, no matter that
3 No matter what time
4 You can't go in there, no matter
5 No matter how hard

a I'm tired.
b who you are.
c it is, call me.
d I try, I still never win.
e I tell her, she never listens!

D Learn and practise. Go to the Grammar Bank.

⏩ page 117 **GRAMMAR BANK**

PRONUNCIATION
/t/ sound in the middle of words

6 A 🔊 **3.10** | Listen to six different speakers saying the sentence below. How many different ways of pronouncing /t/ in the middle of *matter* do you hear?

No matter what they do, they drive me up the wall.

B 🔊 **3.11** | Listen and complete the sentences with the words you hear.

1 ...., you always seem to find me!
2 .... that I'll miss the meeting.
3 I'm not sure I'm free tomorrow, ...
4 ...., I can't seem to stop eating!
5 I know I'll get good service here, ...
6 I'll be there, ...

C Complete the poem *No matter* with your own ideas so that it's true for you.

D Work in pairs. Take turns to read your poem aloud. Do you both pronounce *matter* the same or differently?

SPEAKING

7 A Think of a situation which caused you to feel these emotions. Choose three of the situations to talk about.

amusement annoyance/anger anxiety/nerves desperation excitement fear happiness pride sadness/feeling fed up

B Make notes on the points below for each of your three situations. Think about how you can use the idiomatic phrases in this lesson and *no matter* when telling a partner about them.

- when and where it was
- what happened
- how you felt before and during the situation
- why specifically you felt these ways
- how you reacted and why
- how you feel about it looking back now

C Follow the steps below. Find out if your partners have ever experienced the same thing as you and if so, if they felt the same.

1 Work in pairs. Take turns to tell each other about your first situation.
2 Work with a new partner. Take turns to tell each other about your second situation.
3 Work with a new partner again. Take turns to tell each other about your third situation.

D Work with a final new partner. Tell each other about whose situation you:
- found the most interesting and why.
- can relate to the most and why.
- would like to be in and why.

No matter

No matter how often I ....,
I still can't get it right.

No matter how much I ....,
it still brings me delight.

No matter when ....,
it makes me tear my hair out.

No matter how little I have to ....,
it's a real pain.

No matter who ....,
it makes my day.

3C Carrot or stick?

HOW TO ... | engage with other people's views
VOCABULARY | persuading and motivating
PRONUNCIATION | intonation: responding tactfully

VOCABULARY

persuading and motivating

1 A Work in pairs. What do you think encourages people to do the things below?

- spend a lot of time revising before an exam
- follow rules and laws, even if they don't agree with them
- go to the gym or do exercise
- work hard at a job
- choose environmentally friendly products

B Think about your answers to the questions in Ex 1A. Discuss the questions (1–3) in pairs.

1 Which of your ideas are based on people getting a reward if they do something?
2 Which ideas are based on the fear of something bad happening if they don't do it?
3 Which do you think has a stronger effect on people – the promise of a reward or the fear of something bad?

2 A Read the forum post and the comments. Which of the situations have you experienced? Which of the ideas do you agree with?

B Look at the verbs in bold in the forum post and comments. Which verb or verbs suggest the idea of:

1 persuading someone gently? (x2)
2 tricking someone in order to persuade them?
3 using logical arguments to persuade someone?
4 being the reason why someone does something? (x2)
5 gradually getting someone to accept your opinion?
6 persuading someone by using strong or aggressive arguments?

C Work in pairs. Discuss the questions.

1 When was the last time you reasoned with someone to persuade them to do something?
2 Can you think of any examples of adverts that try to manipulate people by making them feel they will be missing out?
3 What is the best way to coax someone into doing something they are nervous about?
4 What do you think drives some people to work harder than most others?

D Learn and practise. Go to the Vocabulary Bank.

▶ page 136 **VOCABULARY BANK** persuading and motivating

 Max278 ♡ 112 💬 22

I'm studying psychology and have to write an essay on 'carrot and stick' approaches to persuading people. I'd love to know your views – is it better to **coax** people into doing things by offering rewards or **pressurise** them by threatening some kind of punishment if they don't do it?

 LizM ♡ 87 💬 15

@Max278 I'm a teacher, and rewards definitely work better with kids. I try to **reason with** them and get them to see the benefits of working hard. If I can **win** them **over** and gain their trust, they're much more likely to put more time into their studies.

 Pete2000 ♡ 56 💬 5

@Max278 I've just started a new job and I know I have to prove myself, otherwise I'll be out of work. That fear definitely **motivates** me to try hard.

 LM097 ♡ 32 💬 0

@Max278 I'm a student and, for me, the reward is everything. A qualification and a good job – that's what **drives** me to spend long hours at the library!

 Niamo'H ♡ 78 💬 2

@Max278 The promise of a free gift will always **entice** me to buy something, so I guess I can never resist a reward!

 MikeOToole ♡ 11 💬 0

@Max278 I hate it when people try to make me do something by making me feel bad. A lot of adverts **manipulate** people into buying certain products by making them feel they'll be missing out if they don't get them. I think that's wrong.

How to ...

engage with other people's views

3A 🔊 **3.12 | Listen to a discussion between staff in a cinema. Answer the questions.**

1 What do they want to persuade customers to do?

2 What rewards and punishments do they suggest?

3 What do they agree in the end?

B 🔊 **3.12 | Complete the sentences from the conversation with the words in the box. Then listen again and check.**

alternatively	coming	disadvantage	effective
logic	neat	other	practical	sense	suggesting

1 I can see where you're _____ **from**, but **on a** _____ **level**, we can't really start going in to ask people to leave halfway through a film.

2 I can see the _____ **in that**, but **on the** _____ **hand**, we don't want to reduce prices too much, do we?

3 I can see why you're _____ a tough approach, Tali, but … **It might be more** _____ **to** offer a reward rather than a punishment.

4 **That makes** _____ . So, what kind of reward would you suggest?

5 **That's quite a** _____ idea. But **one** _____ **of that would be** that it would be quite expensive for the cinema.

6 Yes, it would certainly win the customers over. _____ , **what about** combining a carrot and a stick – a reward and a punishment?

C Decide if the phrases in bold in Ex 3B are a) engaging with someone else's view or b) making a countersuggestion.

D Learn and practise. Go to the Grammar Bank.

▶▶ **page 118 GRAMMAR BANK**

PRONUNCIATION

intonation: responding tactfully

4A 🔊 **3.13 | Listen to the sentences. At the end of the phrase in bold, does the speaker's voice go down or stay high?**

1 **I can see where you're coming from**, but on a practical level, we can't really start going in to ask people to leave halfway through a film.

2 **I can see the logic in that**, but on the other hand, we don't want to reduce prices too much, do we?

3 **I can see why you're suggesting a tough approach, Tali**, but if they've already paid for their tickets, then it's potentially creating a bit of a conflict.

B Choose the correct words to complete the rule.

We use a **high / low** pitch at the end of the phrase to indicate that we understand someone's point of view, but we **agree / don't agree** with it.

C Work in pairs. Take turns to read out the opinions. Respond by engaging with your partner's idea, then making a countersuggestion.

1 I think we should ban all phones from the cinema.

2 We should put up notices asking people to switch off their phones.

3 We could offer a free snack to people if they switch off their phones.

SPEAKING

5A Read the Future Skills box and do the task.

FUTURE SKILLS

Communication

In a group discussion, it is important to listen carefully to what other people are saying, so you can engage with their ideas. This is sometimes called 'active listening'.

Work in pairs. How can you show people that you are listening to their ideas?

B Work in groups. Read the three situations and choose one to discuss, or think of your own situation.

1 You are flatmates and you also play in a band together. You all work during the day, so you like to do your band practice in the evening, but your neighbour is always complaining about the noise. You want to persuade them to be more tolerant.

2 You work in the same café or restaurant. You are all punctual, but other members of staff are always late for work, which means that you work harder. You want to motivate them to arrive on time.

3 You help look after a community garden in your area. A lot of people enjoy the garden, but there is always a lot of litter, which spoils it for everyone. You want to persuade people to use the litter bins that are already provided.

C Work individually. Think about the situation you chose and think of some possible ways to persuade people. Think about 'carrots' and 'sticks'.

6A In your groups, discuss the situation you chose in Ex 5B. Try to agree on the best way forward.

B Tell the class your ideas. How many groups decided on 'carrots' and how many decided on 'sticks'? Were you good active listeners?

MEDIATION SKILLS

asking the right questions

encourage others to elaborate

▶▶ **page 147 MEDIATION BANK**

3D BBC Street Interviews

Role models

VOCABULARY | describing inspiring people
SPEAKING | describe an inspiring person
WRITING | a biography

Sarmini

Kieran

Camille

Gerry

Tunnvane

PREVIEW

1 Work in pairs and discuss the questions.

1 What kinds of people do you think inspire others? Why?

2 Which of these types of people have most inspired you in your life?

Q1: Who has inspired you in your life?

Q2: What makes a good role model?

VIEW

2A ▶ Watch the interviews. What inspiring people or role models do the people mention? Which person's description of a role model is the most similar to yours? Why?

B ▶ Watch the first part of the interviews again. Complete the descriptions with one word.

1 Sarmini's parents push her to be ....

2 Camille's father gives his family a lot of ....

3 Tunnvane says Shackleton taught her to change her .... if it can no longer be achieved.

4 Gerry says Oprah overcame the .... involved with being a black woman in the USA.

5 Kieran's science teacher helped him to be accepted into ....

6 Kwame's parents were there for him when .... got in his way.

C ▶ Watch the second part of the interviews again. Note down at least one characteristic that each person gives when describing a role model.

Kwame

VOCABULARY

describing inspiring people

3 A Complete the extracts from the interviews with the words and phrases in the box.

> authentically encouraging enthusiastic
> humble limits rubs off on strive
> understanding

1 They make me _____ to be better all the time.
2 She's come from very _____ beginnings.
3 He was really _____ and helped me a lot to get into university.
4 My parents … pushed me to my _____ …
5 … people who live _____ .
6 Being _____ about what you do I think helps.
7 When someone enjoys the things that they do, that _____ other people.
8 … being _____ of the other people, of the individual …

B Match the words and phrases (1–8) in Ex 3A with the meanings (a–h).

a is transferred to
b make a great effort
c being yourself and not what others expect
d from a low social class or position
e giving you confidence
f the edges of my ability
g aware of other people's feelings
h showing a lot of interest or excitement

C Work in pairs. Who do you know that you could describe using the words or phrases in Ex 3A?

My older cousin's love of travel has really rubbed off on me. It's inspired me to explore new places, too.

D Discuss the questions in small groups.

1 Should you always try to live authentically? How can you do this?
2 Do you think your enjoyment of something you like has rubbed off on others? Who? How?
3 How enthusiastic were your teachers at school? Was this important to you?
4 Should we always strive to be better? Is it ever OK not to?

SPEAKING

describe an inspiring person

4 A 🔊 **3.14 |** Listen to someone talking about an inspiring person they know. Answer the questions.

1 Who is the person?
2 What was he like?
3 How was he inspiring?

B 🔊 **3.14 |** Listen again. Number the Key phrases in the order you hear them (1–5).

> ### KEY PHRASES
>
> Someone that/who (has) influenced me greatly is …
> I'd describe … as …
> Some people might say he/she/they … but I see/saw him/her/them as …
> He/She/They inspired me by/to …
> The main thing he/she/they taught me was …

5 A You're going to describe a person you know who has inspired you in your life. Make notes on these things.

- who the person is
- how you know them
- the characteristics of the person
- how the person inspired you
- the most important thing you learnt from them

B Work in pairs. Take turns to describe the person who inspired you, using your notes in Ex 5A and the Key phrases to help you. What do the two people have in common? How are they different?

WRITING

a biography

6 A Work in pairs. How are the people in the box inspiring? Which three do you think are the most inspiring? Why?

> entrepreneurs environmentalists explorers
> humanitarians musicians politicians
> scientists social media celebrities

B Discuss the questions with your partner.

1 What explorers do you know?
2 How did these explorers inspire people?
3 What characteristics do you think an explorer typically has? Why?

C Write a biography. Go to the Writing Bank.

▶▶ page 106 **WRITING BANK**

GRAMMAR

as if/as though

1 Choose the correct options to complete the sentences.

1 I expressed my opinion, and everyone looked at me as though I **am / was** mad.

2 Are you OK? You look as if you **'re / were** ill.

3 Sasha and George soon became close, as if they **knew / had known** each other for years.

4 Nathan stood up, as though he **suddenly remembered / had suddenly remembered** something.

5 I'm so tired! I feel as if I **haven't slept / hadn't slept** for a week!

6 Shay picked up his phone, as if **making / to make** a call.

7 She was staring into space **like / as if** deep in thought.

8 Jack seems **like / though** he's very good at his job.

no matter

2A Complete the online post by adding *no matter* and a relative pronoun.

Alex F_99
Posted 13:54 | 2 days ago

Writer's block

Help! I've got writer's block! I've got an essay to write, but ¹ _____ long I sit here, I can't seem to get started. My mind just keeps wandering. ² _____ I do, I can't seem to focus on the task in hand. I've tried working in different parts of the flat, but ³ _____ I set up my laptop, I have the same problem! This is the first time this has ever happened to me. I can usually at least get started, ⁴ _____ tired I am. And if I get into the essay, I can usually carry on, ⁵ _____ I don't even stop for food. Does anyone have any ideas? I need to get this essay done today, ⁶ _____ !

💬 08   🔁 00   ♡ 16   ✉

B Work in pairs. Have you ever experienced writer's block? How did you solve the problem?

VOCABULARY

3A Choose the correct words to complete the opinions.

1 A lot of online series start out being quite realistic, but they become less **frustrating / convincing** as the story develops.

2 I really don't enjoy documentaries about other people's real-life problems. I find them too **overwhelming / fulfilling**.

3 When I'm tired, I just want to watch something that's light and **disturbing / entertaining**.

4 Most reality TV shows **drive / send** me up the wall! They're so annoying!

5 I don't understand why people enjoy being **scared / terrified** stiff by watching horror movies!

6 A good comedy show is the best thing when you're feeling **low / down** in the dumps.

7 I love watching shows about ambitious people who have a lot of energy and **pressure / drive**.

8 I think cookery shows are great because they **motivate / manipulate** me to try new recipes.

B Do you agree with the statements in Ex 3A? Why/Why not? Tell a partner.

4A Choose the correct options (A–C) to complete the blog post.

Extreme inspiration

A while ago, I started to feel that my life was dull and I was ¹ _____ to death of the daily routines. I felt I needed to do something different – not necessarily something ² _____ or life-changing, just something different. A friend suggested I have a go at one of his favourite extreme sports – street luge. The luge is basically a sledge on wheels that you lie on and use to ride downhill on steep roads. It took some ³ _____ , but eventually I agreed to give it a go. My friend provided some basic training, but even so, as the day approached, I had ⁴ _____ in my stomach day and night. ⁵ _____ what I did, I couldn't relax. What if I was injured in a ⁶ _____ accident? When the day came, excitement took over and I forgot my fears. The experience didn't disappoint – I felt as if I ⁷ _____ as my luge sped down the deserted street. And how has it left me feeling? Definitely more confident and ⁸ _____ to try new things – and maybe inspire others to do the same!

1 A sick	B ill	C fed up
2 A steep	B long	C profound
3 A drive	B coaxing	C manipulation
4 A butterflies	B bees	C flies
5 A Matter	B No matter	C It matters
6 A tragic	B gloomy	C dark
7 A had flown	B am flying	C was flying
8 A sensitive	B devoted	C eager

B 🔊 **R3.01** | Listen and check.

C Work in pairs. What new or extreme activity do you think you might be inspired to try? Why?

image

4

VLOGS

Q: How important is image to you?

1 ▶ Watch the video. What interesting things do people say about image being important to them (or not)?

2 How important is your image to you? Why?

Global Scale of English

LEARNING OBJECTIVES

4A READING | Read a guide to taking legal, social and ethical photos: rules; photography

Pronunciation: *should* in connected speech

Evaluate a proposal: uses of *should*

4B LISTENING | Listen to a talk about place branding: advertising

Pronunciation: contractions: *'ve been, 'll've been*

Give a presentation on a rebranding idea for a place that you know: the continuous aspect

Write a report on creating a rebranding campaign

4C HOW TO … | steer a conversation towards a topic: skills, abilities and experience

Pronunciation: intonation: sounding professional

4D BBC PROGRAMME | Understand a TV programme about why people buy products

Present a product: marketing

Write a product blurb

4A 'Selfie-expression'

GRAMMAR | uses of *should*
VOCABULARY | rules; photography
PRONUNCIATION | *should* in connected speech

READING

1 A Work in pairs and discuss the questions.

1 How many photos do you think you take each week?
2 What do you take them of and why?
3 What would prevent you from uploading an image online?

B Work in pairs. Discuss if it's appropriate to take photographs in the following situations. Does it make a difference if they're selfies?

1 at a museum
2 during a meal with others
3 at the scene of an emergency
4 in the classroom
5 at a historical site
6 in all rooms of a home
7 during a wedding ceremony
8 of a famous person

2 A Read the guide to taking legal, social and ethical photos. Which of the situations in Ex 1B does it say are inappropriate? Why?

B Read the guide again and answer the questions.

1 What should visitors to public places do before taking photos? Why?
2 What does the writer advise when taking photographs of strangers? Why?
3 For what purpose does the writer describe a hypothetical situation of a person being photographed sitting in the street?
4 What is the writer's view of selfies taken at weddings or emergency situations? Why?

3 A Match the words in bold in the guide with the meanings (1–6).

1 do things quickly without thinking of possible problems
2 different from what is normal or expected
3 preferring not to share their personal lives with others
4 very poor
5 wanting to know about something
6 determined not to change your mind

B Do the words you found in Ex 3A create a positive or negative connotation?

C Match the words you found in Ex 3A with their synonyms in the box. Do they have similar or different connotations?

deprived   determined   nosy   secretive   spontaneous   unusual

D Work in pairs. Has the guide taught you anything new about taking photos in the situations in Ex 1B? Which of the rules do you think you need to be more aware of?

GRAMMAR

uses of *should*

4 A Match the extracts from the guide (1–6) with the uses of *should* (a–e). One is used twice.

1 To avoid fines, you **should** always research the laws of places you visit.
2 So, the first question to ask yourself is … '**Should** I be taking this photo?'
3 Checking with a local **should** stop you upsetting anyone.
4 **Should** you do this, it's unlikely you'll be breaking any law.
5 … they **should** never have been taken in the first place.
6 If you **should** get the urge to take a selfie when in public, be absolutely sure it's the right thing to do.

a express likelihood/possibility
b express a criticism of an action
c give advice/a suggestion
d express what is ideal/desired
e express a condition

B Answer the questions about the extracts in Ex 4A.

1 In which extract is a passive form used?
2 In which extract is a continuous form used?
3 Extracts 4 and 6 have the same use. Which do you imagine is more formal in tone? What is the difference in form?

C Learn and practise. Go to the Grammar Bank.

▶ page 119 **GRAMMAR BANK**

Photography: legal, social and ethical rules

With phone cameras at our fingertips, it's not only professionals who are photographers these days. We all are. This means every one of us needs to pay attention to the legal, social and ethical rules that surround the taking of photos, especially in public places.

1. Laws and cultural sensitivities

In most countries, taking photographs in public spaces is legal, as is taking photographs of private property from a public space. However, this isn't the case everywhere. To avoid fines, you should always research the laws of places you visit, and always be mindful of where you are before you start snapping away.

Additional places where photography may be illegal include government buildings, entertainment spaces such as theatres and cinemas, and historical and cultural sites. While this should be made clear to visitors, check if in doubt. Note that some countries have banned photography at popular tourist sites because of **impulsive** visitors causing accidents when taking all-important selfies. Again, ask if you're unsure.

Of course, legalities are only one consideration when taking photos in public spaces. What might be perfectly legal may not be culturally sensitive; something particularly true of historical and cultural sites. So, the first question to ask yourself is not 'How can I get the best photo?' but 'Should I be taking this photo?' Checking with a local should stop you upsetting anyone.

2. Permission

When snapping pictures in public places, it's hard not to capture passers-by in the process, but sometimes we purposely put a stranger front and centre because they make an interesting photo. Should you do this, it's unlikely you'll be breaking any law (in most countries at least), but there are ethical considerations. For this reason, it's best to ask permission. If you're worried that asking permission will cause the person to pose rather than act naturally, which might negatively affect the photo, you could take the photo and then show it to the person and ask permission after the fact. If people refuse to let you use the photo, don't assume they're being **stubborn** – some people are **private** and have the right to be. And remember that taking photos of children you don't know is frowned upon in most cultures.

3. Avoiding exploitative photographs

Being **inquisitive** is considered to be a positive trait in a photographer, as is wanting to learn about social differences and raising awareness of a social issue. However, one unwritten rule in street photography is never to take a photo of someone in a vulnerable state. Another is to always take a photo that truly represents the situation. An image that would break both rules is one of an **impoverished** and hopeless-looking person sitting in the street when in fact they spent much of the day in jovial conversation with passers-by while making a living selling food. I've known photographers to share images like this when they should never have been taken in the first place.

4. Respecting nature

A fundamental rule in nature photography is never to cause harm to wildlife or the environment you come across. Getting close to natural phenomena has been known to cause damage, but more concerning is the harm such a disturbance can cause animals. It can force them into areas they do not want to be, for example, which can affect their food supplies. In some instances, animals rush to get away from people and injure themselves in the process. It's best to keep a safe distance and use the zoom feature on your phone.

5. Selfies

No matter whether you're taking a photograph of yourself or someone else, all the considerations above apply, but there are some additional social and ethical rules to consider when taking a selfie. Putting yourself in the photo takes the focus away from what you're photographing and places it on you. A wedding guest who takes a selfie as the bride walks down the aisle is a classic example. Worse is a selfie taken at the scene of a crime, accident or emergency. It undermines the situation's seriousness and crosses an ethical line. If you should get the urge to take a selfie when in public, be absolutely sure it's the right thing to do. It might not get the reception you expect if you share it with others. People may feel it's, at best, a little **odd** and, at worst, very selfish.

So, as we've seen, it's important to take care when taking photos in public to avoid breaking any privacy laws or social and ethical rules, but as long as we're all mindful of these, there should still be plenty of opportunities to take amazing photos.

PRONUNCIATION
should in connected speech

5 A 🔊 **4.01** | Listen to how *should* and *shouldn't have* are pronounced in each sentence. Choose which pronunciation (a or b) you hear.

1 You should make sure you check first.
   a shud   **b** shub

2 Everything should be OK.
   a shub   **b** shud

3 Should anyone wish to take photos, they must seek permission.
   a shud   **b** shub

4 If they should give us permission, we'll be happy.
   a shud   **b** shug

5 You should post it online.
   a shud   **b** shub

6 They shouldn't have posted it online.
   a shouldn't have   **b** shouldn't 'av

B Complete the information with the words in the box.

> change   difficult   omitted   similar

When two sounds are ¹_____ to pronounce one after the other due to the position of our lips, tongue and jaw, the first or second sound might be ²_____ completely, or we might ³_____ the first sound to one that is the same as or more ⁴_____ to the second one.

C 🔊 **4.01** | Listen again. What happens to the /d/ sound in *should* in the sentences in Ex 5A? In which sentence is another sound omitted? Why?

6 A Complete the prompts with your own ideas.
1 Anyone who likes taking photos should get …
2 A photo should make …
3 I should have remembered to take a photo …
4 I shouldn't have shared a photo/photos …
5 If I should take a really amazing photo, …

B Work in pairs. Take turns to say your sentences in Ex 6A. Pay attention to your pronunciation of *should*.

VOCABULARY
rules

7 A 🔊 **4.02** | Listen to a panellist on a radio panel discussion putting forward a proposal related to photography. Answer the questions.
1 What's the proposal?
2 Is the other panellist for or against the idea?
3 What reasons are given for and against the proposal?

B Decide if the definitions of the words in bold are correct or the opposite in meaning.
1 If photos are **restricted** to one a day, they are limited.
2 If we are **prohibited** from uploading two photos a day, we have permission to do it.
3 If worry about images we post is **eliminated**, we get rid of it.
4 If a rule is hard to **implement**, it's difficult to put into action.
5 If companies have to **impose** a rule, they have to stop people following it.
6 When a company **regulates** a rule, they control it.
7 If a rule **deters** people from posting photos, it makes them do it more.
8 If all photos on social media are **abolished**, people can start to upload them.

C Choose the correct words to complete the proposal.

Phone manufacturers should ¹**deter** / **restrict** the number of photos we can take each day. If they ²**regulated** / **prohibited** us from taking more than a few, we'd become more creative and it would ³**eliminate** / **impose** the need to save photos we never look at again. Of course, manufacturers might not want to ⁴**impose** / **prohibit** such a rule on customers. If they did, they would need to work together to ⁵**abolish** / **implement** such a rule. However, it should be easy to ⁶**regulate** / **implement**, as companies can just stop our devices from working. Of course, we don't want to ⁷**abolish** / **impose** photo-taking completely, just ⁸**deter** / **eliminate** people from taking hundreds.

D Work in groups. What are the pros and cons of the proposals in Ex 7A and Ex 7C? What are your views? Use vocabulary from Ex 7B.

E Learn and practise. Go to the Vocabulary Bank.

▶▶ page 136 **VOCABULARY BANK** photography

SPEAKING

8 A Work in groups. Student A: Go to page 141. Student B: Go to page 142. Student C: Go to page 143. Prepare your proposal.

B In your group, take turns to present your proposals. Then, discuss the benefits and problems of each proposal. Decide on the one you believe would be the most beneficial should it be implemented.

C Share your chosen proposal with the class. Do you all agree?

4B Creating a brand

GRAMMAR | the continuous aspect
VOCABULARY | advertising
PRONUNCIATION | contractions: *'ve been*, *'ll've been*

LISTENING

1 A Think about the cities in the box and what you know about them. Write one word to sum up the image that you think each one has.

> Cairo   Mexico City   New York   Paris   Tokyo

B Work in pairs. Discuss the questions and compare your ideas.

1 Have you been to any of the cities in Ex 1A?
2 Where do your ideas about their image come from?
3 Do you know any cities that have a problem with their image? Why?
4 Do you think a city can change its image or create its own brand? How?

2 A 🔊 4.03 | Listen to a talk about place branding. Choose the best summary of the talk (a–c).

The speaker:

a explains the concept of place branding and gives some examples of places which have benefited from it.

b discusses the advantages and disadvantages of place branding, using examples from around the world.

c shows how cities and countries often choose to use branding rather than trying to solve problems such as crime.

B 🔊 4.03 | Listen again. Are the statements True (T) or False (F)?

1 Cities and countries sometimes use branding to change outdated opinions that people have of them.
2 Unions in New York City funded the branding campaign in the 1970s.
3 New York and Paris both successfully used visual symbols in their branding.
4 Chile has focused on encouraging different groups to all use a similar approach to marketing the country.
5 The speaker mentions El Raval to make the point that even less-known areas of a city can be marketed to tourists.
6 The New York campaign of 2006 was necessary because too many tourists were avoiding Manhattan.

C 🔊 4.04 | It is important to understand the assumptions in a speaker's mind when they ask rhetorical questions. Listen to three rhetorical questions from the talk. Choose the sentence which expresses the assumption behind each one (a–c).

1 a All places are willing to invest in branding and marketing.

b It is difficult for cities and countries to compete and attract tourists and investment without branding and marketing.

c There are other ways apart from branding and marketing that cities and countries can use to attract tourists and investment.

2 a The campaign to promote New York City nearly didn't happen.

b New York needs a new campaign now, to move forward.

c The campaign to promote New York City changed the course of the city's history.

3 a There was a danger that some people might not recognise the image.

b Everyone was sure to recognise the image.

c It is not important for people to recognise the image.

D Work in pairs. Discuss the questions.

1 Which examples of rebranding mentioned do you think are the most interesting or effective? Why?

2 Do you know of any other places that have tried to change their image? Did they succeed?

VOCABULARY

advertising

3A Read the extracts from the talk (1–6). Match the words in bold with the meanings (a–h).

1 The result was the iconic phrase 'I ♥ New York' … which can still be seen on T-shirts and other **merchandise** today.

2 … the huge advantage of such a simple logo like this is that it can be used everywhere, from **billboards** on the walls of buildings to … information **flyers** for tourists.

3 … images of the logo might also appear online and **go viral**, reaching an audience of millions.

4 In 2005, it ran a campaign based around the **slogan** 'Chile: All ways surprising.'

5 Despite the **hype** of the campaign, it was not as successful as hoped …

6 In 2006 there was a **push** to promote other parts of the city and **target** a new generation of tourists

a to direct advertising at particular people

b goods which are sold

c a short advertising phrase that is easy to remember

d large posters advertising something

e to become very popular online and spread to a lot of people

f a big effort to achieve something

g small leaflets which contain information

h intensive publicity to promote something

B Complete the questions with the correct form of the words in bold in Ex 3A.

1 What tourist .... have you bought on holiday?

2 Do you notice huge advertising .... when you are travelling around a city?

3 Can you think of a new product recently that generated a lot of .... ?

4 What makes an advertising .... easy to remember?

5 Why do you think that some videos .... and become extremely popular?

6 Can you think of any advertisements that .... young people?

C Work in pairs. Ask and answer the questions in Ex 3B.

GRAMMAR

the continuous aspect

4A Read the extracts from the talk. Match the verb tenses in the box with the verb forms in bold.

> past continuous   past perfect continuous
> present continuous   present perfect continuous
> future continuous   future perfect continuous

1 … unions **had been running** a campaign called 'Welcome to Fear City'.

2 … the country … **has been using** a less direct and more long-term approach.

3 … cities and countries **are** increasingly **finding** themselves in a similar position.

4 **Will** the campaigns I've talked about still **be running** in twenty years' time?

5 It **was experiencing** financial problems and levels of crime in the city were sky high.

6 It's strange to think that soon people **will have been wearing** those famous 'I ♥ New York' T-shirts for over sixty years.

B Complete the rule with the words in the box. There is one word you don't need.

> complete   duration   result   temporary

The continuous aspect focuses on the .... of an action. It often shows that an action is .... and not ....

C Learn and practise. Go to the Grammar Bank.

▶▶ page 120 **GRAMMAR BANK**

PRONUNCIATION
contractions: *'ve been, 'll've been*

5A 🔊 **4.05** | Listen to four sentences using continuous tenses. What do you notice about the pronunciation of the auxiliary verbs?

B 🔊 **4.06** | Listen and complete the sentences with the words you hear.

1 We .... promoting this area of the city for over ten years.

2 Hopefully, they .... selling a lot of merchandise.

3 Soon, she .... living there for ten years!

4 We can ask them what they .... doing.

C Complete the sentences with your own ideas. Then say your sentences to a partner.

1 Recently, people in my town have been campaigning to ....

2 .... is a place I love. I've been visiting it for ....

3 A restaurant in my town that I love is .... Soon, they'll have been serving food for .... years.

4 One problem in my town is .... I hope it'll have been sorted soon!

SPEAKING

6A You are going to plan and present a rebranding campaign for a place that you know. Think about the place and answer the questions. Make notes for your presentation.

- In what ways could it benefit from rebranding? What people has it been struggling to attract?

- Which people would your rebranding target?
  (businesses, tourists, students, etc.)

- What positive aspects of the place could you focus on?
  (history, heritage, culture, etc.)

- Can you think of a good slogan or logo to promote the place?

- How would you use the branding to promote the new image?
  (merchandise, billboards, etc.)

B Read the Future Skills box and do the task.

FUTURE SKILLS
Communication

In a presentation, we often give factual information that supports our opinion. It is important to present this information in an accurate and objective way.

Look at your notes for your presentation. Which parts are factual and which parts are your opinions? Think about how you can present the factual information in an objective way.

C Work in groups. Take turns to present your ideas to each other. Then discuss the questions.

1 What are the advantages of each campaign?
2 Do any of the campaigns have any weaknesses? What are they?
3 Which campaigns do you think will be the most effective? Why?

D Tell the class which of your campaigns you think will be the most effective and why.

WRITING

a report: creating a rebranding campaign

7A Read the report. What is it about? What does it recommend?

Plan to create a rebranding campaign for Seabay

1 ....
Seabay local authority believes that a rebranding campaign could bring benefits to the town. The aim would be to rebrand Seabay as a modern, fun holiday destination for young people. The town is currently seen as an old-fashioned seaside resort, with little to attract younger visitors. Rebranding would create a new image of Seabay as a fun place to visit, with a range of tourist amenities including entertainment, outdoor activities and shopping. The campaign would take place over three years and the total cost is estimated to be €200,000.

2 ....
Tourist numbers in the town have been falling for the last twenty years and, as a result, unemployment has been growing. Many traditional industries in the area, such as fishing, have also been declining. It is therefore vital that the town attracts a new generation of visitors to bring in much-needed revenue. Creating a fashionable new brand offers a realistic way to target a new generation of visitors and boost the local economy, without completely changing the character of the place.

3 ....
Although a rebranding campaign would offer many benefits for the town, some opposition has been expressed, especially by older residents, who enjoy the peaceful atmosphere in the town and feel that it could be overwhelmed if visitor numbers suddenly increase. There has also been criticism from younger people in the area who would like more focus on attracting modern industries to the town which would offer well-paid work, rather than concentrating solely on tourism.

4 ....
The plan to rebrand the town seems to offer good value for money and a positive way forward for the town. However, it is clear that there is a need for greater consultation with local people to ensure a broad base of support from the population.

B Add the headings (a–d) to the report.
 a Advantages of the plan   c Overview of the plan
 b Conclusions and recommendations   d Opposition to the plan

C Read the report again. Find the formal phrases used to express the ideas below. Which of the phrases you found use passive structures?
1 At the moment, a lot of people think that the town is …
2 We think it will probably cost …
3 The town really needs to attract …
4 Some people have said they are against the plans.
5 We need to ask more local people what they think.

D Write a report. Go to the Writing Bank.

▶ page 106 **WRITING BANK**

4C Presenting yourself

HOW TO ... | steer a conversation towards a topic
VOCABULARY | skills, abilities and experience
PRONUNCIATION | intonation: sounding professional

VOCABULARY

skills, abilities and experience

1 A Read the dictionary definitions of 'humble' and 'brag'. What do you think it means if someone humblebrags?

humble (adj) not considering yourself or your ideas to be as important as other people's

brag (v) to talk too proudly about what you have done, what you own, etc.

B 🔊 **4.07** | Listen and check your ideas. Do you know anyone who humblebrags? Why do you think people find it annoying?

2 A 🔊 **4.08** | Listen to six people talking in job interviews. Decide if each person is humblebragging (H), plain bragging (B) or being neutral (N).

B Read the extracts from Ex 2A and look at the words and phrases in bold. Which ones mean you have a high level of skill? Which mean you have a low level of skill?

1 I'm already **proficient** at computer programming.
2 I'm quite **inexperienced** in Portuguese.
3 Everyone seems to think I'm **competent** in translating.
4 I'm a **trained** teacher.
5 I'm quite **handy with** most tools.
6 I'm happy to work with **unskilled** assistants.
7 I thought the new job would **be beyond** me.
8 I thought I'd be **hopeless** at it.

3 A Think of something you are:

- proficient at/in.
- inexperienced in.
- handy with.
- competent in/at.
- hopeless at.

B Work in pairs. Say your answers to Ex 3A. Can your partner guess your level of skill or experience?

C Learn and practise. Go to the Vocabulary Bank.

▶▶ page 137 **VOCABULARY BANK** skills, abilities and experience

How to ...

steer a conversation towards a topic

4 A 🔊 **4.09** | Listen to two extracts from job interviews and answer the questions.

1 Do you think any of the candidates brag or humblebrag? Give your reasons.
2 After which questions (a–f) do the interviewees steer the conversation to something they want to talk about?
   a Do you have experience of customer service?
   b What do you think is the best way to handle difficult customers?
   c You don't have any formal qualifications in business. Do you think this would be an issue for you?
   d What skills from that job do you think are relevant to a job in sales?
   e What did you enjoy about working in the hotel?
   f There are demanding sales targets each month. How do you think you would cope with this pressure?

B 🔊 **4.10** | Complete the sentences from the interview with the words in the box. Then listen and check.

> broad   can   interesting   just   point   talk   thought

1 That's quite a(n) _____ topic.
2 Perhaps I could just _____ about one incident that I dealt with recently.
3 The most important _____ here is that I'm committed to ongoing training.
4 That's a(n) _____ question.
5 What I _____ say is that in any customer-facing role, the relationship with the customer is the most important thing.
6 I've _____ about this quite a lot.
7 Can I _____ say that I'm an extremely hard worker and I'm highly motivated to do well at my job.

C Which phrases in Ex 4B give the speaker time before they answer? Which ones help the speaker steer the conversation towards things they want to talk about?

D Learn and practise. Go to the Grammar Bank.

▶▶ page 121 **GRAMMAR BANK**

PRONUNCIATION
intonation: sounding professional

5 A 🔊 **4.11** | Listen to three pairs of people talking in interviews. Which speaker (A or B) uses a greater range of intonation? Which speaker sounds more professional?

B Complete the rule with the words in the box.

exaggerate	narrow	neutral	wide

We use a ¹............ range of intonation in informal situations, especially when we want to ²............ or brag. We use a ³............ range of intonation to sound ⁴............ and professional.

C Work in pairs. Take turns to read out the sentences (1–6). Either sound informal and exaggerate, or sound neutral and professional. Can your partner guess which you are doing?

1 I've always had a lot of positive feedback from my colleagues and bosses.

2 I always get on well with my colleagues. I've never been in a situation in which I found it difficult to work with someone.

3 I'm very good at creative tasks. That's one of my main strengths.

4 I always work extremely hard to meet deadlines. I hate missing deadlines!

5 I'm a real people person. I love interacting with customers, even if they are rude or making a complaint. I almost always find a way to resolve the situation so the customer ends up with a smile on their face.

6 I don't have a lot of formal qualifications, but I have a lot of relevant experience from my previous two jobs and I am a very hard worker. If you give me a job to do, I'll make sure it gets done.

SPEAKING

6 A Look at the job adverts (A, B and C). Choose the job you would like to apply for and make notes on the skills and experience you have for that job.

A **Receptionist**   £ Top salary   🕐 Full-time   📍 Local   **Apply**

We are looking for a hotel receptionist for a busy city-centre hotel. The successful applicant will have at least two years' experience and will be a good team player. Good customer service skills are essential.

B **Summer camp assistant**   🕐 Temporary   📍 Local   **Apply**

Are you lively, outgoing and good at working with children? Why not spend the summer as an assistant at one of our summer camps? Applicants must be physically fit and enjoy working outdoors. If you are good at music or art, even better!

C **Project manager**   £ Top salary   🕐 Full-time   📍 Local   **Apply**

A relevant degree and management experience would be helpful. The successful candidate must be prepared to work hard to meet tight deadlines. Knowledge of French, Spanish or German would be an advantage.

B Work in pairs. Tell each other which job you have chosen and turn to page 142 to read the interview questions for your partner.

C Read the Future Skills box and do the activity.

FUTURE SKILLS
Interviewing

In a job interview, it is important to communicate the information about yourself that you want to get across. Sometimes this means that you may have to steer the conversation to the topics that *you* want to talk about.

Look at the examples of how people steer the conversation in Ex 4B again. Then look at the notes you prepared on your skills and experience in Ex 6A. Think about the questions your partner might ask and about how you can steer the conversation and get across the information you have prepared.

---

7 A In your pairs, take turns to interview each other.

B Give feedback to your partner. Answer the questions.

1 How well did they answer your questions?

2 Did they skilfully steer the conversation towards things they wanted to talk about?

3 How professional did they sound when talking about skills and experience?

4 Would you offer them the job? Why/Why not?

MEDIATION SKILLS
taking notes on a written text
relay information in a professional journal

▶▶ page 148 **MEDIATION BANK**

4D BBC Documentary
Branding and behaviour

VOCABULARY | marketing
SPEAKING | a presentation
WRITING | a product blurb

PREVIEW

1 A Work in pairs and answer the questions.

   1 What kinds of products do people use to maintain or improve their appearance?

   2 What other things can people do to maintain or improve their appearance?

B Read the programme information. What kinds of things do you think companies do to persuade people to buy beauty products?

The Truth About ... looking good

The Truth About ... is a documentary series in which reporters and experts carry out an in-depth investigation of issues that affect us all. In this episode, the topic is beauty products and the tactics that companies use to persuade us to buy them.

VIEW

2 A ▶ Watch the BBC video clip. Does it mention any of your ideas from Ex 1B?

B ▶ Watch the video again. Choose the correct words to complete the sentences.

   1 According to Dr Omar Yousef, people **understand** / **don't understand** why they buy products.

   2 In the experiment, the plan is to show consumers **two different products** / **the same product** in different packaging.

   3 In the first part of the experiment, **not many** / **a lot of** customers say they would buy the product.

   4 In the second part of the experiment, the product looks more **natural** / **scientific** and expensive.

   5 The product in the second part of the experiment is **more** / **less** popular with customers.

   6 Consumers **knew** / **didn't know** the real reason for the questionnaire.

   7 The questionnaire measured customers' levels of **anxiety** / **self-esteem** when deciding whether or not to buy.

   8 The luxury product makes people feel **better** / **not so good** about themselves, which makes them more likely to buy it.

VOCABULARY

marketing

3 A Work in pairs. Match the words in bold in the extracts from the video (1–8) with the meanings (a–h).

1 First up, we've put the cleanser in a **no-frills packaging** …

2 The product has been **given a makeover** …

3 When the face cleanser looked more **luxurious** …

4 What we tried to do was to make this product a **status product** …

5 [It] gives it this aura of **credibility**, confidence.

6 They thought this was simply **market research**.

7 … when you observe the **luxury products**, it's likely to drop your self-esteem …

8 … here are these gorgeous people and here is an **aspirational product**.

a products which are very expensive and good quality

b changed to look more attractive

c very plain, simple packaging

d a product which people believe shows they have reached a high level in society

e the quality of deserving to be trusted or believed

f a product which people feel they would like to own

g very expensive and good quality

h a study to find out information about how successful a product might be

B Work in pairs. Ask and answer the questions.

1 Does no-frills packaging put you off buying a product? Why?

2 What luxury products would you be prepared to pay more for? Why?

3 What aspirational products would you most like to buy? Why?

4 What products do you think need to be given a makeover? Why?

SPEAKING

a presentation

4 A 🔊 **4.12** | Listen to the start of a presentation for a new product. What is the product? How will it help people to feel healthier? Do you believe it will work?

B 🔊 **4.12** | Listen again and tick the Key phrases you hear.

> ### KEY PHRASES
>
> This revolutionary new product will …
> … will appeal to customers as …
> We see it as a/an … product because …
> The name … fits the product because …
> Our slogan will be …
> One of its unique features is …

5 A Work in pairs. You are going to present a new product to help people feel good about themselves and try to sell it to the class. Plan your product using the questions below to help you.

- Who is the product for?
- How will it make someone feel good about themselves?
- How is it different from other products on the market?
- What kind of product is it, e.g. a luxury or aspirational product?
- What are its strong points?
- What kind of packaging would be suitable?

B With your partner, plan your presentation. Remember, you need to try to sell your product, so be positive about it! Use the Key phrases to help you.

C Give your presentation to the class. Make notes on your classmates' products and ask questions to find out more.

D Which product was the most popular in the class? Why?

WRITING

a product blurb

6 A Work in pairs. Read the definition of 'blurb'. Which of the features (a–f) would you expect to find in a product blurb?

blurb /blɜː(r)b/ noun [countable]
a short description giving information about a book, new product, etc.

a an emphasis on quality

b criticism of competitor products

c persuasive language

d direct engagement with the reader

e detailed instructions on use

f a focus on the benefits

B Write a product blurb. Go to the Writing Bank.

▶▶ page 107 **WRITING BANK**

GRAMMAR

uses of *should*

1 A Choose the correct words to complete the sentences.

1 I'm so tired today. I should **turn / have turned** my phone off at 10 p.m. last night and not midnight.

2 I regularly feel that I should **be doing / have been done** something more productive, but can't find the motivation.

3 Should **choose someone / someone choose** to offer me chocolate, I will never refuse!

4 When I have a bad day, I tell myself that the next day should **be / be being** better.

5 My offer to do the ironing should not **be taken / take** lightly. I don't offer very often!

6 I should **have posted / have been posted** the first selfie I took and not bothered taking twenty-five more!

B Work in pairs. Which statements in Ex 1A can you relate to? Why? Why not the others?

the continuous aspect

2 A Complete the forum comment with the correct continuous form of the words in brackets.

Fidel@Yolo2
Posted 13:45 | 2 days ago

Town branding: we need your help!

Here at the town council, a team of people [1]............ (currently / work) on developing a brand for our town. This might seem more relevant to companies, but it's something that cities and towns [2]............ (do) for decades in order to appeal to visitors. We need to do the same. This week, the team are publishing a report they [3]............ (work) on for several months and it gives two key suggestions for the focus of the brand. The first is local industry. Our town [4]............ (manufacture) wool products for 150 years next year. We could base our brand on that history. The second suggestion is the diversity of people in the town and the resulting rich culture. We [5]............ (soon / invite) you to join us for a meeting to discuss this in the near future. Until then, please share your thoughts on the two options in the comments below.

💬 31   🔁 9   ♡ 168   ✉

B Tell your partner which of the two ideas in the forum comment you think is the best and why.

3 Complete the sentences with your own ideas to make them true for you. Share them with a partner.

1 Recently, I've been …

2 This time tomorrow, I'll …

3 I hope that by the end of the year, I'll … for a while.

VOCABULARY

4 A Complete the sentences with the words in the box. There are three words you don't need.

| abolish | blurred | competent | deter | hopeless |
| impose | pose | regulate | slogans | |

1 It's easy to create rules to control an industry but not so easy to .... them.

2 Kids under thirteen aren't supposed to use social media but that doesn't always .... them.

3 The best .... used in advertising are short and simple.

4 Few people are brilliant cooks, but most people are .... at making a simple meal.

5 It's better to admit if you're .... at something than pretend you can do it.

6 The government should .... a law on businesses that stops them from messaging staff out of working hours.

B Do you agree with the statements in Ex 4A? Why/Why not? Tell a partner.

5 A Complete the questions with one word.

1 Are you handy .... electronic gadgets?

2 Have you ever tried to use your fingers to zoom .... on a laptop or TV screen?

3 Have you or people you know had a video .... viral?

4 What kind of work are you inexperienced .... ?

5 What advertisement has created a lot of .... in your country in the past?

6 Are all the photos you take .... focus or are some .... of focus?

B Work in pairs. Ask and answer the questions in Ex 5A.

6 A Complete the article with one word in each gap.

Personal branding

When we think of a brand, we usually think of a product, service or company, but did you know that you're a brand, too? Think of a famous brand like Nike and you might think of words like *strong* and *courageous* because of their advertisements in magazines and on [1]............ by the side of the road. There's also the famous slogan which the company [2]............ been using for decades. Your brand is how others perceive you, just in the same way we perceive Nike. So, you should all [3]............ asking yourselves right now, what do you want your brand to be and how can you build it?

Think about your goals and what you hope you [4]............ be doing in five years' time. Consider your strengths and weaknesses and your skills. You might not be proficient [5]............ all skills needed for the job yet, but you should plan ahead for when you are. And remember, you don't want your brand in the future to be affected by things you shouldn't [6]............ posted online yesterday.

B Work in pairs. How would you like people to describe you?

change

5

BBC

VLOGS

Q: What changes have there been in your life recently?

1 ▶ Watch the video. What are the biggest changes that people mention?

2 What changes have there been in your life recently?

Global Scale of English **LEARNING OBJECTIVES**

5A READING | Read an article about a life-changing decision: decision and indecision

Pronunciation: *'d* and *'d have*

Talk about life-changing decisions: mixed conditionals

Write an informal message

5B LISTENING | Understand a radio programme about conservation: the natural world

Pronunciation: word stress

Discuss ideas for helping with animal conservation: the perfect aspect

5C HOW TO … | summarise: social and environmental issues

Pronunciation: intonation when summarising

5D BBC STREET INTERVIEWS | Understand people talking about habits

Talk about the pros and cons of routines: habits

Write a blog post

5A Life-changing decisions

GRAMMAR | mixed conditionals
VOCABULARY | decision and indecision
PRONUNCIATION | *'d* and *'d have*

VOCABULARY

decision and indecision

1 A Work in pairs. Decide on one option in each pair as quickly as possible. Then give your reasons.

1 Tea or coffee?
2 TV series or film?
3 Takeaway or eat out?
4 Singing or dancing?
5 Juice or water?
6 Breakfast or dinner?
7 Vacation or staycation?
8 Love or money?

B How easy was it to make your decisions in Ex 1A? Would you say you're generally decisive or indecisive? Why? Tell your partner.

2 A Do the quiz. Then go to page 141 to read your results. Tell your partner if you agree with your results.

How decisive are you?

Do you decide what pizza you want in a split second or are you undecided for ages – **torn between** your favourites? Take our quiz to find out just how decisive, or **indecisive**, you are. Choose the option that best describes each statement for you.

	Never	Hardly ever	Sometimes	Often	Almost always
1 I make a decision based on instinct and rarely **have a change of heart**.					
2 I write a list of pros and cons before I **reach my decision**.					
3 I am confident in my decisions and don't **have second thoughts**.					
4 Even if I have a real **dilemma**, I can eventually come to a decision that I'm happy with.					
5 I avoid **making decisions on impulse** and with little thought.					
6 I **assess all possible outcomes** before making a decision.					
7 Before making a big decision, I make sure I **sleep on it** to avoid making a mistake.					
8 If I **think better of a decision** once I've made it, I'll change it quickly, without hesitation.					

B Look at the words and phrases in bold in the quiz and answer the questions.

1 Which two words or phrases describe indecision?
2 Which three phrases describe changing your mind or reconsidering a decision?
3 Which word describes a difficult decision where the choices are equally good and bad?
4 Which phrase describes thinking carefully about the possible results of a decision?
5 Which phrase describes making a decision without thinking if it's sensible or not?
6 Which phrase describes finishing making a decision?
7 Which phrase describes delaying a decision to the next day?

C Tell your partner about a time when you did three of the things below. Do you have similar or different ideas and experiences?

1 You were torn between two things.
2 You took ages to reach a decision about something.
3 You made a decision, but had second thoughts after a while.
4 Somebody made you think better of a decision.
5 You had a dilemma.
6 You made a decision on impulse.
7 You assessed all possible outcomes before deciding how to solve a problem.
8 You made a decision but then reversed it because you had a change of heart.

How to make an unpopular decision

It's easy to assume that the biggest decisions we make in life are the ones that take the longest to make, but honestly, I've spent longer debating what type of coffee to have than I did deciding to drop out of uni. I just woke up one morning and realised it wasn't for me. I didn't quit immediately, but my mind was made up and so the following day, I went to the admin office and told them I was leaving and that was that.

Now, telling my family and friends, that was the hard part. My parents had been so thrilled about me being the first person in the family to go to university and they were hugely proud, so you can imagine how much fun it was seeing the disappointment in their eyes when I told them what I'd decided. They tried to cover it up and support my decision, but I could see the strain on their faces as they did. It didn't help that at that very moment, a neighbour popped round and asked how I was enjoying uni. Just what I needed. The guilt I felt about my parents' disappointment was immense, and if I weren't so stubborn, I might have told them I was just joking, but I stuck to my guns and here I am ten years later – still degree-less.

I'd thought telling my friends would be easier, but it wasn't. We'd all headed off to different universities after school, so I waited until everyone returned home in the summer to give them the news. They weren't disappointed, just shocked. I'd always done well at school and had made friends pretty easily, so they couldn't believe that I hadn't taken to university life. 'You've not given yourself time to settle in yet,' they said. (I'd been there eight months.) 'You've just chosen the wrong subject,' they agreed. (I was studying what I'd loved at school.) 'You've just got some bad results,' they assumed. (I'd got consistently high grades.) When I rejected their ideas, it was like I'd rejected them. It was tough, but I knew in my heart what was right for me.

So, how can you make an unpopular decision and stick to it, when all those around you think you've gone mad? Well, firstly, it's important to be sure it is the right decision for you. Think it over, sleep on it but don't overthink it. Trust your instincts. If, once you've made the decision, you feel a weight lifted off your shoulders, then you know it's the right one. Yes, second thoughts will be part of the process, but they're natural. Let those thoughts come and quickly let them go again. Don't hold onto them.

When it comes to telling people, appeal to their logic and their emotions. Firstly, explain the reasons really clearly. Then, describe your feelings both pre- and post-decision. People will be much more likely to understand then. Don't expect people to get on board with your decision immediately though. Give them time to process it and come to terms with it just as you had. Listen to their concerns and address them. Be patient, and people will generally surprise you with their support. If they don't, look for that support elsewhere.

Then, plan your next step. I'm sure you're on the edge of your seats wondering what mine was. Well, that was another decision that shocked everyone. You see, I grew up in a city, surrounded by concrete, so it made no sense to anyone that I would suddenly take myself off to the country to work on a rural sheep farm. But that's what I did, and I don't regret it one bit. It was work that had fascinated me as a child and I saw a job advert for a trainee farm hand so I decided to give it a try. I'm now a farm manager and just as successful as my graduate friends, so I no longer need to prove that my decision was the right one. If I hadn't made the life-changing decision to drop out of uni, I probably wouldn't be as fulfilled as I am today. Standing knee deep in a field of mud at 4 a.m. waiting for a sheep to give birth. Joy!

READING

3 A Read an article about a life-changing decision. What decision did Ashley make? How does he feel about it now?

B Read the article again and answer the questions.

1 What does Ashley say about making minor decisions compared to the decision to drop out of university?

2 How did Ashley know his parents were disappointed when he told them of his decision?

3 How did Ashley feel about his parents' neighbour's visit? Why?

4 How do you think Ashley felt about his friends' comments and ideas? Why?

5 Why do you think Ashley suggests it's best not to think about a decision too much when making it?

6 What does Ashley say we should do if we have doubts about a decision?

7 What does Ashley suggest we do to help people understand our decision?

8 Has Ashley had second thoughts about his decision to drop out of university? Why/Why not?

C Look at the second paragraph. Did Ashley think it was 'fun' to tell his parents that he'd dropped out, or is he using irony to suggest the opposite? How do you know?

D Find three more examples of irony in the article.

GRAMMAR

mixed conditionals

4A Look at the extracts from the article (A and B). Answer questions 1–2 for each extract.

1 Is Ashley referring to a past or present situation after *if*?

2 Is the result he describes in the other part of the sentence past or present? Real or imaginary?

A
> … if I weren't so stubborn, I might have told them I was just joking …

B
> If I hadn't made the life-changing decision to drop out of uni, I probably wouldn't be as fulfilled as I am today.

B Look at the sentences (1–6). Which describe an imaginary past situation and present result? Which describe an imaginary present situation and past result?

1 If I'd got my degree, I'd be some kind of banker now.

2 I wouldn't be with my partner if I hadn't moved to this area.

3 If I weren't so confident about my decisions, I might not have dropped out of uni.

4 If economics wasn't so dull, I might have finished my degree.

5 If I hadn't dropped out of university, I would still be living in the city.

6 We wouldn't be married if we hadn't chosen the same degree.

C Learn and practise. Go to the Grammar Bank.

▶▶ page 122 **GRAMMAR BANK**

PRONUNCIATION
'd and 'd have

5A 🔊 **5.01** | Listen to the sentences. What do you notice about the difference between *'d* and *'d have* in fast connected speech?

1 You'd be more independent if you'd left home.

2 We'd be doing more sport if you hadn't taken up photography.

3 I'd have been bored if you weren't here.

4 She'd have called me if she had my number.

B 🔊 **5.02** | Listen and write the missing words. Then listen and repeat the sentences.

1 I .... a pilot if I'd had enough money for the training.

2 I .... a pilot if I had better eyesight.

3 We .... each other if we lived in the same street.

4 We .... each other if we'd lived in the same street.

C Complete the sentences with your own ideas so they are true for you.

1 If I'd .... in the past, I wouldn't .... now.

2 If I hadn't .... in the past, I'd .... now.

3 If I weren't so ...., I wouldn't have .... in the past.

4 If I were more ...., I'd have .... in the past.

D Work in pairs. Take turns to say your sentences with effective pronunciation of *'d* and *'d have*. Then give further information.

SPEAKING

6A Think about a life-changing, or potentially life-changing, decision that you or someone you know has made. Make notes about these things.

- what the decision was and when
- what the options were
- how the decision was made
- how you/the decision-maker and others felt about the decision
- the outcome of the decision
- what would be different today if the decision hadn't been made
- what might be different in the future as a result of the decision

B Think about how you can use the vocabulary and grammar from this lesson when describing the life-changing decision. Add to your notes.

C Work in groups. Tell each other about the decision you made using your notes to help you.

D Whose decision do you think had, or could have, the most impact on their life? Why? Decide as a group and share your decision with the class.

WRITING

an informal message

7A Imagine you have made the potentially life-changing decision to move home. Work in pairs and discuss the questions.

1 What might be the benefits of moving to a new home?

2 What might be the challenges?

3 What might help a person overcome these challenges?

B Write an informal message about moving home. Go to the Writing Bank.

▶▶ page 107 **WRITING BANK**

5B Conservational change

GRAMMAR | the perfect aspect
VOCABULARY | the natural world
PRONUNCIATION | word stress

VOCABULARY

the natural world

1 A Work in groups. What reasons can you think of why animals become endangered or extinct?

B Read the article and check your ideas.

C Match the words in bold in the article with the meanings (1–8).

1 natural tendencies that make animals behave in particular ways
2 people who are concerned about protecting animals and the natural world (x 2)
3 killing animals in a way that is against the law
4 when animals produce young (x 2)
5 when animals travel long distances as part of their normal way of life
6 animals that are killed for sport
7 animals that kill and eat other animals for food
8 all the animals and plants that live in a particular habitat

2 A Complete the quiz questions with the correct form of the words from Ex 1C.

Can you think of ...

1 a whole _____ that is in danger?
2 three animals that are _____ and kill other animals for food?
3 an animals that is treated as _____ and hunted in your country?
4 a well-known _____ who campaigns to protect animals in the wild?
5 a bird or animal that passes through your country as part of its annual _____ ?
6 a typical animal behaviour that is the result of their _____ ?

B Work in pairs. Answer the quiz as quickly as possible.

C Learn and practise. Go to the Vocabulary Bank.

▶ page 137 **VOCABULARY BANK** the natural world

What leads to extinction?

Animals in the wild have a huge capacity to adapt to change, but sometimes this isn't enough. Around the world, thousands of species of animals are now endangered and hundreds have become extinct. Both natural and man-made factors can lead to the decline of a species. These are the main ones.

Destruction of habitat

Loss of habitat can occur due to natural disasters, human activities or climate change. In some parts of the world, a whole **ecosystem** such as a rainforest may be in danger of being lost. Loss of habitat can result not only in harm to species living in an area, but can also interfere with the **migration** of species that travel through an area.

Pollution

Environmentalists have long warned about toxic chemicals in air, water or on land. Even if the substances don't kill animals outright, they can interfere with **reproduction**, leading to a gradual decline in numbers. The build-up of chemicals in the environment is dangerous even to large **predators**, as they feed on smaller animals which have accumulated chemicals in their bodies.

Human activities

The direct killing of animals by humans can be a problem, for example when animals are seen as **game** and hunted for sport. Sometimes animals' **instincts** can also unwittingly bring them into conflict with humans and lead to injury or death. For example, grazing animals may stray onto agricultural land in search of food and risk being shot by local farmers. The **poaching** of animals is a concern for some species such as elephants – large numbers of these creatures are killed illegally each year for their tusks. Human activities may also have indirect consequences for animal life. Tourists love seeing large animals in their natural environment, but if tourism is not properly regulated, it can have a negative effect on wildlife. Responsible tourism involves working with **conservationists** to prevent too much disturbance to animals, for example during the **breeding** season.

PRONUNCIATON
word stress

3 A 🔊 **5.03** | Listen to the sentences (1–2) and notice the pronunciation of the word pairs in bold. Is the stress on the same syllable or a different syllable in each word pair?

1 It is important to **conserve** this species, so more **conservation** measures need to be taken.
2 About eighteen percent of all birds **migrate** each year, but we don't know the details of all their **migration** patterns.

B 🔊 **5.04** | Listen to four more sentences. Underline the stressed syllable in the words in bold.

1 Some birds have an **instinct** to migrate each year, whereas others have an **instinctive** need to stay in the same territory.
2 Humans have caused a lot of **environmental** damage and **environmentalists** believe we must act quickly to repair it.
3 Some animals now struggle to **reproduce** in the wild because chemicals have interfered with their **reproduction**.
4 **Poaching** has a devastating impact on the number of elephants in the wild, so it is crucial the **poachers** are caught.

C Complete the sentences (1–4) with your own ideas. Then say your sentences to a partner. Which of your partner's sentences do you agree with?

1 It is instinctive for some animals to …
2 I think it is especially important to conserve …
3 I agree with environmentalists that …
4 Illegal poaching is …

LISTENING

4 A Work in pairs. Read the two conservation challenges below. Can you think of ways to help protect the animals?

> In some parts of the world, poachers kill chimpanzees to sell as meat. While there are park rangers to protect the animals, they are not always aware of when the poachers attack.

> In Alaska, polar bears often stray into villages to look for food and they may harm the inhabitants or other animals. As a result, local people occasionally shoot and kill them.

B 🔊 **5.05** | Listen to a radio programme about conservation. Did it mention any of your ideas in Ex 4A?

C 🔊 **5.06** | Listen to the first part of the programme again. Answer the questions.

1 What example of nudging humans is mentioned?
2 What kinds of animals does Ken Ramirez usually work with?
3 What is positive reinforcement?
4 What difference is mentioned between training pet animals and training animals in the wild?

D 🔊 **5.07** | Listen to the second part of the programme again. Complete the summaries of the two research projects that are mentioned.

> In order to protect themselves from danger, chimpanzees [1] _____ around their group to raise the alarm and alert each other by [2] _____ if they sense humans approaching. However, only one or two chimpanzees were responding in this way at the same time, which meant that the [3] _____ were unable to hear them. The trainers installed a system of [4] _____ which ejected rewards in the form of [5] _____ if the chimpanzees created more noise in order to warn each other. This resulted in a massive reduction in the amount of [6] _____ in the area.

> The strategy to keep polar bears away from villages involved training both the bears and the villagers. First, trainers educated the villagers on safe ways to [7] _____ so it wouldn't attract bears. They then encouraged residents to only shoot in the direction of bears when they [8] _____ . To nudge the bears' behaviour, they put [9] _____ leading away from the villages to encourage the bears to search elsewhere. In one village, the number of bear incidents per year fell from [10] _____ to three.

GRAMMAR

the perfect aspect

5A Look at the sentences from the radio programme (1–6). Match each verb form in bold with the tenses in the box. Which examples are passive?

> future perfect   past perfect (x2)
> perfect infinitive   present perfect (x2)

1 In the past, we**'ve discussed** lots of different conservation measures.

2 Nudging **has been used** on humans for some time now.

3 He **had** mainly **worked** with pets and domesticated animals before this.

4 To get the reward, they needed **to have screamed** when humans were approaching.

5 Once the chimps **had been trained** to change their behaviour, poaching in the area was reduced by eighty-six percent.

6 If we change animals' behaviour to solve one problem, **will we have caused** another problem in five years' time?

B Choose the correct words to complete the rules.

1 We use the perfect aspect to show that an action is **completed / in progress**. The exact time of the action is **sometimes / always** mentioned.

2 We can use the present perfect with *for* or *since* to show that an action started in the past and is **still / no longer** relevant.

3 The past perfect shows that an action happened **before / after** another action in the past.

4 We use the future perfect to look **back / forwards** from a time in the future.

5 We use the **future perfect / perfect infinitive** after verbs like *seem* and *appear* and modals like *need* and *ought*.

C Learn and practise. Go to the Grammar Bank.

▶▶ page 123 **GRAMMAR BANK**

6 Choose the correct verb forms to complete the questions (1–3). Then ask and answer them in pairs.

1 What **had you learnt / have you learnt** about animal behaviour in this lesson?

2 How do you think the trainers felt when they saw that the animals seemed **they had learnt / to have learnt** to change their behaviour?

3 In twenty years' time, what other animals do you think **have benefited / will have benefited** from 'nudging'?

SPEAKING

7A Work in pairs. Read about the conservation challenge facing elephants in Africa. Think of ways to help with the animals' conservation. Use the questions below to make notes.

1 What solution would you suggest?

2 What are your reasons for choosing this solution?

3 How would your solution be effective?

> Elephants in parts of Zambia embark on an annual migration at the start of the dry season to areas where they can more easily find water. For most of their journey, which is in a national park, rangers are able to protect them from poachers. However, the elephants' route takes them through one particular jungle area where it is difficult for park rangers to operate. This route is the one they have always followed and has been passed down through the generations, from older elephants to younger ones. As they pass through this danger zone, large numbers of the animals are killed by poachers each year for their tusks.

B You are going to roleplay a meeting to discuss solutions to the problem. In your pairs, look at your notes in Ex 7A again and answer the questions (1–3).

1 How can you organise your ideas into a logical, structured argument?

2 Which are the most significant points you want to share in the meeting?

3 How can you highlight the significant points, for example by giving reasons or examples?

C Read the Future Skills box and do the task.

FUTURE SKILLS
Teamwork

In a meeting, it is important for people to have clear roles and work together to reach a decision. The chairperson makes sure that everyone's arguments are heard and that a decision is reached. Another person should take notes, to make sure there is a clear record of what is discussed. Other participants should focus on thinking of and responding to ideas.

Work in pairs. Can you think of any useful phrases the chairperson, note-taker and other participants could use?

Chairperson: That's an interesting point. Does anyone else have … ?
Note-taker: Sorry, I didn't quite catch that.
Other participants: This is only a suggestion, but …

8A Work in groups. Choose a chairperson and a note-taker and discuss your ideas. Take turns to make your arguments, highlighting the significant points. The chairperson should help the meeting reach a decision on the best solution.

B Share your group's solution with the class. Which group's solution do you think will be the most effective? Why?

C Turn to page 142 and read how Ken Ramirez and his team tackled the problem. Was it similar to your ideas?

5C Effecting change

HOW TO ... | summarise
VOCABULARY | social and environmental issues
PRONUNCIATION | intonation when summarising

VOCABULARY

social and environmental issues

1 A Work in pairs and discuss the questions.

1 What are some common social issues around the world?

2 What are some possible ways of raising awareness about these issues? Make a list of ideas.

B 🔊 **5.08 |** Listen to four local news reports. Match speakers 1–4 with the actions (a–d) and issues (e–h).

Actions	Issues
a wore outfits at an event	**e** homelessness
b organised a demonstration	**f** inequality
c creation of a computer game	**g** plastic pollution
d took a journey	**h** climate change

C Work in pairs. Rank the awareness-raising activities in Ex 1B according to how effective you think each one is. Share your ideas with another pair. Do you agree?

2 A Read the extracts (1–6) from the news reports. Decide if each pair of words in bold means something similar (S) or different (D).

B 🔊 **5.09 |** Listen to the extracts from the news reports and choose the words you hear.

C Complete the table with the words in bold in Ex 2A where possible.

Problems related to poverty	
Problems related to the environment	
Problems related to people's rights	
Solving social issues	

NEWS REPORTS

1 In addition, he is raising money for a **commercial / non-profit** organisation that seeks to protect coastlines and waterways from the harmful effects of **contaminated / polluted** water.

2 A computer game developed ten years ago is continuing to raise awareness of **homelessness / the homeless** around the world.

3 In the game, players imagine they have become **employed / jobless** and are down to their last $1,000.

4 A group of protestors stopped traffic in the city centre this morning as part of a **campaign / series of activities** to raise awareness of climate change.

5 The group are concerned about the increased number of lorries in the area which **absorb / emit** harmful **greenhouse gases / toxins**.

6 The annual **appeal / fundraiser**, famous for its sometimes outrageous fashion, saw several outfits **advocating / supporting** social change – in particular addressing **equality / inequality** experienced by **the advantaged / the disadvantaged**.

3 A Complete the opinions with the correct form of words from Ex 2A. More than one answer might be possible.

1 It's unfair that wealthy famous people ask ordinary people to donate to TV ....

2 Governments can eliminate .... by providing free accommodation.

3 Everyone should support at least one .... organisation with time or money if they can.

4 There's no point trying to reduce the pollution .... by cars.

5 Environmental activism should prioritise the plastic in our .... oceans.

6 .... among people can never be achieved. There will always be some kind of .... in the world.

B Work in pairs. Do you agree or disagree with the opinions in Ex 3A? Why/Why not?

C Learn and practise. Go to the Vocabulary Bank.

▶▶ page 138 **VOCABULARY BANK** social and environmental issues

How to ...
summarise

4 **A** Work in pairs and discuss the questions.

1 Look at your list of awareness-raising ideas from Ex 1A. What are the pros and cons of each?

2 Do the negatives of any of these activities outweigh the positives? Why/Why not?

B Read an article about ways to raise awareness of a social or environmental issue. Which ideas on your list does the writer mention? Which idea do you think is most likely to be effective? Why?

The first step to effecting change: raising awareness

Raise people's awareness of your issue and change their attitude. Try these activities.

1 Start a petition where people sign their names to say they agree with social action. Present the petition to people in power.

2 Organise a local public debate, inviting speakers with different views to discuss the issue, and the general public to watch.

3 Organise a concert to make people aware of the issue while also entertaining them.

4 Start a social media campaign to make people more aware of it.

Whatever you decide to do, make sure the activity engages people rather than annoys them.

5 **A** 🔊 **5.10** | Listen to committee members of a charity debating how to raise awareness of homelessness in their area. What suggestions do they make? Which one do they decide is best? Why?

B 🔊 **5.11** | Listen to extracts from the conversation. Complete the sentences (1–4) with a word you hear.

1 You _____ that the council aren't doing anything.

2 In a _____, it's where you get a load of people together to sleep rough for the night in the town centre.

3 So you're _____ we shouldn't do anything to upset anyone?

4 _____, it's a choice between getting lots of attention but annoying people and risking little attention but upsetting no one.

C 🔊 **5.11** | Listen again. Match the summaries (1–4) in Ex 5B with their purpose (a–d). Does the speaker use the original speaker's words or their own?

a to keep an explanation short by summarising key points

b to summarise what has been discussed so far

c to check understanding of what a speaker said

d to check understanding of what a speaker has inferred

D Learn and practise. Go to the Grammar Bank.

⏩ page 124 **GRAMMAR BANK**

PRONUNCIATION
intonation when summarising

6 **A** 🔊 **5.12** | Read and listen to a summary of the article in Ex 4B. Mark ' / ' where the speaker pauses. Does the speaker's voice go up or down before each pause?

> So, in a nutshell, to get people to change their habits you first need to raise their awareness of the problem. To do this, you can organise a petition, a debate, a concert or a social media campaign.

B 🔊 **5.13** | Listen to an activist talking about a petition and make notes on the key points she mentions.

C Work in pairs. Take turns to summarise the ideas the activist makes in Ex 6B. Use effective intonation.

SPEAKING

7 **A** Work in groups. Choose an issue which you feel is important. Use your ideas from Ex 1A to help you.

B On your own, think of different ways that you could raise people's awareness of this issue and effect change.

C Read the Future Skills box and answer the question.

FUTURE SKILLS
Collaboration

Collaboration involves different types of interaction, such as initiating, clarifying, brainstorming, summarising, questioning/challenging and consensus building.

How might we need to act differently during different interactions?

8 **A** In your groups, plan an awareness-raising campaign for your issue. Follow the steps (1–4).

1 Brainstorm ideas.

2 Evaluate each idea, clarifying, questioning, challenging and summarising each one.

3 Select the best ideas.

4 Decide how and when each idea will happen.

B Work with another group.

- Take turns to present your campaign.
- Listen to each other carefully and summarise key points to check your understanding.
- Ask further questions to find out more.

C Whose plan do you think will be the most effective? Why?

MEDIATION SKILLS
presenting the components of an argument
simplify a complicated argument

⏩ page 150 **MEDIATION BANK**

5D
Habits

VOCABULARY | habits
SPEAKING | a discussion about the pros and cons of routines
WRITING | a blog post

David

Loona

Becki

Abdullahi

PREVIEW

1 Work in small groups. Look at the different areas of life in the box and answer the questions.

> exercise   food and drink   getting ready in the morning
> meeting friends   shopping

1 In which areas of your life do you follow a similar routine most days?
2 In which areas do you like to change and do things differently?

Q1: In what ways are you a creature of habit?

Q2: Is being a creature of habit a good or a bad thing?

VIEW

2 A ▶ Watch the interviews and answer the questions.
   1 Which areas of life in Ex 1 do the people mention?
   2 Which people think that having strict routines is:
      a a good thing?   **b** a bad thing?   **c** both?

B ▶ Watch the first part of the interviews again. Which person might say each of the following?
   1 The measurements have to be exactly the same every day.
   2 I do certain things in exactly the same order every day.
   3 I'm not keen on making plans.
   4 My routines make me feel secure.
   5 The actions feel natural and automatic.

C ▶ Watch the second part of the interviews again. Are the statements True (T) or False (F)?
   1 David thinks that having plans that are too fixed may prevent you from changing if the situation changes.
   2 Becki thinks she ought to try new experiences, but she is unwilling to change.
   3 Abdullahi believes that having some strict routines helps him feel in control of his life.
   4 Emma doesn't think that routines can help you when things go wrong in your life.
   5 Loona believes that routines can prevent you from doing things in new and different ways.

Emma

VOCABULARY

habits

3 A Work in pairs. Read the ideas from the interviews. Match the phrases in bold (1–6) with the meanings (a–f).

1 I'm not really a **creature of habit**.
2 I [don't] really **plan ahead** too much.
3 … you might not have a **back-up plan**.
4 [It] also can be a bad thing because it gets you **stuck in a rut**.
5 It gives you **a sense of comfort**.
6 It allows you to **go outside your comfort zone**.

a think about things in detail before they happen
b do something that is unfamiliar to you, and which you feel slightly nervous about
c be in a situation where you are unable or unwilling to try new things
d a feeling of calm and lack of stress
e someone who follows the same routines every day
f an alternative approach if a situation changes

B Complete the sentences with the correct form of the phrases in bold in Ex 3A.

1 If you're organising an event, it's important to .... and make decisions about the details.
2 My dad is definitely a .... He hates any changes to his routine!
3 It's always important to have a .... in case something goes wrong.
4 I try new things every week so I don't get ....
5 I like to .... from time to time, even if it does make me feel anxious.
6 Looking at photos of my friends and family gives me a ....

C Work in pairs. Which of the sentences in Ex 3B are true for you?

SPEAKING

a discussion about the pros and cons of routines

4 A Read the two opinions about routines. Decide which one you agree with more and make notes on your opinions and reasons.

> To be successful in life, you need to have strict routines.

> Routines destroy everything that is fun, exciting and creative in life.

B 🔊 **5.14** | Listen to part of a discussion about one of the opinions in Ex 4A. Which opinion do the people discuss?

C 🔊 **5.14** | Listen again and tick the Key phrases you hear.

KEY PHRASES

Let's be honest, …
If you think about it, …
When you put it that way, I'd have to say …
That's not the way I see it at all.
The big downside of … is that …
You have to admit that …

5 A Work in small groups. Discuss the two opinions in Ex 4A. Use the Key phrases to help you.

B In your groups, discuss who is and isn't a creature of habit. Do you agree overall that being a creature of habit is a good or bad thing?

WRITING

a blog post

6 A Read the title and first paragraph of a blog post. What changes to the topics in the box do you think the writer will discuss?

> clothes   entertainment   exercise   food   friends   travel   work

Stuck in a rut?

Have you ever felt that your life was just one long, endless routine? That's what happened to me last year. I suddenly realised that every week of my life was exactly the same as the previous one – same job, same meals, same people, same places. It was beyond mundane! So, I decided to tackle the problem head on and make some big changes.

B Work in pairs and compare your ideas.

C Write a blog post. Go to the Writing Bank.

➤➤ page 108 **WRITING BANK**

GRAMMAR

mixed conditionals

1 A Read the situations and correct one or two mistakes in each mixed conditional sentence.

1 I made the decision to go to university. I've got a good job now.

I wouldn't have had a good job now if I hadn't made the decision to go to university.

2 I'm not interested in animals. I didn't become a vet.

If I would have been interested in animals, I would become a vet.

3 I moved to the capital three years ago. Now I have a lot of friends.

If I hadn't moved to the capital three years ago, I probably wouldn't have had a lot of friends now.

4 There aren't many job opportunities for actors. I decided not to study drama.

I might study drama if there had been more job opportunities for actors.

5 I didn't join my friend's band. I'm not a famous musician.

I would be a famous musician if I joined my friend's band.

6 I don't have any rich relatives. I wasn't able to borrow money to set up my own business.

If I would have had rich relatives, I would be able to borrow money to set up my own business.

B Work in pairs. Are any of the sentences in Ex 1A true for you? Can you change any to make them true for you?

the perfect aspect

2 A Complete the conversation with the correct perfect form of the verbs in brackets

Mia: Er, what are you wearing, Callum? You really need to change your style! You ¹_____ (have) that jacket for at least ten years! Haven't you got something smarter?

Callum: What's wrong with it? This jacket ²_____ (always / admire) by my friends! I was really upset last week when I thought it ³_____ (steal). Luckily, I found it again!

Mia: Hmm. I'm sure it was nice when you bought it. But you seem ⁴_____ (forget) that fashions change.

Callum: That's true, but I don't want to spend loads of money each year replacing perfectly good clothes. You must spend hundreds of pounds every year. Just think about how much you ⁵_____ (spend) by the end of this year, and I bet that by next summer, most of those clothes ⁶_____ (throw away). I prefer to spend my money on other things, like trips and meals out. And I can still wear clothes that I like!

B Work in pairs. Are you more like Mia or Callum? In what ways?

VOCABULARY

3 A Choose the correct words to complete the questions.

1 Have you ever made a plan and then had a change of **heart / belief**?

2 When was the last time you bought something **on / for** impulse? What was it?

3 Which **instincts / ecosystems** do you think it is most important to protect? Why?

4 Do any birds or animals **reproduce / migrate** to your country at certain times of year? Where do they come from?

5 How can governments encourage businesses to provide **diversity / equal** opportunities for people?

6 If you organised a **fundraiser / hardship**, who would you give the money to?

B Work in pairs. Ask and answer the questions in Ex 3A.

4 A Choose the correct options (A–C) to complete the blog post.

Social factors drive human development

In the natural world, animals ¹_____ and changed in response to their ²_____ . We know that animals are continuing to evolve in response to events such as ³_____ and climate change. But what about humans? If we ⁴_____ in the past, we ⁵_____ more like our ape-like ancestors. But are we still evolving now, and how will we evolve in the future? Scientists believe that social factors may be driving evolution now. Compared to the past, when there were huge differences between rich and poor, there is generally more ⁶_____ now, and fewer people are employed in jobs requiring a large amount of physical strength. As a result, there is some evidence that human bones are slowly becoming weaker. Also, in the past, twins were at a disadvantage because they were generally smaller and weaker than single babies. However, with modern healthcare and ⁷_____ schemes, fewer families suffer physical and financial ⁸_____ and there is evidence that the number of twins in the population is increasing. It is, however, unclear how humans may evolve in the future.

1 A had evolved	**B** have always evolved	**C** will have evolved
2 A environment	**B** reproduction	**C** instinct
3 A fossil fuels	**B** landfill	**C** deforestation
4 A didn't evolve	**B** wouldn't have evolved	**C** hadn't evolved
5 A would have looked	**B** would still look	**C** had looked
6 A equality	**B** diversity	**C** inequality
7 A homeless	**B** welfare	**C** shelter
8 A pollution	**B** equal opportunities	**C** hardship

B 🔊 **R5.01 | Listen and check.**

C Which characteristics do you think would be the most useful for future humans? Why?

oops!

6

VLOGS

Q: Tell me about a recent mistake you made and how you felt about it.

1 ▶ Watch the video. Which mistakes did you identify with the most?

2 What mistake have you made recently? How did you feel?

6A Algorithm

GRAMMAR | inversion
VOCABULARY | algorithms
PRONUNCIATION | sentence stress: inversion

READING

1 A Work in pairs and answer the questions.

1 Is it possible for algorithms to make mistakes? Why/Why not?

2 Which of the decisions below do you think an algorithm could make better than a person? Why?

- how much money someone can afford to borrow if they want to buy a flat or a new car
- how likely it is that your house or flat will be burgled, so how much insurance you should pay
- which series you should watch next on a streaming platform
- how much money an individual should receive from the government if they are unable to work
- how likely a particular individual is to commit a crime
- where in the countryside new homes should be built
- which job candidates to invite for an interview

B All the decisions in Ex 1A are often made for us by algorithms. Why do you think some people might be concerned about this?

2 A Read the article about algorithms. Which decisions in Ex 1A do the people mention? Which of your ideas from Ex 1B does it mention?

B Read the article again. Are the statements True (T) or False (F)? Correct the false sentences.

1 Hana and Jasmine are both concerned that human errors can be included when algorithms are created.

2 Aidan and Jasmine agree that it is best not to rely on algorithms at all.

3 Hana and Aidan have different views about how well algorithms deal with people's individuality.

4 Aidan and Jasmine both had a positive attitude to algorithms in the past.

5 Hana and Jasmine both believe that people are unlikely to question data from algorithms.

C Work in pairs. Discuss the questions.

1 Which person's views do you have the most sympathy with? Why?

2 Have you had any personal experiences with decisions made by algorithms? What happened?

VOCABULARY

algorithms

3 A Look at the verbs in bold in the article. Match them with the meanings (1–8).

1 to deal with information

2 to put information into a computer

3 to arrive at a result that is incorrect

4 to predict something that will happen in the future

5 to produce information after analysing data (x2)

6 to control or influence something (x2)

7 to make a feeling stronger

8 to decide which group a person or thing belongs in

B Complete the sentences with the correct form of the words in Ex 3A.

1 Computers are much better than humans at .... large amounts of data quickly.

2 If you .... the data into a computer correctly, it will always .... the information you need.

3 It is still possible to .... a sum, even if you use a calculator.

4 It is impossible for a computer program to .... future weather patterns.

5 When people express similar opinions to me, it .... my own beliefs.

6 A person's age usually .... how comfortable they feel about using modern technology.

C Work in pairs. Discuss which sentences in Ex 3B you agree with. Give examples to support your ideas.

Should we trust algorithms?

We are all aware that algorithms are increasingly being used to make a range of decisions about our lives. If we apply to take out a mortgage or borrow money to buy a car, an algorithm will **dictate** how much the bank will lend us. When we go onto social media, an algorithm will **determine** what adverts we see, which may influence the choices we make about which products to buy, which films to watch or which books to read. Never before have machines had so much power over our lives. But should we be concerned that computer programs influence and control us in this way? Three people give their opinions on the benefits and dangers of the impact of algorithms.

Hana Baker

I work for a charity representing people with disabilities. The majority of our clients are unable to work because of the challenges they face, so they receive money from the government to pay for their daily needs. In the past, decisions about whether someone was eligible to receive money, and the amount they could get, were always made by a human being. When algorithms started being used to make the decisions, a lot of our clients found their monthly income was reduced considerably and life became really tough for them. But the worst thing was that there was no way of challenging the decision – you can't argue with a machine.

I get the fact that a computer has much greater ability than a human to **process** huge amounts of data, but it seems too simple to think all you have to do is **input** the data and the computer will always **output** the correct decisions. Human lives are more complex than that, and a computer can't empathise with the particular circumstances of someone's life. I also think people tend to trust the algorithm because they think a machine is more objective and better at understanding the data than a human, so they think a machine is less likely to **miscalculate** than a human. But they forget that the algorithm is only as good as the people who designed it. If the algorithm is badly designed, it will generate decisions that are skewed. And this can really impact people's lives in a negative way. Under no circumstances should a computer be making such important decisions.

Aidan Reed

I've always been a big user of social media as a way of keeping in touch with friends and also keeping up with world events. I've never minded the fact that you get adverts popping up for all kinds of things, from clothes to drama series and music. I quite often liked the things that come up and it was quite nice to have personalised recommendations, even if it was from an algorithm rather than from a real person. But then I gradually became aware that everything that was being offered to me was closely tied to my profile – if you like these brands of clothing, the chances are you'll like this one, too. Not only had the algorithm **categorised** me as a certain 'type' of person, but it was also actively encouraging me to stay within this type. I realised that if I stuck to the recommendations, I would never try anything new or different. People are more than just profiles, but computers can never understand this. So, I now make a point of ignoring what the algorithms **generate** for me. We need to think for ourselves and make up our own minds. Only then can we be sure that we are not being controlled by machines.

Jasmine Campbell

I work in the police and I've always been concerned about algorithms used in so-called predictive policing. The idea behind predictive policing is that you can **forecast** where and when crimes may take place and who the criminals are likely to be. Basically, you input data about where crimes are typically committed, and what kinds of people have been arrested and charged with committing them. The algorithm analyses all this data, then comes up with its predictions. It sounds good in theory, but the problem is that the data you're putting in is open to bias. For example, let's say the police arrest more people from certain social groups or particular age groups, because of their own prejudice. The data reflects this bias, so the algorithm will then **reinforce** the prejudice and reflect it in its predictions. It becomes a vicious circle. And it's difficult to argue with the output from an algorithm. Everyone assumes it must be right because it's a machine and we think it's less likely to make mistakes than a person, but that isn't always the case, especially if mistakes or prejudices are built into the algorithm. Clearly, algorithms can be useful, but in no way do I think they are perfect. I personally think we should be aware of their limitations and weaknesses.

GRAMMAR

inversion

4A Complete the sentences from the article with the phrases in the box. Check your answers in the article.

> can we   do I think
> had the algorithm categorised
> have machines had
> should a computer

1 Never before .... so much power over our lives.
2 Under no circumstances .... be making such important decisions.
3 Not only .... me as a certain 'type' of person, but it was also actively encouraging me to stay within this type.
4 Only then .... be sure that we are not being controlled by machines.
5 In no way .... they are perfect.

B Choose the correct alternatives to complete the rules.

When we use some adverbials at the ¹**beginning / end** of a sentence, we change the order of the ²**subject and verb / verb and object**. We put the auxiliary verb ³**before / after** the subject.

C Learn and practise. Go to the Grammar Bank.

▶▶ page 125 **GRAMMAR BANK**

PRONUNCIATION
sentence stress: inversion

5A 🔊 **6.01** | Listen to the sentences. Is the first part of the sentence stressed or unstressed? Why?

1 In no way do I think that algorithms are perfect.
2 Under no circumstances should a computer be making such important decisions.
3 Never before have computers had so much power over our lives.

B Complete the sentences (1–3) with your own ideas. Then work in pairs and take turns to say your sentences. Remember to stress the adverbials.

1 In no way do I agree that …
2 Under no circumstances would I …
3 Never before have …

In no way do I agree that a computer should choose the best candidate for a job.

SPEAKING

6A You are going to have a debate about algorithms. Read the statement below. Student A: You will argue in favour of the algorithm. Read the ideas below and add some more ideas of your own. Student B: Turn to page 141 and follow the instructions.

> Debate: An emotionally intelligent algorithm would be an incredibly powerful tool that we could trust with the most complex decision-making in society, i.e. at work, school, in government, etc.

Ideas for:

Algorithms:
- are still quite new – they will improve and become more sophisticated.
- can be programmed to 'learn' from each decision they make.
- can handle complex decision-making, e.g. in legal and medical cases.
- ....
- ....

Humans:
- are not perfect at decision-making (they can be affected by prejudices, emotions, tiredness, a 'bad day').
- are limited by their own personal experience, which is narrower than the experience of an algorithm.
- don't necessarily learn and change after making mistakes.
- ....
- ....

B Work with another student on your side of the debate. Compare your ideas and prepare your arguments. Try to include inversion in your arguments for emphasis.

C Read the Future Skills box and do the task.

FUTURE SKILLS
Communication

When you put forward an argument, someone else will often put forward a counterargument. It is important to predict their counterarguments and listen to them carefully, so that you can respond in a clear and detailed way.

Look at your arguments in Ex 6B. What counterarguments might people present? How can you respond to these?

7A Work with another pair on the opposing side of the debate. Present your arguments (for and against) to each other. Remember to present counterarguments and to respond to counterarguments.

B Hold a vote in your group to find out if you agree with the statement in Ex 6A. Discuss which arguments most influenced you.

C Tell the class how your group voted and why. Does the rest of the class agree or disagree with the statement?

6B Online blunders

GRAMMAR | passive structures
VOCABULARY | talking about mistakes; phrases with *right* and *wrong*
PRONUNCIATION | intonation to show attitude

VOCABULARY

talking about mistakes

1 A Work in pairs. What kinds of mistakes do people sometimes make while communicating online? Make a list of ideas.

B Read the comments about online gaffes. Are any of your ideas mentioned? Which mistake do you think was the worst? Why?

2 A Match the words in bold in the comments with the meanings (1–8).

1 thought something was true even if they weren't certain (x2)
2 was incorrect (x2)
3 in a way that was unplanned or unintended
4 in a way that was wrong
5 made a mistake
6 wrongly thought someone/something was someone/something else
7 made someone believe something that isn't true
8 correct something that is wrong

B Complete the sentences with the correct form of the phrases in Ex 2A. More than one answer may be possible.

1 I .... sent a message about a friend to that very same friend.
2 I once made a mistake worse when I tried to .... the situation.
3 I've .... a stranger in the street .... a friend and waved at them.
4 I've been .... by a spam email or message.
5 When people first meet me, they often .... something about me that's not true.
6 I once wasted time when a measurement I made .... by quite a lot.
7 I .... when I uploaded a photo of a friend without their permission and they weren't happy.

C Work in pairs. Tell your partner if you've ever made any of the mistakes in Ex 2B. What happened?

D Learn and practise. Go to the Vocabulary Bank.

▶▶ page 138 **VOCABULARY BANK** phrases with *right* and *wrong*

Online gaffes: you're not alone!

When Jenny D shared her work mistake on social media this week, many of you replied with your own errors. Here are some that made us chuckle.

 @JennyD ◻11 ♺2 ♡23 ✉

This week, I **accidentally** invited all 3,000 staff at my company to an end-of-year celebration lunch with 'free food and drink'. The invitation was meant for my immediate team only, so when I had hundreds of acceptances, I quickly realised what I'd done. I've tried to **rectify** the situation by deleting the invitation and sending out a new one, but I suspect extra people are still going to turn up.

 @TommyBoy ◻8 ♺5 ♡34 ✉

Oh dear, I know how you feel! I **slipped up** hugely when I was an intern at a large multinational company. I **mistakenly** sent out a confidential internal email to every single customer. I expected my boss to ask me to pack up my desk and leave, but luckily, she supported me.

 @Mr_C_S ◻17 ♺3 ♡17 ✉

Oh no! In my case, I uploaded a photo to social media of me and my friends on a night out, but I **mistook** my girlfriend's name **for** my ex's name and tagged my ex by mistake. My girlfriend didn't see the funny side.

 @LucyB ◻19 ♺5 ♡44 ✉

Last week, I made it into the local newspaper when I advertised a sofa for sale that I said 'needed to be gone today' and somehow managed to upload a photo of my children rather than the sofa. Strangely, no one made an offer!

 @Sarah ◻16 ♺7 ♡31 ✉

I ordered a plant for the corner of my living room and **was mistaken** on two counts. I **made the assumption** the plant was real when it wasn't, and I **presumed** it was measured in metres and would almost reach the ceiling. I **was off** by quite a lot. It was measured in centimetres and was meant for a doll's house.

 @PaulLondon ◻16 ♺3 ♡44 ✉

My dad got invited to a 60th birthday party, but the wording on the invitation **misled** him into thinking it was a 60s-themed birthday party. He turned up in 1960s clothes with a long-haired wig and everything. Everyone else was in a suit or dress.

LISTENING

3 A 🔊 **6.02** | Listen to two colleagues discussing a mistake. What was the mistake? How did it happen? What might the outcome be?

B 🔊 **6.03** | Listen to the first part of the conversation again. What emotion is Liam experiencing? Which of these things help you to infer this? How?

> pitch   sentence stress   speed
> volume   word choice

C 🔊 **6.04** | Listen to the rest of the conversation again. Choose the correct feelings.

1 Anita is **disappointed / impressed** when she sees Liam's drawings.

2 Liam feels **confused / embarrassed** about sending the email to the wrong people.

3 At first, Anita is **disappointed / horrified** that Liam sent the email.

4 Liam is **disgusted / worried** that he sent the email without checking the recipient's name.

5 Anita sounds **calm / frustrated** when analysing the situation.

6 In response to Anita's analysis, Liam feels more **excited / optimistic**.

7 Liam feels **motivated / resigned** when talking about the forthcoming weekend.

D Work in pairs. How serious do you think Liam's mistake was? What do you think Liam's line manager Diane should do or say in the meeting with him?

PRONUNCIATION
intonation to show attitude

4 A 🔊 **6.05** | Listen to the pairs of sentences. For each feeling (1–6), which intonation (a or b) conveys it correctly?

1 frustration	4 desperation
2 enthusiasm	5 surprise
3 criticism	6 annoyance

B 🔊 **6.06** | Listen and repeat each sentence with the appropriate intonation.

C Work in pairs. Take turns to choose one of the two feelings in brackets and say the sentence in the appropriate way. Guess which feeling your partner chose.

1 The email's just arrived. (joy / worry)

2 I got sixty-five on the test. (excitement / disappointment)

3 Where's he going now? (annoyance / curiosity)

4 I can't believe I did that! (anger / disbelief)

GRAMMAR

passive structures

5 A 🔊 **6.07** | Listen to the meeting between Liam and Diane. What's the outcome?

B 🔊 **6.08** | The first sentence in each pair is an extract from Liam's chat with Anita in Ex 3A. Listen to extracts from his conversation with his manager and complete the more formal second sentences.

1 I'm worried they might fire me.
   I was worried I ....

2 I'd ended up with some time on my hands.
   … I found myself with some time that needed ....

3 … they might have accidentally been sent to the whole team.
   … I .... sent them to the whole team.

4 I'm an idiot. And after they'd promised me a promotion soon, too.
   I'm disappointed in myself, especially after having .... a promotion.

5 Maybe I'll get a telling off and no more.
   … be advised that this an official verbal warning, but no further action ....

6 I don't suppose she enjoys the senior managers calling her on a Friday afternoon.
   No one enjoys .... by senior managers on a Friday afternoon, least of all me.

6 A Look at the extracts from Liam's conversations in Ex 5B. Underline the passive form in each pair. Are they more commonly used in the informal or formal extracts?

B Match the passive forms you underlined in Ex 6A with the reasons they are used (a–e). More than one answer might be possible.

a to avoid changing the subject from one thing (e.g. *I*) to another (e.g. *you*)

b to maintain a level of objectivity and therefore formality by avoiding *I* or *We*.

c to avoid admitting wrongdoing or placing blame on someone

d The agents aren't important or are obvious to the listener.

e The focus is on the receiver of the action, not the agent.

C Look at the passive forms you underlined in Ex 6A again and answer the questions.

1 Which verbs are in the infinitive form, with or without *to*? Which are in the *-ing* form?

2 Which verbs refer to the present or future? Which refer to the past?

3 How is the infinitive form different in the present/future and past?

4 How is the *-ing* form different in the present and past?

D Learn and practise. Go to the Grammar Bank.

▶▶ page 126 **GRAMMAR BANK**

7 Work in pairs. Student A: Go to page 141. Student B: Go to page 143. Follow the instructions.

SPEAKING

8 A Work in groups of three. You are going to tell each other about a mistake you have made in informal and more formal contexts. Student A: Go to page 142. Student B: Go to page 143. Student C: Go to page 143. Read and plan your role play.

B Work in your groups. Take turns to tell each of your partners about your mistake.

1 Student A, tell Student B, your friend. Then tell Student C, your teacher.

2 Student B, tell Student C, your friend. Then tell Student A, your manager.

3 Student C, tell Student A, your friend. Then tell Student B, the company customer service operator.

WRITING

an email of complaint

9 A Work in pairs and discuss the questions.

1 What kinds of things do people typically complain about to companies?

2 Have you ever had to complain about something to a company? What was it?

3 What kind of information do you expect to find in an email of complaint? In what logical order?

B Read the email. What is the writer complaining about? What is she asking for?

C Match the formal phrases (1–7) in bold in the email with their purpose (a–g).

a describe something as not fulfilling its purpose or role

b state the purpose for writing

c make a request while appealing to the reader's sense of what's right

d present an additional issue with the product/service/event

e politely state that a response is expected

f appeal to the reader's sense of empathy

g refer to an attachment to the email

10 A Think about a time that you were disappointed by something you paid for. Use the ideas below to help you. Tell a partner what it was and why it disappointed you.

> a meal out   a product bought in a shop
> a product bought online   an event
> poor customer service   public transport

B Plan to write an email of complaint to the people responsible stating why you are writing, what the problems were and what your desired outcome is.

C Write your email of complaint. Then, work with a new partner. Read each other's emails. Are the emails polite but firm? Do you think they will achieve the desired outcome? Why/Why not?

To: sales@cookybakery.com
From: C. Fisher
Subject: problems with cake

To whom it may concern,

[1]**I am writing to express my considerable disappointment with** a cake ordered online from your bakery last month.

The cake had been scheduled to arrive on Thursday of this week, but was instead received late yesterday afternoon, over 24 hours late and just two hours before the start of the surprise 30th birthday party it was intended for. This caused considerable concern for myself and the other party organisers as we sought to find out where the cake was.

Unfortunately, its eventual arrival did not put our minds at ease. As soon as the cake box was opened, it became clear that it did not meet our expectations. When placing my order online, I provided instructions as to the wording on the cake and it is very disappointing that the cake maker was unable to correctly spell a fairly common name despite the fact that it had been written out for them. [2]**To make matters even worse**, we could see from the colour of the cake that it was chocolate flavoured, not lemon flavoured as requested. [3]**Please see the attached** order form for confirmation. As a result, an alternative cake had to be purchased in haste from a local supermarket.

[4]**I am sure you understand my frustration at** having spent a considerable amount of money on a cake which was late, and when it did arrive, [5]**was not fit for purpose.** [6]**I have no doubt that you will feel able to offer me a full refund** and [7]**I look forward to hearing from you soon regarding this matter**.

Regards,

Cassie Fisher

6C In dispute

HOW TO ... | negotiate in a dispute
VOCABULARY | buildings and homes
PRONUNCIATION | sounding assertive

VOCABULARY

buildings and homes

1 A Look at the photos. What problems do you think the couple experienced when buying their new home? Read the news story and check your ideas.

B Read three comments about the news story. What problems do the people mention?

2 A Look at the words and phrases in bold in the news story and comments. Find:

1 two positive adjectives.
2 two negative adjectives.
3 two nouns relating to problems with homes.
4 a phrase meaning that a building has fallen down.
5 a verb meaning to have a view of something.

B Work in pairs. Discuss the questions.

1 How do you think Cal and Claire felt when they first saw their new house? Why?
2 Talk about any problems you or people you know have had with their home. Use vocabulary from Ex 2A.

C Learn and practise. Go to the Vocabulary Bank.

▶▶ page 139 **VOCABULARY BANK**
buildings and homes

Cal Hunter and Claire Segeren were planning to buy a flat in the centre of Glasgow, in Scotland. Claire was travelling at the time, so Cal attended the auction in Glasgow on his own. Unfortunately, Cal struggled to understand the auctioneer's strong accent and accidentally bought a house an hour and a half from the city. Not only was the home in the wrong location, but it was also in very bad condition. It wasn't completely **in ruins**, but it was pretty **derelict**! There were **cracks** in some of the walls and a lot of the wood was **rotten**. However, Claire and Cal were determined to make the most of their new home, so they moved into a caravan in the garden and set about renovating it. Two years later, they still haven't moved in!

Comments

 Caroline 22
9 hrs ago

I can imagine how Cal and Claire felt. I rented a flat last year after viewing it online, but without actually visiting it. In the photos, the bathroom looked **luxurious**, but in fact it was dark and damp and some of the walls were covered in **mould**!

 ♡ Like ♀ Comments ↷ Share

 Jess2000
6 hrs ago

I realise Cal and Claire have had to do a lot of work on their house, but really, they should count themselves lucky. They're both young and they own their own house. There's no way I could afford to buy even a flat in the city where I live.

♡ Like ♀ Comments ↷ Share

 Jack DD
5 hrs ago

I really feel for Cal and Claire. I wanted to rent a small cottage on the outskirts of Manchester. I found one that looked lovely and **cosy** inside. I was hoping it might have lovely views over the countryside, but unfortunately, when I got there, it **overlooked** a really ugly factory at the back, which completely spoiled it!

 ♡ Like ♀ Comments ↷ Share

How to …
negotiate in a dispute

3 A 🔊 **6.09 |** Listen to a conversation between neighbours. What are they in a dispute about?

B 🔊 **6.09 |** Complete the sentences from the conversation with the words in the box. Then listen again and check.

> acceptable   arrangement   compromise
> don't think   happy   offer

1 This isn't really ....
2 I .... **it's fair that** I should have to be exhausted just so that you can give a good performance.
3 **Maybe we could come to an** .... **about** when I practise.
4 **That sounds like a good** ....
5 **I'd be** .... **with that**.
6 **I can** .... **you** two free tickets to the gig.

C Complete the table with the phrases in bold in Ex 3B.

Complaining	Making an offer	Accepting the offer
It isn't reasonable to expect me to …	What I can do is …	That's acceptable to me.

D Learn and practise. Go to the Grammar Bank.

▶▶ page 127 **GRAMMAR BANK**

PRONUNCIATION
sounding assertive

4 A 🔊 **6.10 |** Listen to the sentences. How does Alyssa sound when she complains to her neighbour?

a angry and upset   **b** unsure of herself   **c** firm and confident

B 🔊 **6.10 |** Listen again. Then choose the correct words to complete the rule.

To sound confident and assertive, we speak at a **loud** / **normal** volume and we use a **broad** / **narrow** range of intonation. Our intonation **rises** / **falls** at the end of the sentence.

C Complete the sentences with your own ideas. Then work in pairs and practise saying them to sound assertive.

1 I'm not happy that …
2 It isn't really acceptable that …
3 I don't think it's fair that …

SPEAKING

5 A Work in pairs. You are going to roleplay a dispute between a landlord and a tenant. Student A: Go to page 142. Student B: Go to page 143. Follow the instructions.

B Tell the class about your disputes and what you agreed.

> **MEDIATION SKILLS**
> summarising agreements and expectations
> accurately report the outcomes of a meeting
>
> ▶▶ page 151 **MEDIATION BANK**

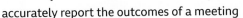

6D BBC Comedy
Tech fail

VOCABULARY | technology
SPEAKING | problem solving
WRITING | a set of instructions

PREVIEW

1 A Work in pairs. Put the common technology problems in order 1–6 (1 = most annoying, 6 = least annoying). Are there any other technology problems you find irritating?

> battery runs out quickly
> devices won't connect
> forgotten password   pop-up ads
> slow internet connection
> spam in your inbox

B Read the programme information. What do you learn about the BBC's new IT system?

W1A

W1A is a mockumentary series set in the BBC offices in the W1A postcode area of London. The series follows Ian Fletcher, Head of Values, as he attempts to help shape the BBC of the future. In this episode, Ian attends training for the organisation's new integrated software system, Syncopatico, which allows devices to 'shake hands', i.e. share information when in close proximity to each other. Ian then works with his new, not always effective, assistant Will to try to solve a problem with the system.

VIEW

2 A ▶ Watch the BBC video clip. What four technical problems occur?

B ▶ Watch the video again. Are the statements True (T) or False (F)?

1 The purpose of Syncopatico is to connect everyone and everything at the BBC.
2 Will has the knowledge he needs to solve the problem with the system.
3 Will suggests swapping devices with Ian to solve the problem.
4 Ian knows that Will isn't to blame for the problem.
5 Ian is curious about someone else's document on Will's device.
6 Ian thinks it's 'cool' that the system lets you print anywhere in the building.

SPEAKING

problem solving

5 A 🔊 **6.11** | Listen to two team leaders discussing a problem at their company. What is the problem? What suggestion do they agree on?

B 🔊 **6.11** | Listen again. Which phrase in the Key phrases box is not used?

> **KEY PHRASES**
>
> Another issue seems to be …
> I'd say that … is/are the main issue.
> If I were in charge, I'd …
> One thing to consider is …
> We/They need to take into account (the fact that) …
> What about … ? That might help to …

VOCABULARY

technology

3 A Read the extract from the video. Decide if the definitions for words and phrases (1–7) are correct.

> Welcome to your ¹**virtual PA**. One ²**unified system** that changes the game, ³**integrates** your world, ⁴**syncs** you **with** everything and everyone around you without you doing anything. Syncs you to the BBC itself in real time, ⁵**wirelessly**, continuously and ⁶**in real time**. Eleven years ⁷**in development** … I give you Syncopatico.

1 digital secretary
2 created with one part
3 separates things to be more effective
4 working in different ways
5 without the need for cables
6 as fast as information arrives
7 being created

B Work in pairs. Tell each other about a piece of software that you have used, using vocabulary from Ex 3A.

4 A Complete the phrases (1–8) with the verbs in the box.

> adjust   disable   drain   jam
> print   put   recharge   update

1 .... a document/a report on paper
2 .... your phone on airplane mode/silent mode/mute
3 .... your settings/clock/volume so they work how you want
4 .... your apps/software so they're the latest version
5 .... your battery when it's low
6 .... your battery of power
7 .... the printer (with too much paper)
8 .... a feature/a setting so it doesn't function

B Which of the actions in Ex 4A cause problems? Which provide solutions?

C Work in pairs. Tell each other about the last time you did or experienced some of the actions in Ex 4A. Why?

6 A Read the case study on page 141 and make notes on the points (1–3).

1 What is the main issue?
2 What aspects need to be taken into account when solving this issue?
3 What solution(s) would you suggest to satisfy the needs of everyone?

B Work in small groups. Discuss the situation and the three points in Ex 6A. What solution(s) do you suggest? Use the Key phrases to help you.

C Present your solution(s) to the class. Whose is likely to be the most effective? Why?

WRITING

a set of instructions

7 A Work in pairs. Imagine you do not have access to your phone. Which of the activities below would you find it most difficult to do without your phone? Why? What would be an alternative solution?

- sending messages
- getting directions
- listening to music
- accessing bus or train tickets
- paying for things
- translating or looking up words

B Work in pairs. Imagine your phone battery is running very low and you cannot recharge it until you get home. What could you do to stop it from running out before you get home?

C Write a set of instructions. Go to the Writing Bank.

▶▶ **page 108 WRITING BANK**

GRAMMAR

inversion

1 A Choose the correct verb forms (a, b or c).

1 Under no circumstances _____ work on my days off.
   a I will   **b** do will I   **c** will I

2 Only after I go to bed _____ relax each day.
   a am I able to   **b** do I able to   **c** I'm able to

3 Not only _____ pizza, I love pasta, too.
   a I do love   **b** do I love   **c** love I

4 Never _____ to a more beautiful place.
   a I have been   **b** did I been   **c** have I been

5 In no way _____ of algorithms grading students.
   a I approve   **b** do I approve   **c** I do approve

B Are the statements in Ex 1A true for you? Tell a partner.

2 A Complete the sentences so they are true for you.

1 Only when I _____ , will I _____ .
2 Under no circumstances do I _____ .
3 Not only have I _____ , I've also _____ .
4 Never before have I _____ .

B Share your sentences in Ex 2A with your partner. Are any of them similar?

passive structures

3 A Complete the sentences with the correct passive form of *give*.

1 School students seem to _____ harder tests in recent years.
2 Students should _____ a grade for effort as well as for the quality of their work.
3 We all hope _____ a lot of money one day!
4 Nobody likes _____ orders.
5 _____ a gift for no reason is far nicer than _____ one for your birthday.

B Do you agree with the statements in Ex 3A? Why/Why not? Tell a partner.

VOCABULARY

4 A Complete the sentences with the words in the box.

> accidentally   assumption   mistook   off   track

1 I made the _____ that the shoes I ordered were adult size but they're for kids.
2 I _____ ordered the wrong sized trousers.
3 I _____ a stranger in the street for a friend and waved madly at him!
4 I know it's not finished yet, but do you think I'm on the right _____ ?
5 I calculated it to be 1.5 m long, but I was _____ by about 30 cm!

B Work in pairs. When was a time you made a wrong assumption? What happened?

5 A Choose the correct words.

Algorithms can [1]**process** / **miscalculate** a lot of data in a short space of time, but they can't predict the future better than humans. Data from the past is [2]**input** / **output** into the algorithm, and the algorithm uses it to [3]**forecast** / **reinforce** the future, but of course the past isn't the future. The algorithm can [4]**dictate** / **miscalculate** the prediction as a result. To [5]**determine** / **process** future predictions, we can use whatever an algorithm [6]**inputs** / **outputs** to help us, but we need human intelligence to ultimately make the right decision.

B Work in pairs. Do you think computer intelligence will one day overtake human intelligence? Why/Why not?

6 A Complete the news report with the words in the box.

> cracks   crumbling   derelict   luxurious   rotten

A couple in North Carolina in the USA who bought a totally [1] _____ mansion for $155,000 have just had it valued at $900,000. The property had serious problems, with [2] _____ in the roof letting in water, [3] _____ brickwork and floorboards so [4] _____ that no one could enter the dining room. Nine months of renovations later, much of which they did themselves, the couple are now owners of a [5] _____ six-bedroom property.

B Work in pairs. Would you be happy to take on a project like the couple in Ex 6A? Why/Why not?

7 A Complete the article with one word in each gap.

Supermarket substitutions

Supermarket customers might expect every item in their online order to [1] _____ delivered, but the reality is that some items are unavailable on the day of delivery. The ordering system tries to suggest sensible substitutions, but it seems that it can slip [2] _____ , suggesting replacements that are completely unsuitable. The employees who pack the shopping have the chance to put the situation [3] _____ by selecting something more appropriate, but they are often pushed for time so might stick with the system's suggestion. The result is some very strange and confusing substitutions. Shoppers claim to have [4] _____ given cooking oil instead of milk, peach shampoo instead of peaches and cheese instead of pizza. Not only [5] _____ one customer receive dog food instead of bread sticks, but they also got toilet cleaner instead of orange juice. Needless to say, these substitutions rub customers up the [6] _____ way, with many complaining on supermarkets' social media feeds.

B Work in pairs. What strange substitutions do you think a supermarket system might suggest for these items?

> bread   cream   fish   red pepper
> vegan ready-meal   vitamin C tablets

trends

7

VLOGS

Q: Tell me about a recent trend in your country.

1  Watch the video. Which trends that people mention are the most surprising?

2 What trends are popular in your country at the moment?

Global Scale of English | LEARNING OBJECTIVES

7A LISTENING | Understand a talk about language: explaining meaning

Evaluate newly created words: adverbials

Pronunciation: pausing: adverbials

Write a comment on a blog post

7B READING | Read article extracts on the globalisation of food: trends; food and drink

Pronunciation: consonant-to-vowel linking with fronting

Discuss food and drink trends and habits: fronting: reasons, causes and explanations

7C HOW TO ... | exaggerate: shopping; describing clothes

Pronunciation: sentence stress: exaggeration

7D BBC STREET INTERVIEWS | Understand people talking about the past

Discuss attitudes to the past and present

Write a blog post

7A The word on the street

GRAMMAR | adverbials
VOCABULARY | explaining meaning
PRONUNCIATION | pausing: adverbials

VOCABULARY

explaining meaning

1 A Read the article about word trends in three different decades. Can you guess the correct decade from the box for each section (A–C)?

> 1970s   1980s   1990s   2000s   2010s

B Choose the correct word or phrase to complete each sentence. Use the words in bold in the article in Ex 1A to help you.

1 To **sum up** / **signify**, we find the new proposals on working hours completely unacceptable.

2 Can you **capture** / **spell out** exactly what you mean?

3 Let me give you a few more examples to **define** / **illustrate** my point.

4 In karate, wearing a white belt **signifies** / **spells out** that you are a beginner.

5 It's hard to **define** / **specify** the word freedom.

6 It's important to choose your words carefully, to **signify** / **convey** the exact meaning you want.

7 Her description really **defines** / **captures** the atmosphere of the forest at sunrise.

8 Can you **specify** / **signify** what kind of animal you saw?

C Complete each sentence with one word. Then share your ideas with a partner.

1 .... sums up how I feel today.

2 .... is something that is easy to specify.

3 .... is very hard to define.

4 .... conveys how I feel about my work or studies.

5 .... captures the mood of this decade.

6 .... signifies something important to me.

Words of the decade

As each decade comes along, new words come into use to describe new objects, actions or feelings, or to reflect fashions or concerns of the time.

A In this decade, computer words were coming thick and fast. The word 'spreadsheet' **specified** a particular type of computer program. 'Email' was the new method of communication and the term 'snail mail' **spelled out** how slow traditional mail seemed in comparison. The adjective 'stressed-out' came in to **illustrate** the idea of being overworked and under too much pressure.

B This was the first real decade of the internet. The word 'website' neatly **sums up** the decade, as this was the time when a large amount of information suddenly became available online. And one of the disadvantages of the internet is demonstrated by the word 'spam', which **signifies** any unwanted or nuisance email. Meanwhile in the world of work, the phrase 'dress-down Friday' **captured** the idea of a new, more relaxed attitude to work, in which Fridays were seen as a gateway to the weekend, so people wore more casual clothes.

Spam!

C In this decade, social media really took off. The word 'tweet', associated only with birdsong in the past, came to **define** a new way of communicating on the platform Twitter. And the decade also saw the emergence of the word 'selfie', which, for many people, **conveys** not only the idea of a photograph, but also how social media has made many of us obsessed with our own image.

LISTENING

2 A Work in pairs. Discuss the questions.

1 Can you think of any words that have become more or less popular in your language in recent years?

2 Why do you think the words we use change in popularity over time?

B 🔊 **7.01 |** Listen to part of a talk about how words become more or less popular over time. Complete the main points.

1 Words become more and less trendy in a similar way to ....

2 Researchers studied the popularity of words using a(n) ....

3 It is possible that words become more or less popular due to their use by different ....

4 Historical events, ... and social issues can all affect how frequently words are used.

C 🔊 **7.01 |** Listen again and answer the questions.

1 What period of time did the study use to look at how words become more and less popular?

2 What does the speaker say about the popularity of baby names?

3 Why does the speaker mention words to do with space?

4 What examples of words that became popular brand names does the speaker give?

5 According to the speaker, what can we learn about the nature of fashion and trends in general from this study?

GRAMMAR

adverbials

3 A 🔊 **7.02 |** Complete the sentences from the talk with the adverbials in the box. Listen and check.

after a while   decidedly   in a detailed way
interestingly   on an almost yearly basis

1 So, we're all familiar with the idea that there are fashions or trends in clothes and other consumer goods, with things rising to either the height of fashion or becoming completely unfashionable ....

2 Marcelo Montemurro and his team from the University of Manchester used a computer database to track the use of words ....

3 .... , the cycle of popularity for words has recently become longer by a few years.

4 .... , they start to look more unusual and attractive again.

5 So people start to choose them again, in much the same way as styles of clothing come back into fashion after a period of being .... unfashionable.

B Look at the adverbials in Ex 3A again. Answer the questions.

Which one:

1 refers to a period of time? (a time adverbial)

2 gives information about frequency by answering the question 'how often?' (a frequency adverbial)

3 describes how something happens or is done? (an adverbial of manner)

4 makes the meaning of an adjective or adverb stronger or weaker? (an intensifying adverb)

5 shows the speaker's attitude and makes a comment on a whole sentence? (a sentence adverbial)

C Choose the correct words to complete the rules.

1 Adverbials add extra information to a sentence about time, frequency, manner, etc. They can be a single word or a **phrase / whole sentence**.

2 Adverbials of time, frequency and manner usually come **before / after** a verb and its object, but they can also come at the beginning of a sentence for emphasis.

3 Sentence adverbials show the speaker's attitude and make a comment. They usually come at the **end / beginning** of a sentence.

4 Intensifying adverbs come **before / after** an adjective and make the meaning of that adjective stronger or weaker.

D Learn and practise. Go to the Grammar Bank.

▶▶ page 128 **GRAMMAR BANK**

PRONUNCIATION
pausing: adverbials

4 A 🔊 **7.03 |** Listen to the sentences from the talk and notice the adverbials in bold. Choose the correct rule (a or b).

1 **Surprisingly**, this pattern was fairly regular.

2 They used a computer database to track the use of words **in a detailed way**.

3 They tend to have periods of great popularity, then fall out of favour **for a while**.

4 **Interestingly**, the cycle of popularity for words has recently become longer.

5 **After a while**, they start to look more unusual and attractive again.

a We pause after an adverbial at the beginning of a sentence.

b We pause before an adverbial at the end of a sentence.

B Complete the sentences with your own ideas. Then work in pairs and take turns to say your sentences. Remember to pause after the adverbials where appropriate.

1 Undoubtedly, I use the word .... a lot.

2 I use the word .... infrequently.

3 At the moment, a popular name that I like is ....

4 Interestingly, my language has a lot of words for ....

SPEAKING

5 A Read the tips on how to create your own new English word. Complete them with the correct headings (a–d).

   a Make a noun into a verb
   b Use a word from your own language
   c Join words together
   d Use prefixes or suffixes

How to create your own English word

1 ....

English is full of portmanteau words such as 'screenager' (a combination of the nouns 'teenager' and 'screen'). Think of two more words and combine them to make a new one!

2 ....

There are plenty of words that have been imported into English from other languages, for example English uses the French phrase 'déjà vu' and the German word 'kindergarten'.

3 ....

If you can 'bike' into town, what other forms of transport could you use as a verb?

4 ....

Take an existing word and change its meaning slightly by adding a new beginning or ending. You can 'de-clutter' your life, so might you be able to 'de-gadget' it? You can 'oversleep', so might it be possible to 'undersleep'?

B Work in groups. Use one of the tips in Ex 5A and create your own new word in English. Think about how to explain the meaning and think of examples of how it could be used.

C In your groups, take turns to present your word to the class.

D Discuss and evaluate all the words in your groups and choose your favourite. Tell the class which word you chose and why. Which words did the class like best?

WRITING

a comment on a blog post

6 A Read the blog post. What is the writer's opinion about emojis?

 Ed_Jacobs2007 • Follow
2 days

Call me old-fashioned, but does anyone else hate the way people use emojis in messages? It's so confusing that everyone seems to use them in a different way. Some people use them 'seriously', to tell me that they're feeling amused, angry or upset. Others use them in a jokey or ironic way, to mean the opposite of what they show. Another annoying aspect of them is when somebody sends you an emoji that your phone doesn't recognise because it's from a different kind of phone or it's too old, so you just see one of those boxes with a question mark. Please can we ditch emojis and return to using just words to say what we mean?

💬 49 comments   ↪ share   ♡

B Read the comments on the blog post (A and B). Which one:

   1 agrees with the writer?
   2 disagrees with the writer?
   3 corrects a point that the writer makes?

A **JennyW** • Follow
2 hrs ago

Emojis are definitely a lot less clear than words! I sometimes think people use them when they can't be bothered to think of the proper words to use. One thing that drives me mad is when people send a simple message and then a whole string of emojis! What am I supposed to focus on – the words or the emojis? Are the emojis saying the same thing as the message, or are they expressing some ironic comment on it? And how am I supposed to understand what they really mean? Yes, emojis can be fun, but let's not forget that it's the words that are important.

💬 reply   ↪ share   ♡

B **SamTylerxoxo** • Follow
2 hrs ago

I actually love emojis and all the different ways that people use them. And why shouldn't they be used in a jokey or ironic way? People often say things like, 'Ha-ha, very funny!' to mean the opposite, so what's wrong with using emojis in a similar way? To me, it's just people being creative and having fun. And it simply isn't true that there's no way of finding out what emojis mean. There are plenty of lists online of emojis and their 'official' meanings, a bit like dictionaries that give us the 'official' meanings of words.

💬 reply   ↪ share   ♡

C Look at the comments again. Are they formal or informal? Answer the questions to help you decide.

   • Do the writers use full forms or contracted forms?
   • What kinds of phrases do they use – formal or informal?
   • Do they write in an impersonal way, or address the reader directly?

D Write a comment on a blog post. Go to the Writing Bank.

▶▶ page 109 **WRITING BANK**

7B Food fads

GRAMMAR | fronting: reasons, causes and explanations
VOCABULARY | trends; food and drink
PRONUNCIATION | consonant-to-vowel linking with fronting

VOCABULARY

trends

1 A Read the dictionary definition. What food fads do you remember from the past? Think about health foods, foreign foods, cooking techniques, etc. Make a list.

> **fad** noun [countable] /fæd/
> something that people like or do for a short time, or that is fashionable for a short time

B Work in pairs. Share your ideas. Did you take part in these fads? Why/Why not?

C Read the text extracts on food fads. Which one (A–D) describes:

1 one cause of food fads?
2 the danger of food fads?
3 a food fad the writer was glad disappeared?
4 examples of food fads from the past?

A The **surge** in popularity of a new so-called 'superfood' or a supposedly fantastic new diet can quickly attract attention. However, **switching** to a new diet which omits or increases the quantity of a particular food or food group can cause an imbalanced diet, resulting in a loss of much-needed nutrients.

C Who remembers the cronut? This delicious pastry (a cross between a donut and a croissant) **exploded** onto the food scene when a New York bakery started selling it in 2013. On seeing queues around the block, other bakeries made similar products, but the cronut failed to **transform** from a trend to a **consistent** part of our diets. 'No!' our tastebuds cried when we couldn't find them in every bakery anymore. 'Thank goodness', our waistlines and hips replied.

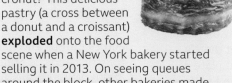

B Food trends are nothing new. Just in my lifetime, we've had the **shift** from eating at the table to eating in front of the TV, the rise of chocolate fountains, and their subsequent **decline** as we all **reverted to** eating chocolate cold, and more recently the **evolution** of the avocado from Mexican food ingredient to what we put on toast in the mornings. These things come and often go. Will demand for avocados **shrink** or **remain steady** in the future? That's yet to be seen.

D Social media is a huge **catalyst** for food fads these days. People compete to share images of themselves eating whatever the latest trendy food is before anyone else, just to appear cool and fashionable.

2 A Match the words and phrases in bold in the extracts in Ex 1C with the meanings (1–8).

1 increase dramatically (x2)
2 decrease (x2)
3 stay the same
4 always happening in the same way
5 the change of something over time
6 move from one thing to another (x3)
7 return to something
8 the cause of a change

B Which words in the box have the same noun and verb forms? Use a dictionary to help you.

> decline   evolution   explode
> shift   shrink   surge   switch
> transform

C Choose the words you think describe current food trends. Work in pairs and share your ideas. Do you agree? Why/Why not?

1 The consumption of avocados is **declining / surging**.
2 A lot of people are **reverting to / switching to** different diets.
3 Laboratory-grown meat will result in **the evolution / shrinking** of the meat industry.
4 Concerns over health are a **consistent / catalyst for change** in the food industry.
5 There'll soon be **an explosion / a transformation** of local artisan food on the market.
6 Our demand for sugary foods and drinks **remains consistent / is declining**.

D Learn and practise. Go to the Vocabulary Bank.

▶▶ page 139 **VOCABULARY BANK** food and drink

READING

3 **A** 🔊 **7.04** | Listen to two summaries of the information in the extracts in Ex 1C. Which summary (A or B) achieves the following points for making an effective summary?

1 mentions all the main points from the texts
2 omits minor or irrelevant points
3 connects and orders the main points logically
4 links ideas between the points
5 is put into the speaker's own words

B You're going to summarise texts on the topic of the globalisation of food. First, read the article extracts (1–3) below and then choose the author's main point in each one (a or b).

Text 1   **a**   Pizza found all over the world is a great example of food globalisation.

        b   There are some mouth-watering toppings added to pizza around the world.

Text 2   **a**   Food globalisation is caused by exploration, migration and technology.

        b   Globalisation has issues, but many dishes may not exist today without it.

Text 3   **a**   Food appropriation occurs when one culture takes credit for another culture's food.

        b   There are things we can do to appreciate, not appropriate, food from other cultures.

C Read the extracts again and answer the questions. Make notes of your answers. Use your own words.

1 What does the author say about pizza and local tastes in Text 1?
2 Why does the text mention the pea pizza, the squid pizza, etc. in Text 1?
3 How do fish and chips exemplify the author's main point in Text 2?
4 What benefits and issues related to globalisation does the author describe in Text 2?
5 How do chefs and supermarkets appropriate food from different cultures according to the author of Text 3?
6 What two tips does the author give for avoiding cultural appropriation in Text 3?

4 **A** Plan to give an oral summary of the extracts in Ex 3B in your own words, using the information in Ex 3A and Ex 3C to help you. Decide how to bring the main points and a few key details together in a logical way.

B Work in pairs. Take turns to give your oral summaries. Did your partner achieve the points in Ex 3A?

---

1 Go around the world and ask people what their favourite food is, and pizza must surely be up there in the top three dishes mentioned. It's a hugely popular international food thanks to globalisation. Naturally, when any food travels abroad, it can find that it's changed to suit the local palate, and that's certainly true of pizza. I'm not sure the original creator of the dish could have foreseen the variety of toppings that would end up on their beloved crust.

In Brazil, for example, green peas are a topping on pizza, sometimes alongside carrots and raisins. (I bet there's no need to hide the greens for children on that plate of food.) In Japan, you can find squid on pizza, and in the UK, the Full English Breakfast pizza contains eggs, meat, tomatoes, mushrooms and even baked beans – all the ingredients of a traditional breakfast in pizza form.

Packed full of coconut trees, it makes sense that Costa Rica is home to the pizza with a coconut topping. Similarly, tandoori chicken is commonly eaten in India, so why not have a tandoori chicken pizza topping? Less logical though is the banana curry pizza on the menu in one pizzeria in Sweden. It's not immediately something you associate with European cuisine, but it's actually a best-seller.

These toppings are wide and varied, but they're also a symbol of globalisation. Spread by migrants in the nineteenth and twentieth centuries, later to all four corners of the globe by international businesses, pizza is changed to suit local tastes while still representing the country it originated from.

2 Since globalisation is a main feature of cultural exchange and a key catalyst of economic development for most countries, it has had an enormous effect on the food we eat. Many of our staple foods are not indigenous to our own countries but were instead introduced from faraway lands hundreds of years ago. The tomato, for example, originated in Central and South America, making its way across Europe and Asia in the 1500s, and later to Africa and the Middle East in the 1700s and 1800s. Without this spread across the globe, salads in the USA, pizza in Italy and shakshuka in North Africa would be entirely different dishes, or not exist at all.

Sometimes, it's entire dishes that migrated as a result of globalisation. Take fish and chips. For many, there's nothing more British than eating deep-fried fish in batter with chips out of paper and yet this dish was actually introduced to the country in the 1800s by migrants from Spain and Portugal.

Today, the key catalysts of globalisation are improved technology, economic integration removing trade barriers between countries, social media and increased competition between food companies. Seeing as this allows us to enjoy new and exciting foods from around the world, globalisation is clearly beneficial, but there are potential negative effects, too. A loss of local culture, the surge in consumption of fast food and a negative impact on the environment are all criticisms aimed at the globalisation of food.

GRAMMAR

fronting: reasons, causes and explanations

5 A Complete the sentences with a word or phrase. Then, find them in the extracts in Ex 3B and check your answers.

1 ...., it makes sense that Costa Rica is home to the pizza with a coconut topping.

2 .... globalisation is a main feature of cultural exchange … it has had an enormous effect on the food we eat.

3 .... this allows us to enjoy new and exciting foods from around the world, globalisation is …

4 ...., the profile of the dominant culture is raised and the value of the minority culture is lessened …

B Answer the questions about the words/phrases in the gaps in Ex 5A.

1 What is their purpose?

2 Can the clause where these words appear stand alone, or is it dependent on the other clause?

3 Which of the clauses where these words appear can also come second in the sentence?

4 What other words can replace the first word in sentence 2?

C Learn and practise. Go to the Grammar Bank.

▶▶ page 129 **GRAMMAR BANK**

---

3 When it comes to food, cultural appreciation of another country's dish can very easily become cultural appropriation, when members of a dominant culture in a society adopt the food of a minority culture in the society without acknowledging that minority culture, often making money as a result. Supermarkets and restaurant owners in particular can fall foul of this. They sometimes add new ingredients to the food, too, claiming it 'elevates' it in some way. As a result of this supposed elevation, the profile of the dominant culture is raised and the value of the minority culture is lessened, albeit unintentionally.

So, when the big new food trend explodes, and it happens to be something from another culture, how can we, as food consumers, appreciate it without appropriating it? The first thing is to never diminish the food by claiming it's some kind of exotic oddity. Just because the food is different to food in our own culture doesn't mean it's unusual in another culture. We should use consuming food from other cultures as an educational experience, learning about its origins, the techniques used in growing or making it and its importance as part of the culture's diet.

Secondly, we should also try to purposely purchase the food from premises owned by people from the same culture as the food, or buy cookbooks written by people from that culture. That way, we know the food is 100 percent authentic, made in exactly the same way it's traditionally produced and that those people are the ones who will profit.

PRONUNCIATION
consonant-to-vowel linking with fronting

6 A 🔊 **7.05** | Listen and notice how the words in bold link in fast speech. Why do you think this is?

1 **As everyone** on social media was eating *pho*, we decided to do the same.

2 **Since it's** fashionable to bake these days, I'm trying my hand at making bread.

3 **As a result of increased** globalisation, we have a huge choice of food at our disposal.

4 **Because of** the increase in veganism, fewer people are eating meat.

B Complete the prompts with your own views on food.

1 Since it's ...., I don't often have ....

2 As I don't like ...., I hardly ever ....

3 Because of a love of ...., you can often find me ....

C Work in pairs. Take turns to share your ideas in Ex 6B. Use connected speech appropriately.

SPEAKING

7 A Read the information about the BBC Radio programme. Is veganism a trend in your country?

Vegans

More and more people are giving up animal or animal-derived foods and turning to vegan diets. Mary-Ann Ochota explores the reasons behind this trend, and its impact.

B 🔊 **7.06** | Listen to an extract from the programme. Why did the woman from Kenya become vegan? What has its effect been for her?

C Work in pairs and discuss the questions about the rising trend of veganism.

1 To what extent do you think the points in the box have contributed to the trend?

> a desire for increased sustainability
> health and well-being   increased globalisation
> a need for convenience   social media

2 What do you think the impact of the trend is now and might be in the future?

3 Is the trend and its impact generally positive or negative? Why?

4 Do you think this is a short-term or long-term trend? Why?

8 A Work in groups. What are the biggest food trends in your culture right now? Make a list.

B In your groups, discuss the questions in Ex 7C about the food trends on your list in Ex 8A.

C Present your group's ideas in Ex 8B to the class. Did you all pick out similar trends?

7C Pre-loved

HOW TO ... | exaggerate
VOCABULARY: shopping; describing clothes
PRONUNCIATION: sentence stress: exaggeration

VOCABULARY

shopping

1 A Work in pairs. Is it common for people to buy and use second-hand items in your country? Why/Why not? Which particular items are popular?

B Read the first part of the infographic. What do you learn about the ownership of second-hand items? What reasons do you think are behind this trend?

C Read the second part of the infographic. What reason is given for buying each of the second-hand items listed?

2 A Complete the definitions with the words in bold in the second part of the infographic.

1 If something has had a previous owner, it's ....
2 If something is ...., it's expensive.
3 If something is ...., it's fashionable.
4 If something is fashionable and expensive, it's .... or ....
5 If something is in bad condition after a lot of use, it's ....
6 If something is ...., it's of a good enough quality.
7 If something is ...., it's old but high quality.

B Think about your answers to these questions. Think about how you can use the words in Ex 2A where possible.

1 Which of the items in the infographic would you buy second-hand? Why?
2 What else would you buy second-hand? Why?
3 Why would you not buy the other items in the infographic second-hand?
4 Some people say that at least fifty percent of what we own should be second-hand. Do you agree? Why/ Why not?

C Work in pairs and discuss the questions in Ex 2B. Do you have similar or different ideas?

D Learn and practise. Go to the Vocabulary Bank.

▶▶ page 140 **VOCABULARY BANK** describing clothes

Trends

31% Increase in second-hand items for sale on auction websites

$64 billion Estimated value of second-hand fashion in USA in 2025

2029 Year second-hand fashion will be worth more than fast fashion

$218 billion Estimated value of global second-hand clothes market in 2026

There's no point wasting money on children's clothes when kids grow so fast. Sell the **decent** clothes that don't fit them anymore and spend the money on **second-hand** replacements.

All couples want to look **classy** on their wedding day, but by buying a pre-loved outfit and giving it a second chance to fulfil its purpose, you can save money and be kind to the environment.

With so many people selling off **fancy** exercise equipment they've used just a handful of times, there's no need to pay full price for something new. Look for used items in excellent condition on sale locally for a great price.

The latest tech can be **costly**, so visit retailers and ask for items which have been opened, used or displayed in store. They're often in great condition and considerably cheaper.

When setting up a new home, visit markets, antique shops and second-hand stores for cheap second-hand furniture. With a little bit of work, it's easy to make **shabby** items look homely and brand new.

Visit **vintage** stores for fashion from the past to help you look fashionable, save money and reduce unwanted waste. From classic T-shirts to **trendy** suits to leather jackets that look lived in, you'll find items to match your style.

How to ...
exaggerate

3 A **7.07** | Listen to a conversation between two friends in a vintage clothes shop. Tick (✓) the things Theo would buy. What is Maisie looking to buy?

- trainers
- jeans
- denim jacket
- leather jacket
- band T-shirt

B **7.07** | Choose the words Theo and Maisie used in Ex 3A. Listen and check.

1 You take **a while** / **forever** to find something you want.
2 My feet are **hurting** / **killing** me and I'm **hungry** / **starving**.
3 There's **nothing** / **something** better than shopping at a vintage store.
4 I bet they cost a **fortune** / **lot**.
5 They're about **two** / **ten** sizes too small though.
6 I've told you a **few** / **million** times before, I don't like denim jackets.
7 This scruffy thing? I want one that's been lived in for a few years, not a few **centuries** / **decades**!
8 What if I bump into the previous owner in the street and they say 'Hi'? I'd **die of** / **feel** shame.
9 I wouldn't be seen **anywhere** / **dead** in a pop band T-shirt.
10 Then you'll be literally **green with envy** / **jealous**.

C Work in pairs. Why does the speaker use the words you chose in Ex 3B, and not the alternatives? What is the effect?

4 A Match the correct phrases in Ex 3B (1–10) with their type (a–c).

a exaggerated actions or states
b exaggerated size or quantities
c exaggerated comparisons or likenesses

B Learn and practise. Go to the Grammar Bank.

▶▶ page 130 **GRAMMAR BANK**

PRONUNCIATION
sentence stress: exaggeration

5 A **7.08** | Listen to the sentences. Which word is stressed the most? Why?

1 Anya's going to kill me when she finds out what I bought.
2 This shirt costs an absolute fortune!
3 I'd never be seen dead in those shoes.
4 A year old? It looks a hundred years old.

B Complete each sentence so it's an exaggeration of something true for you.

1 I have a ton of _____ at home which I never use/wear.
2 My _____ was/were killing me after _____ .
3 I'd never be seen dead in _____ .
4 There's nothing better than _____ .
5 I'd die of embarrassment if _____ .

C Work in groups. Take turns to read out your sentences in Ex 5B. Stress the most appropriate word. Which person do you have the most in common with?

SPEAKING

6 A Read the Future Skills box and discuss the question.

FUTURE SKILLS
Leadership

Leaders need to persuade others to believe in their ideas. To be persuasive, we can do these things.
1 Provide logical and emotional reasons for the idea.
2 Mention opposing or potential issues and dismiss them with valid reasons.
3 End by drawing positive conclusions.

Think of a time you persuaded someone or were persuaded by someone. What persuasive techniques were used?

B Work in pairs. You are going to try to persuade your partner to buy some vintage items. Student A: Go to page 143 and look at your items. Student B: Go to page 142 and look at your items. Follow the steps (1–3).

1 Think of ways to persuade your partner to buy the items, using exaggeration to help you.
2 Student A: Show Student B your items and try to persuade them to buy them. When your time is finished, find out which items Student B would be happy to purchase.
3 Student B: Show Student A your items and try to persuade them to buy them. When your time is finished, find out which items Student A would be happy to buy.

C Who was more persuasive in your pair? How?

MEDIATION SKILLS
synthesising information
compare, contrast and synthesise information in texts

▶▶ page 152 **MEDIATION BANK**

Past and present

VOCABULARY | memories
SPEAKING | a discussion about attitudes to the past and present
WRITING | a blog post

Samuel   Tilly

PREVIEW

1 Work in pairs. Do the quiz and compare your answers. Which of you thinks and talks about the past more?

Are you nostalgic about the past?

How often do you …	often	sometimes	never
look at old photos?			
think about things in the past that you miss?			
talk about past events with friends and family?			
think that things seemed better in the past?			

Q1: What kind of things make you feel nostalgic?

Q2: What was better about life when you were younger?

VIEW

2 A Watch the interviews, then work in small groups. Do any of the people feel nostalgic about the same things as you?

B ▶ Watch the first part of the interviews again.

Which person mentions:
1 doing an activity in the present and recalling doing the same thing as a child?
2 spending time with people they knew in the past?
3 watching films and videos of themselves in the past?
4 how the changing seasons make them think of the past?
5 how songs remind them of doing something with a parent?
6 three particular smells that remind them of their childhood?
7 being reminded of people who live in distant places?

C ▶ Watch the second part of the interviews again. Note down one thing that each speaker feels was better in the past.

VOCABULARY

memories

3 A Work in pairs and read the sentences. Which ones are taken from the interviews?
1 That smell just **took me back** to my childhood.
2 It **reminds me of** driving in the car with my mum.
3 It **brings back memories of** family holidays.
4 Seeing old movies **transports me back** to my childhood.
5 I'd love to **recapture** that feeling of freedom.
6 Looking at old photos can help you **relive** experiences and feelings.
7 He likes **reminiscing** about his time at school in Scotland.
8 I don't think it's ever possible to **recreate** a past feeling.

B Look at the words and phrases in bold in Ex 3A. Which ones are used to describe a memory that is caused by something in the present? Which ones are generally talking about remembering something?

C Work in pairs. Talk about things that make you feel nostalgic. Use some of the words and phrases in Ex 3A.

Tara   Seb   Eloise

Lauren   Allan   Joy

SPEAKING

a discussion about attitudes to the past and present

4 A Work in pairs. Read the opinions about the past. Explain in your own words the ideas they express.

> The past is gone and the future is still a dream. Only the present exists.

> Our past is never really gone. It is part of us and we carry it with us to inform our present.

> The past only exists in our minds, and we change it to create the memories we want to remember.

B 🔊 **7.09** | Listen to part of a discussion about the opinions in Ex 4A. Which two opinions do the people discuss?

C 🔊 **7.09** | Listen again and tick the Key phrases you hear.

KEY PHRASES

It's certainly true that …
I'm not sure I go along with that idea because …
… is definitely important because …
If you … too much, you might …
Focusing on … allows you to …
It's easy to see … as …

D Work in groups. Discuss how each of the opinions in Ex 4A might be true and decide which opinion you agree with the most and why. Use the Key phrases to help you.

WRITING

a blog post

5 A Work in pairs. Tell your partner about a particularly happy memory from your past.

B Read the blog post. What kinds of memories does the person want to hear about?

 SA   ✎ 2 reviews   ⦿ GB   A day ago

Positive memories

Last week, a friend of mine came out with a quote suggesting that the past is gone, and we should forget about it. He was arguing that getting stuck in the past prevents you from really enjoying the present. But, as someone who loves poring over old photos and being transported back to fun times with friends or family, this struck me as completely wrong. My experience is that revisiting happy times in the past can bring joy to the present, making you feel close to people you perhaps don't see that often now, and lifting your mood. What better on a dull, rainy afternoon than flicking through photos of that amazing holiday you had a couple of years ago and reliving the fun, or listening to music that recaptures that crazy first week of university? And I can't be alone in this. What happy memories do you enjoy reliving?

6 A You are going to write a blog post about a happy memory. Think about a happy memory you have and make notes on the following.

- where you were and who you were with
- what happened
- how you felt at the time
- what takes you back and reminds you of the memory
- how you feel when you relive it

B Write your blog post.

C Share your blog posts with the class. Whose memories are similar to yours? Which did you most enjoy reading about?

GRAMMAR

adverbials

1 A Rewrite the sentences using the correct adverbial in brackets in a suitable place.

1 It's important to talk to people when they're upset. (in a sensitive way / carefully)

2 We finally reached our destination. (always / two hours later)

3 We eat out in restaurants. (very rarely / decidedly)

4 The hotel was disappointing. (quietly / incredibly)

5 No one was injured in the crash. (amazingly / pretty much all day)

6 I work from home. (quite / three days a week)

B Write sentences about yourself using the adverbials in the box. Read your sentences to a partner and give more information.

> from time to time   in a generous way
> incredibly   last summer
> to my astonishment

fronting: reasons, causes and explanations

2 A Read the pairs of sentences and underline the reason, cause or explanation in each one.

1 I passed all my exams. I worked so hard.

2 I was ill in the summer. I wasn't able to work.

3 I left the organisation. I was disappointed by the job.

4 Hana is a talented painter. She hopes to become a professional artist.

5 Alex kept applying for jobs. His friend's success had inspired him.

6 We decided not to go for a walk. The weather was bad.

B Rewrite each pair of sentences in Ex 2A as one sentence. Front the reason, cause or explanation and use the words in brackets below. Where no word is given, use an *-ed* participle clause. You may need to make extra changes to the sentence.

1 Since I worked so hard, I passed all my exams. (since)

2 _____ (illness)

3 _____

4 _____ (as)

5 _____

6 _____ (result)

VOCABULARY

3 A Choose the correct words to complete the opinions.

1 I find it easier to understand complex ideas if writers use stories to **illustrate** / **define** their points.

2 I often find it difficult to **signify** / **sum up** exactly how I'm feeling.

3 I think that in the future, technology will **transform** / **decline** the way we eat.

4 I avoid foods like butter and cheese because I know they contain a lot of **nutrients** / **cholesterol**.

5 I would never spend a lot of money on designer clothes. They're far too **costly** / **shabby**.

6 For me, clothes should always look good together. When I wear trousers, I always wear a **loud** / **matching** top, never one in a completely different colour.

B Do you agree with the statements in Ex 3A? Why/Why not? Tell a partner.

4 A Choose the correct options (A–C) to complete the article.

Tourism trends

The world of travel is changing. We look at four current trends.

Solo travel Holidays used to be for families, couples or groups of friends, but [1]_____ , there has been a [2]_____ towards travelling alone. Many people are now keen to explore new cultures [3]_____ , without the distraction of friends or family members.

Eco travel [4]_____ concerns about climate change, a growing number of people are seeking out trips that they consider to be ethical or sustainable. [5]_____ these travellers are keen to reduce their carbon footprint, they may wish to avoid flying to their destination. Eco holidays also often include some form of volunteering, which [6]_____ a willingness to give back to the communities they are visiting.

Healthy food Whereas in the past, many tourists were happy to [7]_____ a snack in the street, there is now a trend towards trips with healthy food options. A growing number of tourists now [8]_____ that they are more likely to stay in hotels serving fresh, [9]_____ food.

Automation The rapid [10]_____ of new technologies is bringing a range of changes in the tourism industry. Customers use chatbots to help them book their trips online, and some top-end hotels are also introducing robot receptionists to greet guests.

1 A usually	**B** in recent years	**C** decidedly
2 A shift	**B** decline	**C** surge
3 A generally	**B** interestingly	**C** in a relaxed way
4 A As a result	**B** Because	**C** Influenced by
5 A As	**B** Motivated by	**C** As a result of
6 A sums up	**B** signifies	**C** defines
7 A grab	**B** pull	**C** hold
8 A capture	**B** specify	**C** illustrate
9 A junk	**B** nutrient	**C** organic
10 A catalyst	**B** switch	**C** evolution

B 🔊 **R7.01 | Listen and check.**

C Which of the trends in the article do you think are the most positive? Why? What other trends in tourism are you aware of in your country?

the future 8

B B C

VLOGS

Q: Do you generally feel optimistic or pessimistic about the future?

1 ▶ Watch the video. Are most of the people optimistic or pessimistic? What reasons do they mention?

2 How do you feel about the future?

Global Scale of English
LEARNING OBJECTIVES

8A READING | Read an extract from a story about a dystopian future: dystopian and utopian societies

Pronunciation: pausing when conceding a point

Have a debate on technology and dystopia: concession

8B LISTENING | Understand a radio discussion about future technologies: science and technology

Pronunciation: contractions and weak forms: the future perfect

Evaluate solutions to future problems: future forms

Write an opinion essay

8C HOW TO … | maintain and end a discussion: money

Pronunciation: intonation: ending a discussion

8D BBC PROGRAMME | Understand a science-fiction TV drama

Give a summary: machines

Write a continuation of a narrative

8A Dystopias and utopias

GRAMMAR | concession
VOCABULARY | dystopian and utopian societies
PRONUNCIATION | pausing when conceding a point

READING

1 A Work in pairs and answer the questions.

1 What do you imagine life is like in each of the societies in the photos?

2 Which society would you prefer to read about or see in a film? Why?

B Read the information about the BBC Radio programme. How would you define *dystopia* and *utopia*? Why do you think people prefer dystopian fiction to utopian fiction?

The Why Factor B B C

Dystopian fiction is hugely popular right now, in books, on TV and in film. Shabnam Grewal explores what it is about dystopias that makes them so appealing to us, and why we prefer dystopian fiction to utopian fiction.

C 🔊 **8.01** | Listen to an extract from the programme. How are *dystopia* and *utopia* defined? How similar are these definitions to your own definitions in Ex 1B?

2 A Read an extract from a forthcoming book. Would you like to read the whole book? Why/Why not?

B Read the extract again. Using ideas mentioned in the extract, and your own knowledge, what can you infer about these things?

1 the physical state of the city

2 the life the main character leads

3 protests and violence in the streets and their cause

4 the main character's view of the past

5 the Volters

6 what happened to cause the current situation

7 why thoughts could be problematic in the future

C Work in pairs. Share your ideas from Ex 2B. Give reasons to support your inferences.

D Work in pairs. Do you think that this kind of dystopian future is a possibility? Why/Why not?

The sun, already dimmed by pollution, sinks low as I make my way home. I pass once verdant but now decaying trees; symbols of both the city and the lives of its residents today. The street that was always a hive of activity is deathly quiet as people scurry home, heads down, avoiding all contact. I glance to my left and see dusty curtains twitch slightly as a woman peeks out to see what she can spot. Once it was out of curiosity. Now it's both out of **paranoia** that people are watching her, and the desire to see something that will gain her bargaining power.

I pull up my collar with my grime-stained hands and think back to the days when neighbours would smile and wave, chat, ask for advice or offer to help out a neighbour in need. The days when we had dreams and money to burn. It wasn't **paradise**. There were bad times as well as good. We had to follow rules and contribute to society, but we had personal freedom and a sense of community. Despite a few small disagreements, there was **harmony** in our neighbourhood. Today, knowing we're under constant **surveillance**, all we do is avoid each other and, of course, avoid the attention of the Volters.

Speaking of which, I spot two Volters either side of me, scanning everyone who passes to check we are home before **curfew** and are not getting involved in any **social unrest**. They needn't bother. There's been no such trouble for months, not with the lack of **justice** that exists now. I speed up to pass the Volters quickly, glancing at them as I do. Their metal frames cast a shadow over the street in more ways than one, but I can't blame these machines. It was those who once programmed them who must accept responsibility. There's a fine line between opportunity and threat, and those men and women crossed it for a little more money, a little more power. Their **greed** wasn't the only cause either. The rest of us must accept our part in it, too. We all turned a blind eye for the sake of a touch more convenience, when we should have been more cautious. We're all now paying the price for our stupidity with **oppression**.

With the Volters now behind me, I slow down as I spot my home in the distance. 'Home', I chuckle bitterly to myself. Home was once a safe haven – a place of **tranquillity** to rest after a hard day's work. A warm and loving place, full of life, laughter, and when I look back now, **innocence**. That might sound like **idealism**, but it was infinitely better than the place it is today. It's now little more than a shelter from the cold and rain, where hope left, and fear moved in. I shake my head to clear my thoughts. I've heard there's talk of brain implants. If it's true, all these thoughts I have will need to be a thing of the past.

VOCABULARY

dystopian and utopian societies

3 A Complete the table with the words in bold in the book extract in Ex 2A.

Describing dystopias	Describing utopias
....	....
....	....
....	....
....	....
....	....

B Match the words in Ex 3A with the meanings (1–12).

1 a state of being peaceful
2 watching people
3 selfish desire for more (e.g. power)
4 a time people must be inside
5 being together in peace
6 unreasonable belief you can't trust others
7 people being treated fairly
8 protests or violent behaviour
9 an extremely pleasant place
10 an unrealistic belief in perfection
11 the lack of knowledge of bad things
12 when a group of people are treated unfairly

C Work in pairs. Think of a fictional dystopian or utopian society. Use the words in Ex 3A to help you describe it. Do you think people would always choose to live in a utopia?

GRAMMAR

concession

4 A Read the forum discussion about the book extract. How many commenters are positive about it? How many are unsure or not interested?

 kay92 **Admittedly**, it doesn't sound like the happiest of settings for a story, but personally I love anything dystopian and I can't wait to find out more about this particular world and the person who's narrating it.

 nessieblue You're right **@kay92**, it doesn't sound that cheery, but **at the same time**, the best stories are those where the main characters fight against oppression and win in the end. I'll definitely be giving it a go when it's released.

 samrocks It has potential, but I'll wait to see what reviewers say about it once they've read the whole thing.

 ice2006 **Although** it'll no doubt be a big seller, it's not for me. I prefer my stories served with a big side dish of positivity thank you very much.

 foxylox I'll definitely be reading this, **even though** it sounds like a lot of stories that have gone before it.

 akeem99 You said it **@foxyloxy**. Nothing original here. I'm out.

 cal3 **True though that seems** **@akeem99**, we've only seen a tiny extract. I'm willing to take a chance on it.

 wildcat Me too, **@cal3**. **While** there are a lot of books in this genre, it gets my attention.

B Look at the words and phrases in bold in the forum discussion and select their purpose (a, b or c).

a add strength to a speaker's point of view
b give an example to support a speaker's point of view
c introduce a point of view that the speaker disagrees with, but admits is true

C Look at the words and phrases in bold again. Do the commenters usually start with their opinion or the concession that an opposing opinion is true? Why do you think this is?

D Learn and practise. Go to the Grammar Bank.

▶▶ page 131 **GRAMMAR BANK**

PRONUNCIATION
pausing when conceding a point

5 A 🔊 **8.02 |** Listen to the sentences. Mark the pauses you hear with ' / '.

1 Even though it's said that young people don't read anymore, many of them do.
2 Fiction can be shocking, but at the same time true stories can be more shocking.
3 Admittedly, dystopian stories don't sound positive, but they can be very uplifting.
4 True as that may be, not everyone has the same taste in fiction.

B 🔊 **8.02 |** Listen again. Which word or phrase is stressed most in each sentence? Why do you think this is?

C Complete the sentences with your own ideas.

1 Even though … are popular, …
2 Admittedly, … , but I'm optimistic/pessimistic about …
3 While my favourite … is, …
4 Interesting though … is, I feel that …

D Work in pairs. Tell each other your sentences in Ex 5C. Pause and stress key words appropriately.

SPEAKING

6 A Work in pairs. You are going to have a debate. First, read the infographic. Would you describe these statistics as positive, worrying, surprising or something else?

B Work with another pair. Decide which pair (Pair A) will argue for the statement below and which pair (Pair B) will argue against it. Then, go to page 142 and read the five extracts. Use this information to help you put together your argument with supporting ideas.

Because of our use of technology, we're already living in a dystopian world.

C Pair A and Pair B: Work together and debate the topic.

- Pair A: You have one minute to summarise your argument for the statement.
- Pair B: You have one minute to summarise your argument against the statement.
- Both pairs: Discuss and respond to each other's arguments.

7 A Have a class vote to find out if most people agree or disagree with the debate statement in Ex 6B.

B Read the Future Skills box and do the task. Share your reflections with a partner.

FUTURE SKILLS
Self-management

Regular reflection helps us to recognise what we have learnt from our experiences and how that affects future goals and activities. Useful questions are:
- 'Have I put maximum effort in? Where can I put in more effort in the future?'
- 'How did I benefit? How can I use this in the future?'
- 'What was my personal goal? Did I achieve it? How does this change future goals?'

Answer the questions about today's lesson.

Our use of technology today

13
Number of new social media users every second

4.8
Average number of hours spent on a mobile phone daily

147
Number of minutes the average person spends on social media daily

770 million
Number of CCTV surveillance cameras worldwide

2 million
Number of smartphones sold around the world each day

4.62 billion
Number of people on social media

8B The science we need

GRAMMAR | future forms
VOCABULARY | science and technology
PRONUNCIATION | contractions and weak forms: the future perfect

VOCABULARY

science and technology

1 A Work in pairs. Can you think of any useful things that should be invented? Why would we need them?

B Read the forum post and comments about things people think should be invented. Which invention would you most like to have? Why?

Czilling ♡ 32 💬 12 ↪

I wake up every morning and I know I've been dreaming, but I can never remember my dreams. I would love a device that could **monitor** my brain as I sleep and **convert** my thought patterns into a story that I could read in the morning. Does anyone have any other ideas for things they think should be invented?

Neil M ♡ 2 💬 0 ↪
Self-cleaning clothes – clothes that can **detect** dirt and **activate** their own cleaning process to **eliminate** it, so I'd never have to do any washing!

Agwe_B ♡ 6 💬 1 ↪
A car that could **generate** its own power – so no need to fill up with fuel or **recharge** the battery. Of course, it wouldn't **emit** any harmful pollutants!

Samalik2016 ♡ 14 💬 1 ↪
A way to **modify** our favourite foods so they have the same flavour but don't contain anything that's bad for us. That would really **revolutionise** our diets and our health!

C Choose the correct word to complete the adverts. Use the words in bold in the posts in Ex 1B to help you.

1 *Breathe Safe*
A revolutionary new T-shirt that **monitors** / **converts** levels of air pollution around you and **activates** / **eliminates** an alarm when they get too high, so you know to go indoors.

2 *Chew4Ever*
Do you get fed up with the fact that chewing gum loses its flavour after only a few minutes? We have **modified** / **recharged** the way we flavour our gum, so it continues to taste good all day long. It will save you money and will also **generate** / **eliminate** a lot of waste from discarded chewing gum!

3 *CosyToes*
Do your feet get cold in the winter? These amazing socks **convert** / **detect** when your feet are starting to get cold, then use solar energy to **monitor** / **generate** heat to keep them warm!

4 *RainPower*
One of the problems with having solar panels on your roof is that in some countries it isn't always sunny. Now the *RainPower* device uses new technology to **recharge** / **convert** the energy from falling rain into electricity, so you can provide clean energy for your home without **emitting** / **modifying** any damaging contaminants.

5 *EverCharge*
It's a real pain having to **activate** / **recharge** the batteries in all your devices. These brand-new *EverCharge* batteries will **revolutionise** / **eliminate** your life because they simply never run out of power!

2 A Work in pairs. Discuss whether each product in Ex 1C is a great idea, possibly useful or just ridiculous. Explain your reasons.

B Learn and practise. Go to the Vocabulary Bank.

▶▶ page 140 **VOCABULARY BANK** science and technology

LISTENING

3 A Work in groups. Think of three inventions or discoveries in the past that changed people's lives in a positive way. Tell the class your ideas.

Electricity changed people's lives by allowing them to …

B 🔊 8.03 | Listen to a radio discussion about simple inventions that could change the world in the future. What three inventions are mentioned?

C 🔊 8.03 | Listen again. Match each statement with one of the three inventions, the fabric (F), the app (A) or the shower (S).

1 A lot of small benefits would make a big difference when all added up.
2 This addresses a problem that is growing in many countries.
3 Most people wouldn't be motivated to use it.
4 The technology can be used on a small or large scale.
5 There are many different ways in which the technology could be used.
6 It could improve people's health.

4 A How likely is it that each invention will be developed, according to the comments about the radio discussion (1–6)? Match each invention in Ex 3B with two comments.

1 It's already in use, so it's almost certain that many of us will be using this technology within ten years.
2 It will probably be cheaper to produce in ten years, so it's likely that it will be used in products that we buy.
3 It's very unlikely that the technology will ever be widely available.
4 It would possibly encourage sellers to offer healthier options.
5 It will definitely cut down on a lot of waste.
6 It's impressive because it will undoubtedly produce energy in a way that doesn't harm the environment.

B Work in pairs. Discuss the questions.

Which of the inventions:

1 would you most like to have in your home or daily life? Why?
2 do you think could bring the most benefits to people? In what ways?
3 have potential disadvantages? What are they?

GRAMMAR

future forms

5 A Choose the correct forms to complete the sentences from the radio discussion.

1 … within the next ten years, these technical issues **will be addressing** / **will have been addressed**.
2 I'm also hopeful that the costs **will have come down** / **are coming down** by then.
3 So, my guess is we **will have used** / **won't be using** food-scanner apps any time soon.
4 I think by then, architects **will be building** / **will have been building** these kinds of systems into new homes for a while.

B Work in pairs. Look at the correct forms in Ex 5A again. Match them with the future forms in the box. Which sentence in Ex 5A uses a passive form?

future continuous   future perfect   future perfect continuous

C Complete the rules with the correct future forms from Ex 5B.

We use the:

1 .... for an action that will be in progress at a time in the future.
2 .... to talk about the length of an action from a time in the future.
3 .... for an action that will be completed by a time in the future.

D Learn and practise. Go to the Grammar Bank.

▶▶ page 132 **GRAMMAR BANK**

PRONUNCIATION
contractions and weak forms: the future perfect

6 A 🔊 8.04 | Listen to the sentences. Underline the parts of the words in bold that are pronounced as contractions or weak forms.

1 I'm optimistic that scientists **will have found** a way around this issue.
2 These devices are a great idea and I'm sure **they will have become** very popular within a few years.
3 Hopefully, this invention **will have been developed** soon.
4 It's a serious problem, but experts predict **it will have been solved** in the next few years.

B Choose the correct words to complete the rules.

1 In future perfect forms, we **never** / **usually** pronounce *have* and *been* as weak forms in natural speech.
2 We usually pronounce *will* as a contraction after a **noun** / **pronoun**.

C Complete the sentences with your own ideas. Then work in pairs and take turns to say your sentences. Remember to use contractions and weak forms as appropriate.

1 I hope that within the next few years, I'll have …
2 By the end of next year, I'll have been …
3 In the next ten years, I think … will have been …

SPEAKING

7 A Think of three possible future technologies or inventions that we might be using by 2100 and make notes. Use the ideas in the box and the questions below to help you.

> energy   environment   food
> medicine   travel

- What problems will need to be solved?
- What new technologies will scientists have developed?
- What new machines or devices will people be using?

B Work in pairs. Present your ideas to each other and justify your predictions. Then choose three ideas to present to the class.

C Take turns to present your predictions to the class and explain how likely you think they are to be developed by 2100. Make notes on all your classmates' predictions as you listen to the presentations.

8 A Read the Future Skills box and do the task.

FUTURE SKILLS
Critical thinking

When we discuss different ideas, it is useful to compare them in detail, to decide which is best. To do this, you need to think carefully about each idea and consider its strengths and its weaknesses.

Look at your notes in Ex 7C. What different structures and phrases can you use to compare your classmates' predictions? Make a list.

'One reason I think this prediction is more likely to come true is …'

'I think this idea is less likely because …'

B Work in groups. Discuss and compare all the predictions. Decide on the two that you think are the most likely.

C Tell the class your ideas and reasons. Then hold a class vote to choose the technology that is most likely to be invented.

WRITING

an opinion essay

9 A Read the statement in the essay question. Do you agree or disagree with it? Why?

'Governments should fund research into new technologies, rather than relying on private companies to do it.'

To what extent do you agree with this opinion?

B Read an essay responding to the question. What is the writer's opinion on the topic? Does the writer mention any of your ideas in Ex 9A?

¹ .... The world faces many significant problems, such as pollution, climate change and the challenge of feeding a growing global population. Solutions must be found to these problems so that people can continue to live successfully on this planet, without causing any further damage or destruction. Because these problems affect us all, it seems fair that governments should pay for it, rather than relying on private companies.

² .... It often requires the use of large laboratories with costly, state-of-the-art equipment. It is also often necessary to employ large teams of scientists to work on projects. Most companies cannot afford to spend millions of dollars on these kinds of facilities.

³ .... Some research projects might take several years to come up with any significant results or discoveries. In other cases, exploring a promising idea might require a lot of time and effort, but might, in the end, lead to the realisation that the idea cannot be developed any further. It is impossible for private companies to fund long-term projects as they need to produce and sell products quickly, in order to pay for the research.

In conclusion, I believe that governments should invest a significant portion of their spending to fund research in order to find solutions to the major problems that affect us all.

C Read the essay again. Complete it with the correct sentence at the beginning of each paragraph (a–c).

a Research requires long-term investment.
b New technologies are vital to the future of us all.
c Research into new technologies is expensive.

D The sentences in Ex 9C are called topic sentences. Answer the questions.

1 What is their function?
2 How many ideas and examples does the writer use to support and expand on each topic sentence?

10 A Work in pairs. Discuss the essay question below. Do you agree or disagree with the statement? Why?

'Science will eventually find solutions to climate change, so individuals don't need to change the way they live now.'

To what extent do you agree with this opinion?

B Plan your essay and make notes on your arguments, opinions and reasons.

C Write your essay. Remember to use topic sentences supported by ideas and examples to help present your arguments.

8C Spend or save?

HOW TO ... | maintain and end a discussion
VOCABULARY | money
PRONUNCIATION | intonation: ending a discussion

VOCABULARY

money

1 A Work in pairs. Discuss the questions.

1 Are you generally a saver or a spender?
2 How important do you think it is to plan financially for the future?
3 How important is it to live in the moment?
4 Is it possible to achieve a balance between living in the moment and planning for the future?

B Work in pairs. Read what two people say about money. What are the advantages and disadvantages of each person's approach?

I'm really interested in the FIRE movement. It stands for Financial Independence, Retire Early, and I think it makes a lot of sense. Who wants to work until they are seventy? Basically, I keep a careful eye on my **expenditure** and I **put aside** as much money as I can each month. I buy the **essentials** such as food, cover the household bills, then give myself a small **allowance** each month to spend on clothes and going out. Apart from that, I save as much as I can. So, no holidays and no expensive nights out. Some people might think I'm **stingy** because I don't give expensive presents, but I'm focused on building up my savings so I can retire as soon as I can.

My motto is 'Work hard, play hard.' I've got a **steady job** and I'm well paid. I don't see the point in being **frugal** and holding on to your money – just enjoy it! I don't think twice about **splashing out on** a new outfit or a meal in a nice restaurant. Life is for living! I usually manage to **blow** my salary well before the next one is due. Most months I do overspend, so I have a small **overdraft** at the bank. But I don't see this as a problem. Maybe I'll be able to save more in the future, when I'm older, but while I'm young, I want to enjoy my life!

2 A Decide if the meanings of the words and phrases in bold are correct or incorrect. Correct the ones that are incorrect. Use the texts in Ex 1B to help you.

1 Your **expenditure** is the amount of money you spend each month.
2 If you **put** money **aside**, you spend it on things that you want.
3 **Essentials** are extra things that you don't need to buy, but want to buy.
4 An **allowance** is an amount of money that you can spend.
5 If you are **stingy**, you are generous with your money.
6 A **steady job** is one that is not certain or secure.
7 If you are **frugal**, you are careful about how much money you spend.
8 If you **splash out on** something, you buy something expensive.
9 If you **blow** your salary or savings, you keep some and don't spend all your money.
10 If you have an **overdraft** at the bank, you have a negative amount of money in your account.

B Work in pairs. Tell your partner about:

1 three essentials that you buy every week.
2 something you splashed out on recently.
3 someone you know who is very frugal and tries to save every penny they earn.
4 a steady job that you would like to have.
5 someone you know who always blows their salary.
6 something you would stop buying if you wanted to reduce your expenditure.
7 how much allowance you give yourself each month to buy clothes.
8 someone you know who is stingy.

C Learn and practise. Go to the Vocabulary Bank.

▶▶ page 140 **VOCABULARY BANK** money

How to …
maintain and end a discussion

3 A 🔊 **8.05** | Listen to a discussion between friends about their attitudes to money. Match each person (1–3) with a summary of their views (a–c).

1 Alina
2 Oscar
3 Beth

a believes it is a good idea to save money now in order to have a better future

b thinks that it is best to spend your money and enjoy life while you are young

c believes it is possible to have a good time and also save some money each month

B 🔊 **8.05** | Complete the extracts with the words in the box. Listen again and check.

> as   dare   frankly   great   guess
> looking   makes   see   the coin   with

1 Well, ... Alina, I think it's a stupid idea!

2 .... I see it, the future is completely unpredictable.

3 But the other side of .... is that it's very easy to waste all the money you earn in your twenties.

4 I guess that's one way of .... at it, but on the other hand, …

5 That .... two of us.

6 I can .... what Oscar's saying.

7 I .... say most young people could save a small amount each month.

8 I'm .... Alina here.

9 It's been .... talking to you.

10 I .... we're all different.

C Work in pairs. Which words and phrases in Ex 3B:

a introduce a personal opinion?

b express agreement with another person?

c express disagreement, or introduce an opposing opinion?

d summarise the discussion and bring it to an end?

D Learn and practise. Go to the Grammar Bank.

▶▶ page 133 **GRAMMAR BANK**

PRONUNCIATION
intonation: ending a discussion

4 A 🔊 **8.06** | Read and listen to three extracts from the discussion in Ex 3A. Which person ends with a flat tone and falling intonation (1–3)? Why?

1 Isn't that when people try to save as much as they can while they're young, so they can retire early?

2 I guess that's one way of looking at it, but on the other hand, if you focus all your efforts on the future, there's a danger you won't enjoy the present. I'm all for living in the moment and enjoying life while you can!

3 Well, you'll never convince me that I should give up all the things I enjoy. But it's been great talking to you. I guess we're all different.

B Work in pairs. Take turns to say the extracts in Ex 4A. Can your partner hear the difference in tone and intonation when you want to end the discussion?

SPEAKING

5 A Do you ever give money to charity? If so, how do you decide how much to give?

B Read the opinions about giving away money. Which opinions do you agree/disagree with most strongly? What arguments and examples can you use to support these opinions?

> I work hard for every penny I earn, so I don't believe in giving any of it away. If other people don't have enough, that's not my responsibility.

> I think it's important to give when you can, for example when there's been a big natural disaster. But if I don't have any spare cash, I don't give, and I don't feel bad about it.

> For me, we should only keep as much money as we need for essentials. I support a few charities and whenever I have money left over at the end of the month, I give it away.

> I believe most people could live quite comfortably on ninety-nine percent of the money they have, so I put aside one percent of my income each year and give it away.

> In my opinion, the most practical and cost-effective way I can help other people is to get a well-paid job and become as rich as I can, then give away most of what I've earned. That's my life plan!

C Work in groups. Discuss and compare your ideas. Use phrases from this lesson to maintain and end your conversation.

D What ideas do the people in your group share? Tell the class.

> **MEDIATION SKILLS**
> co-developing ideas
> contribute to collaborative decision-making
>
> ▶▶ page 154 **MEDIATION BANK**

8D BBC Entertainment

Science fiction

VOCABULARY | machines
SPEAKING | a summary
WRITING | a continuation of a narrative

PREVIEW

1 A What science-fiction films, series or books do you know? Which are your favourites? Why?

B Work in pairs. Discuss the questions.

In a sci-fi story, how might …

1 people travel through space and time?
2 a company deliver goods to different parts of the universe?
3 factories be run and organised?
4 machines select people for different jobs?

C Read the programme information. Have you watched any similar TV series?

BBC

Doctor Who

Doctor Who is a long-running BBC science-fiction drama series. It was originally intended as a family show, but it also has a lot of adult fans. The main character, the Doctor, and her assistants travel through space and time in a spaceship that looks like an old-fashioned police telephone box and have a series of adventures in the different places they visit. In this episode, an unexpected delivery leads the Doctor and her assistants to visit Kerblam, the biggest retailer in the galaxy.

VIEW

2 A ▶ Watch the BBC video clip. Does it mention any of your ideas from Ex 1B?

B ▶ Watch the video again and answer the questions.

1 Why does the Doctor decide they all need to go to Kerblam?
2 How do they decide to gain access to the building?
3 Why do the Doctor and her assistants have to be scanned?
4 What are 'organic workers'?
5 Why does the Doctor swap tags with Graham?
6 What job is Graham given?

B B C

VOCABULARY

machines

3 A Work in pairs. Complete the sentences (1–7) with the words and phrases in the box.

> conveyor   delivery bot   fully automated
> robots   scan   shuttle   teleport

1 The postman who delivers the parcel to the Doctor is a _____ .
2 The receptionist at Kerblam says she didn't know that a _____ was arriving today.
3 The Doctor says that some of her best friends are _____ .
4 The receptionist describes the processes at Kerblam as _____ , but people-powered.
5 The workers _____ the products and send them in to the packing stations.
6 Once the customer's order is packed, it goes on the _____ .
7 From Dispatch, the postmen retrieve the parcels and _____ them direct to the customers.

B Match the words and phrases in 1–7 in Ex 3A with the meanings (a–g).

a using only machines, not humans.
b move something by breaking it down into tiny pieces and transporting it very quickly over long distances
c a machine that looks like a human and delivers parcels
d read information on something using a special device
e a spacecraft that makes regular journeys to and from the same destination in space
f machines that can move and do some of the work of a person, usually controlled by a computer
g a moving part of a machine that you can put things on to carry them along

C Work in pairs. Discuss the questions.

1 Where do people scan goods on a day-to-day basis?
2 Do you think delivery bots that look like humans will ever exist? Why?/Why not?
3 Do you think it will ever be possible to teleport people or things? Why/Why not?

SPEAKING

a summary

4 A 🔊 **8.07** | Listen to a summary of a science-fiction film. Do you know the film?

B 🔊 **8.07** | Listen again and tick the Key phrases you hear.

> **KEY PHRASES**
>
> The plot is fairly straightforward/fiendishly complicated, etc.
> Nothing is as it appears to be.
> They face the difficult task of …
> It's a race against time because …
> The tension rises as …
> In a twist at the end, …

C Think of a science-fiction film or series you know and plan your summary. Use the Key phrases to help you.

D Work in groups. Give your summaries and discuss the films or series. Which have you already seen and enjoyed? Which would you like to see? Why/Why not?

WRITING

a continuation of a narrative

5 A Look at the different ways in which science fiction can be produced and enjoyed. Which of these do you find the most enjoyable? Why?

> animations   comic books   films   novels   TV series

B Which of the statements (1–3) do you think is true for all of the science-fiction media in Ex 5A?

1 They all consist of futuristic scenarios.
2 They all narrate a sequence of fictitious events.
3 They all adhere to scientifically possible theories.

C Write a continuation of a narrative. Go to the Writing Bank.

▶▶ page 109 **WRITING BANK**

GRAMMAR

concession

1 A Match the sentence beginnings (1–6) with the endings (a–f).

1 Although I live in the city,
2 I support healthy eating. That
3 Hard as something may
4 While my friends and I have similar views,
5 Setting goals can focus you. At the
6 Vegetables are good for you.

a seem, we should always believe we can do it.
b said, I think it's good to treat ourselves, too.
c They're so boring to eat though.
d same time, they can put pressure on you.
e we disagree on a few things.
f I much prefer country life.

B Do you agree with the statements in Ex 1A? Why/Why not? Tell a partner.

2 A Choose the correct words to complete the sentences.

1 **That said / Although** technology helps us, it causes problems, too.
2 **At the same time / Even though** we might fail at something, we'll always learn something.
3 We can try to get on with everyone. There are always some people we don't connect with **although / though**.
4 As fun **as / while** travelling seems, it can be very tiring.
5 Tea has far more benefits than coffee. **While / That said**, I drink much more coffee.
6 **Admittedly, / Even though** staying fit takes time, but we should all make time for it.
7 **However / While** we enjoy being sociable, it's nice to have time to ourselves, too.
8 Having a list of goals can be motivating. **At the same time / True though**, it can put too much pressure on us.

B Work in pairs. Which statement in Ex 2A do you agree with the most? Why?

3 A Complete the sentences with your own ideas.

1 An activity everyone should try is .... That said, ...
2 Even though I don't .... very often, I find it very ....
3 Fun though .... is, it's not for everyone.
4 An app I'd recommend is .... , although ....
5 One of the most .... people I know is .... He/She's sometimes .... though.
6 It's always nice to .... at the weekends, even though I should probably be .... instead.

B Work in pairs. Take turns to share your ideas in Ex 3A. Expand your ideas a little each time.

future forms

4 Add one word to each sentence to make it grammatically correct.

1 I'll sitting here waiting for you when you come out.
2 By ten o'clock, we'll been waiting for an hour.
3 The concert will ended by the time we get there.
4 I hope that by the time I'm thirty, I'll have running my own company for at least a year.
5 Hopefully, the food will have delivered by the time you get home.

5 A Choose the correct verb forms (a, b or c).

1 This time next week, we .... on a beach in Italy.
   a have laid   b 'll be lying   c 'll have been lying
2 Meet me at 2 p.m. I'll .... my work by then and will be ready to go.
   a have been finishing   b be finishing   c have finished
3 In March, my parents will .... for fifty years!
   a be married   b have been married   c have finished
4 Soon you .... at that screen for over three hours. Take a break!
   a 'll have been looking   b 'll be looking   c 'll have looked
5 Come back at midday. Your car .... by then.
   a will have fixed   b will be fixing   c will have been fixed
6 I can't meet you at 1 p.m. I'll .... to the airport to pick up a client at that time.
   a have travelled   b have been travelling   c be travelling
7 I've just realised that I'll .... for this company for five years in March!
   a have been working   b worked   c be working
8 Haven't you finished that yet? You'll .... it for over a month soon.
   a be doing   b have been doing   c have done

B Work in pairs. Does each sentence in Ex 5A talk about a future action in progress, a finished future action or the length of an action seen from a future time?

6 A Complete the questions with the correct future continuous, future perfect or future perfect continuous form of the verbs in brackets.

1 What .... (you / do) by the time you go to bed tonight?
2 What .... (you / do) this time tomorrow?
3 Who .... (you / talk) to at eight o'clock tomorrow morning?
4 For how long .... (you / study) English by the end of this course?
5 What goals .... (you / achieve) by the end of the year?
6 For how long .... (you / live) in your current home next year?
7 Where do you think .... (you / live) in ten years' time?
8 What job do you think .... (you / do) in ten years' time?

B Work in pairs. Take turns to ask and answer the questions in Ex 6A.

VOCABULARY

7 A Match the words in the box with what is being talked about (1–6).

> curfew   greed   oppression   paranoia
> social unrest   surveillance

1 'Everyone's talking about me.'
2 'I don't have the same rights as other people.'
3 'We can't go outside after 9 p.m.'
4 'He has lots of money, but he wants more!'
5 'Cameras are recording our every move.'
6 'People on the streets are protesting angrily.'

B Work in pairs. What might people say when talking about these things?

> harmony   innocence   justice   paradise

8 A Choose the correct words to complete the article.

Medical technology of the future?

Technology changes all the time, which means we can't always predict [1]**hazardous / state-of-the-art** developments in the future. However, it's very possible that technological devices which [2]**convert / monitor** our daily health may well completely [3]**modify / revolutionise** the medical industry in the future. They would allow us to quickly [4]**detect / recharge** any problems that are arising so that we could deal with them fast. For example, we could have smart contact lenses that check a person's blood sugar level, allowing them to adjust their medication and [5]**activate / eliminate** any negative effects of diabetes before they occur. Or there might be a tool that parents add to their smartphones to look into their child's ears to spot infections and so on. The tool would [6]**emit / generate** information that can be sent directly to the child's doctor.

B Work in pairs. Can you think of a medical invention that would revolutionise medicine in the future?

9 A Complete the sentences with one word. The first letter is given.

1 I don't have long-term work. When I get a s............ job, I'll save more.
2 I put a............ money each month for a holiday.
3 I know someone who is very f............ and thinks carefully about every purchase.
4 I save money by avoiding p............ restaurants and eating in cheap ones.
5 I look for products which are d............ so I get a cheaper price.
6 I love to s............ out on nice things for myself.
7 My friend's too s............ to give money to charity.
8 I b............ most of my salary as soon as I get it.

B Work in pairs. Is each sentence true or false for you? Why?

10 Complete the sentences with the words in the box.

> activate   allowance   economical   essentials
> innocence   overdraft   overpriced   recharge
> recyclable   user-friendly

1 When children watch the news, they lose some of their ....
2 I don't have enough money in my bank account for this. I'll have to use my ....
3 If you open that door, it'll .... the fire alarm.
4 Five euros for a bottle of water? That's .... !
5 The packaging is .... so it can be used again.
6 We need a more .... heating system. This one wastes a lot of energy.
7 I need to .... my phone battery. It's run out.
8 We don't buy luxuries, only the ....
9 I didn't have an .... when I was a child. My parents only gave me money if I needed it.
10 These instructions aren't very .... I can't understand them at all.

11 A Choose the correct options (A–C) to complete the article.

Technology utopia

A technology utopia is a utopia where technology is used to solve all of the world's problems. In this utopian world, technology [1]............ the pollutants which factory chimneys [2]............ into gases which are not [3]............ to the environment. Technology [4]............ hunger and disease. It gets rid of unemployment, and so everyone earning a steady income can then pay for food and energy [5]............ , and no longer has to be [6]............ just to survive. Technology creates [7]............ transportation and communication systems which are available to all, no matter where they live in the world. Basically, technology creates a world of peace and [8]............ . Admittedly, achieving this kind of utopia is probably near impossible, [9]............ if we can invest in technology that will help us to solve global problems rather than help people make money, we might just be able to create a technology [10]............ .

	A	B	C
1	activates	generates	converts
2	emit	modify	recharge
3	hazardous	user-friendly	recyclable
4	revolutionises	eliminates	puts aside
5	allowances	overdrafts	essentials
6	cost-effective	pricey	frugal
7	hazardous	energy-efficient	handheld
8	harmony	paranoia	oppression
9	while	because	but
10	paradise	justice	innocence

B 🔊 **R8.01** | Listen and check.

C Work in pairs. Do you think a technology utopia is possible? Why/Why not?

1B a proposal: transforming a city space

1 A Read the proposal to change an area in a city. What changes does it suggest? Why?

> 1 ....
> The aim of this proposal is to transform the existing George Square area to create an urban space that encourages people to feel relaxed and to better interact with each other.
>
> 2 ....
> The current square contains too many inactive edges. For example, there are no shops or cafés and the old warehouses on one side consist of blank walls with no windows. The area in the centre of the square used to be a green space, but it is currently a car park, with no space where people can socialise. As a result, the square has an unfriendly feel. People passing through it tend to walk quickly and often fail to interact with each other.
>
> 3 ....
> The plan is to demolish the old warehouses. These will be replaced by two rows of small shops, with apartment blocks above. The hotel on the south side of the square will be refurbished and reopened to the public. Cafés and seating areas will also be built in on all sides of the square. The former park will be restored, with seating areas and a water feature, to create a relaxing blue space.
>
> 4 ....
> The changes proposed above will modernise the square and create more active edges. This will encourage people to socialise and interact with each other more. It will also create a blue space where people can relax and unwind.

B Complete the proposal with the correct headings (a–d). How do the headings help the reader?

   a The existing area   **c** Introduction
   b Conclusion   **d** Proposed changes

C Find formal sentences and phrases in the proposal to match the informal sentences and phrases (1–6). Which ones use passive verbs? Which use reduced relative clauses?

   1 I'm writing this proposal to …
   2 Because of this, the square feels unfriendly.
   3 People who walk through it …
   4 Instead of these, we will have …
   5 We will restore the old park, …
   6 The changes I am suggesting …

2 A Read the task below and plan your ideas. Use the ideas you discussed in Ex 4C on page 13 to help you.

> A local authority of a town or city you know wants to transform an urban area to make it more sociable and friendly. They would like ideas from members of the public about what changes to make. You have been asked to write a proposal to help with their decision-making.

B Write your proposal. Include headings to structure your proposal and use formal language.

2B an article: rivalry

1 A Read the article. How did the sibling rivalry it describes benefit an industry?

Sibling rivalry can boost an industry

Sibling rivalry is known to help develop problem-solving and social skills, but combine it with business rivalry and it can result in huge success. Such success, in fact, that international brands can be born.

That's what happened with the Dassler Brothers. In 1919, the brothers formed a shoe company in a small town in Germany. Their business took off in 1936 when they persuaded Jesse Owens to wear their running shoes at the Berlin Olympics. He did so and won four gold medals.

Unfortunately, ª**owing to** a dispute, the brothers' relationship broke down so badly that in 1948 they decided to go their separate ways. Rudolf opened a shoe factory on one side of the river and Adolf opened a shoe factory on the other side. It can never be proven that it was sibling rivalry that fuelled both companies' international success. ᵇ**Nevertheless**, it must surely have helped. The brothers were no longer cooperating but were trying to outdo each other.

The dispute affected the whole town. At one time, one person in every family worked at one of the factories. This created even more allegiances and rivalries, ᶜ**yet**, no one knows exactly why the two brothers fell out – not even their own grandchildren do.

The brothers now lie at opposite ends of the same cemetery. They never made up, and their companies – Adidas and Puma – remain rivals today.

B Work in pairs and answer the questions. Do you think the brothers' rivalry helped to drive the trainer industry or do you think other factors were involved?

C Look at the linking words and phrases in bold (a–c) in the article. Answer the questions (1–2).
   1 Which introduces a reason?
   2 Which introduce a contrast between ideas?

D Look at the highlighted words and phrases in the article. What idea does each one refer back to?
   'Such' refers back to 'success', i.e. huge success.

2 A You are going to write an article about a rivalry. It could be a business rivalry, a sporting rivalry or another type of rivalry.
- Research the rivalry and make notes about it in your own words.
- Select the most interesting ideas to include.
- Decide on the main point of the article and what to include in each paragraph.

B Write your article. Remember to use linking words appropriately.

C Read at least one other person's article. What is the writer's main point? Do you agree with it?

2D a reflection

1 A Read the reflection. What is the person reflecting on? Does he generally feel positive or negative about the experience?

Last month, I took my driving test for the first time. I'd had around thirty driving lessons, but I'm not the most natural driver in the world, so applying for and taking my test was a slight risk. However, I really wanted to be on the road and independent before the summer. Sadly, I failed.

In the run-up to the test, I'd practised the key skills that I had to demonstrate – parking, reversing and, of course, the emergency stop. I'd taken two driving lessons that week and I'd also gone out in my mum's car with her or my dad by my side every day. I drove around different parts of the town several times, so I knew the roads inside and out. All this gave me confidence.

What didn't help were the nerves I suffered on the day. They kicked in as soon as I woke up and just got worse as the day wore on, but I did nothing to try to combat them. Looking back, it all came down to that. The nerves caused me to lose concentration at times and as a result I made too many mistakes for the examiner to pass me.

All in all, I'm pleased that I gave the test a try and got to the end without passing out! I certainly learnt more about myself and how nerves can affect my performance. Next time, I'll definitely implement some techniques for dealing with my anxiety before the test, so I can maintain my focus and show off my driving skills adequately. Then, hopefully, I'll pass.

B Read the reflection again. Put the topics in the order the writer writes about them (1–4). What does he say about each thing?

  a What went well.   ....

  b What was learnt for similar future situations.   ....

  c What the challenge was and what the goal was.   ....

  d What went less well.   ....

2 A Prepare to write your own reflection about an experience you had which you learnt from. Make notes on the points in Ex 1B. Decide on the order of information.

  B Look for useful phrases in the reflection in Ex 1A that you can use in your own essay.

  C Write your reflection.

3A a review: fiction

1 A Read the review. What is the author reviewing? Does she recommend it? Have you ever seen it?

Tears in rain

[1]One of the most memorable monologues in film history appears in the 1982 film *Blade Runner*. Directed by Ridley Scott and starring Harrison Ford and Rutger Hauer, this sci-fi film tells the futuristic story of a world where synthetic humans known as replicants live among humans. While the film wasn't a hit when first released, it soon gained a large following due to its imagery and is now a cult classic.

[2]The scene known as 'Tears in rain' comes near the end of the film. Cop Deckard is searching for replicant Batty. Replicants are programmed to die after four years to protect humanity, but Batty is desperate to live. When Deckard finds Batty, he chases him across rooftops and ends up hanging off the top of a building. Deckard now has the same fear of death that Batty has, but Batty chooses to save Deckard's life, something Deckard has refused to do for Batty.

[3]What makes this scene special is the profound forty-two-word speech that Batty gives next. He reminisces about the things he has seen and experienced in his short life and recognises these memories will be lost like 'tears in rain'. Hauer conveys nostalgia, anger and sadness while the sound effects of heavy rain add to the drama.

[4]The 'Tears in rain' scene undoubtedly helped *Blade Runner* to achieve success. Although the white dove flying free at the end lacked realism for me, it is a scene which will remain with the viewer for some time.

B Match the paragraphs (1–4) with the purposes (a–e). One paragraph has two purposes.

  a Say what is good about the scene.

  b Give an overall recommendation.

  c Give background details to the film.

  d Say what is bad about the scene.

  e Explain what leads up to and what happens during the scene.

C The writer refers to the following things to support her recommendation. What does she say about each one to support her view of the scene?

  1 the popularity of the film today

  2 the acting

  3 the script

  4 the sound effects

  5 the appearance of a dove

2 A Think of a scene from a book, film, game, TV show or play you know. Prepare to write a review of it. Make notes on these things:

  • background details about the book/film/game/TV show or play

  • what happens in the scene

  • what's good about it (e.g. story, script, acting, lighting, soundtrack, special effects)

  • what's bad about it (e.g. story, script, acting, lighting, soundtrack, special effects)

  • your overall view of it and your recommendation

  B Write your review. Make references to different elements of the scene.

  C Swap reviews with a partner. Does your partner's review encourage you to see the scene for yourself? Why/Why not?

3D a biography

1 A Read a short biography of Ernest Shackleton, who Tunnvane said inspired her in the interviews on page 40. Do you think he was inspiring? What characteristics might you use to describe him?

Ernest Shackleton 1874–1922

Ernest Shackleton was an Anglo–Irish explorer who attempted to reach, and later circumnavigate, the South Pole. He was born in Kilkea, Ireland, on 15 February 1874 to Anglo–Irish parents, but soon moved with his family to London. Shackleton joined the Merchant Navy aged sixteen. In 1901, Shackleton joined the National Antarctic *Discovery* Expedition, but was sent home after falling ill. In 1907 he led the National Antarctic *Nimrod* expedition and reached a point ninety-seven nautical miles from the South Pole.

Shackleton returned to the Antarctic a third time to lead a crew on board *Endurance*. However, his ship got stuck in ice for ten months and was eventually crushed. Shackleton and his crew spent five months on melting ice floes before they were forced into their lifeboats. They sailed for sixteen days across dangerous waters before reaching the uninhabited and inhospitable Elephant Island.

After four months on the island, Shackleton and five crew members sailed 1,300 km from Elephant Island to the south side of South Georgia. They then had to traverse the island, something which had never been done before, to reach help. Four months later, after four attempts, Shackleton returned to Elephant Island to rescue his crew.

On 5 January 1922, during Shackleton's fourth expedition to Antarctica, he died on board his ship stationed at South Georgia. He was forty-seven years old. Although attitudes to his failed *Endurance* expedition were not positive at the time, Shackleton is now widely admired for his leadership skills and his ability to keep his entire crew alive in extreme and challenging circumstances.

B Read the biography again. Number the information in the order it appears in the biography.

a Notable moments in the person's life in chronological order ....

b The person's legacy ....

c The person's birth and early years ....

d The end of the person's life (if not alive) ....

e One-line summary of who the person is/was ....

2 A You are going to write a short biography of a famous person who has inspired you. Think about the people in Ex 6A on page 41. Make notes on the points in Ex 1B above.

B Write your biography.

C Read your biography several times.

1 Check there is no missing information or irrelevant information.

2 Check the information is organised and linked logically.

3 Check the accuracy of your grammar, vocabulary, spelling and punctuation.

4 Make any necessary changes to improve your biography.

D Share your biography with the class. Read other students' biographies. Which person sounds the most inspiring? Why?

4B a report: creating a rebranding campaign

1 A Read the information and comments about a plan to create a rebranding campaign for Heathfield, a rural area. Answer the questions.

1 What is being suggested?

2 Who is in favour of the plan?

3 Who is against it?

Minutes of the Heathfield council meeting
(24/10/2022)

After much discussion, it was agreed that:

- the council should approach a reputable marketing company to create a rebranding campaign for Heathfield. The aim would be to modernise the image of the area and attract more tourists.
- a budget of £150,000 would be set aside to pay for this campaign over a period of two years.

Dear Madam,

We are a group of business leaders in the Heathfield area and wish to express our concern at falling tourist numbers. Revenue from tourism is vital to this area and we believe there is an urgent need for the local council to take action to promote tourism and attract more visitors, which would lead to the creation of jobs and other economic benefits.

Dear Editor,

Your newspaper has recently suggested that our local area rebrand itself in order to attract tourists. I must express my objections to this idea. I have been living in this area for over forty years and I believe there is already too much tourism, which brings problems such as litter, noise and difficulties parking in local towns and villages. I am sure I am not alone in thinking …

Heathfield Local Residents' Committee
Online petition [23 signatures so far]

We call on the Heathfield local council to invest in attracting employment opportunities for local people rather than funding a rebranding campaign that would attract more tourists.

Sign here

B Write a report about the plan in Ex 1A. Use the headings below in your report. Use formal language and structures.

Overview of the plan

Advantages of the plan

Opposition to the plan

Conclusions and recommendations

C Swap reports with a partner. Do you agree with your partner's conclusions and recommendations?

4D a product blurb

1 A Read the product blurb. What kind of product is it advertising? What is the name of the product?

Shiny, strong, healthy-looking hair not only makes you look amazing, it makes you feel amazing, too. And we believe that only the best natural ingredients can produce the best results. That's why here at SuperShine we have teamed up with an international research laboratory to combine the beauty of nature with the expertise of scientists and created a shampoo we know will produce the results you want. Using top-quality, 100 percent natural ingredients, we have blended the perfect mix of cleansers and essential oils into a luxurious, creamy shampoo. SuperShine gently cleanses and nourishes your hair, removing grime and adding in rich, moisturising oils to leave it looking and feeling fabulous. What's more, unique ingredients in SuperShine protect your hair from the dust and dirt we encounter in our daily lives, so it stays looking better for longer. And because we believe that beautiful hair shouldn't cost the Earth, we've produced a luxury product just for you at a no-frills price. Try SuperShine for a natural, healthy shine that will keep on lasting.

B Read the blurb again. What does it say about:

1 the effect the product will have on your appearance and mood?

2 the input of science into the product?

3 the source of the ingredients?

4 the way the product works?

5 a feature of the product that other similar products don't have?

6 the price of the product?

C Product blurbs often repeat key positive words and ideas to reinforce the message. Look at the blurb again and note down words and ideas that are repeated.

2 A Prepare to write your own marketing blurb for a product that will help someone look or feel good about themselves.

- Think about the features of a product blurb in Ex 6A on page 53.
- Make notes on the topics in Ex 1B above.
- Decide on key positive words and ideas you want to repeat.
- Use phrases from the blurb in Ex 1A.

B Write your blurb.

C Swap blurbs with a partner. Would you like to try your partner's product? Why/Why not?

5A an informal message

1 A Read the email. Who is writing to whom and why? How would you describe the tone?

Hi Emi,

My cousin Neil gave me your email address and suggested I get in touch. I believe you recently decided to move into a flat in my building. So, congratulations and welcome to your new home! I'm sure you'll love it here. It's in a really great location and the residents are really friendly (and a bit nosy too sometimes, but let's forget about that!).

I'm sure you're really busy getting settled in, but when you get a chance, why don't we meet up? I can show you around the area and we can grab a coffee at my favourite coffee place round the corner. I can also introduce you to some of the neighbours so you feel more at home here.

What do you think? Reply here or message me on 0098 493284 and let me know.

Tomasz

B Read the email again. Find examples of the following ways in which Tomasz tries to create a rapport with Emi.

1 using first names

2 showing empathy to the recipient's situation

3 showing you value the recipient's time

4 asking for input

5 using humour

6 using informal language, e.g. phrasal verbs, contractions

C Read Emi's reply. In what ways does she mirror the email she received? Why does she do this?

Hi Tomasz,

Thanks so much for your email. I really appreciate the warm welcome and offer to show me around. I'd love to take you up on that if that's OK. I think I need to hear more about these nosy neighbours at the very least, but a trip to a good nearby coffee shop would be great, too. I'm free any time this weekend. Let me know when you are.

Looking forward to meeting you!

Emi

2 A Alex, a friend of a friend, has recently decided to move to your neighbourhood. Write him a welcome email. Build a positive rapport, using as many techniques in Ex 1B as possible.

B Write a short reply from Alex. Mirror the style of the email you're replying to.

5D a blog post

1 A Read the rest of the blog post. Which of your ideas from Ex 6B on page 65 does it mention?

So, I headed to the gym. I'd always been slightly scornful of people who 'do exercise' – they're always so ready to tell you how amazing it makes them feel. But, surprisingly, I found they're right! Believe me, exercise really can change your life. I started by just lifting a few weights and doing a gentle run once or twice a week. I'd say definitely take it steady and take it one step at a time. But I started to feel the benefits quite quickly and not just in terms of increased fitness and energy. The most surprising thing was how it filtered into other areas of my life. Because I felt good, I found I wanted to eat healthier food, and because I had more energy, I found time to catch up with old friends and meet some new ones. It was like a positive spiral in my life. So, I guess my advice to others would be to just make one change to start with, and make it something you want to do. Don't waste time on things you don't enjoy because you won't commit to them. Take it steady and start small. Do what I did and set yourself some goals and try to stick to them, and then relax and enjoy wherever it leads you. Get out of that rut!

B Complete the phrases for giving advice with the words in the box. Use the blog post to help you. Can you think of any other phrases for giving advice?

> guess   say   set   small
> waste   what

1 I'd .... definitely …
2 I .... my advice to others would be …
3 Don't .... time on …
4 Start ....
5 Do .... I did and …
6 .... yourself some goals and try to stick to them.

2 A Write a blog post about your experience of making a change in your life. Give some advice to others about what they can do. Use phrases for giving advice.

B Share your blog post with the class. Whose story is the most inspiring? Which pieces of advice do you think are the most useful? Why?

6D a set of instructions

1 A Read the instructions to prevent your phone battery from dying. Are any of your ideas from Ex 7B on page 77 mentioned? Have you ever had to do any of these things?

Ways to prevent your battery dying

If your phone battery is running out and you can't recharge it until you get home, just follow these steps to save battery power.

1 Turn down the brightness of your screen
If your phone has an auto-brightness feature, turn it on so your screen automatically adjusts to your environment, i.e. it's dim in sunlight and bright in the dark. If you don't have auto-brightness, you can reduce the brightness of your screen manually.

2 Switch on airplane mode
It's a good idea to put your phone on airplane mode when you don't need to access your messages. That way, your messaging apps won't keep looking for and downloading messages.

3 Turn off wi-fi
If you have wi-fi turned on but you're not using a recognised wi-fi network, your phone will continually identify nearby wi-fi hotspots and try to connect to one. Stop this from happening, and save battery power, by turning your wi-fi off.

4 Turn off push notifications and location services
Notifications and location services can be really convenient, but this convenience comes at a cost as they keep running in the background and eat up your battery. Disable these features unless you feel they're absolutely necessary.

5 Turn off background updates
Apps run background updates without you even knowing it, which both drains the battery and uses data if you're not on wi-fi. Disable this feature so that apps only update when you open them. You may need to wait a second or two longer to access them, but you'll be glad when your battery lasts that little bit longer.

B Find examples of the following features in the set of instructions in Ex 1A.

1 clear cause-and-effect explanations
2 direct engagement with the reader
3 use of imperative verbs
4 encouraging language

2 A Prepare to write a set of instructions for using an app, website, piece of software, device or gadget. Think about the following points and make a plan.

- the focus of the instructions and the title
- the steps you want to outline and their subheadings
- what information you will include under each subheading
- the features listed in Ex 1B
- what useful phrases in the instructions in Ex 1A you can use in your own tips

B Write your set of instructions. Use your plan in Ex 2A to help you.

C Share your instructions with the rest of the class. Whose set of instructions would be the most useful for you?

7A a comment on a blog post

1 A Read a blog post about language. What is the writer's main point?

  a Everyone should learn to speak English.

  b Language is becoming too globalised.

  c There is no such thing as a universal word.

• • •

RyanB
3 hrs ago

I know we live in a globalised world, but can we please keep the joy of different languages? So many words are now international, it's making travelling and visiting different countries boring. Wherever you go, it seems that people watch *football*, eat *burgers* and drink *cappuccino*. You can get a *taxi* or hop on the *metro* in pretty much any city in the world and everyone thinks that things are OK! Please let's not all start speaking the same language – let's keep languages different, so we can all enjoy the challenge of having to learn at least a few words when we travel to a new country!

 5

♡ Like   💬 Comments   ↪ Share

B Work in pairs. Do you agree with the writer in Ex 1A? Give your reasons.

C Write a comment responding to the blog post in Ex 1A. Agree or disagree with the writer and correct points the writer makes which you think are wrong.

8D a continuation of a narrative

1 A Read a narrative of the next part of the *Doctor Who* clip you watched in Ex 2A on page 100. Where are Ryan and the Doctor at the end of the narrative? What do you think happened next?

Ryan and the Doctor turned to follow the TeamMate down a narrow corridor. Like most parts of the building, it was fully enclosed by metal walls, with no windows or natural light. The silence was broken only by the regular clunk of the TeamMate's metal feet on the smooth floor. They headed slowly but steadily downwards, following signs towards the packing stations. The Doctor seemed confident and excited, looking around her and taking everything in. But Ryan, privately at least, was beginning to doubt that they would ever get to the bottom of the mystery note that had been delivered with the Kerblam parcel. Finally, they arrived at the packing stations and were delighted to see that they were manned by 'organic workers' or real people! The TeamMate assigned them to their individual stations, explained the packing process to them, then turned and walked away with a cheery wave, its bright artificial eyes shining in the dim light as it made its way back along the corridor. Right. Now it was time to really get to work and find out what that note was all about and who needed help.

B Read the narrative again. Which of the following features does it include?

- an account of the main events
- descriptions of the place
- descriptions of the people or robots
- descriptions of the sounds
- information about how the people were feeling
- references to previous events in the story

2 A Prepare to write the next paragraph of the narrative. Think about what you would like to happen next and make notes on the features in Ex 1B.

B Write your paragraph. Include vocabulary and phrases from the text in Ex 1A where possible.

C Swap paragraphs with a partner. How similar or different are your versions of what happens next? How do you think the story finally ends?

GRAMMAR BANK

1A describing past and present habits

REFERENCE ◀◀ page 10

used to/would

We use *used to* and *would* to talk about past habits. These are repeated past actions and events that took place in the past, but which don't happen now.

We **used to** meet up on Saturdays and cycle into town.

Joe **would** stop by on his way home from work.

We also use *used to* to talk about past states, but NOT *would*.

I **used to** have longer hair.

Notice that we use *get used to* to say that we are becoming familiar with something. We use *be used to* to say we are already familiar with something and it is no longer new to us.

I**'ve got used to** working the night shift.

I**'m used to** having just six hours' sleep a night.

will

We use *will* to describe present habits.

He**'ll** get up early every morning and go for a run.

When we stress the word *will*, it expresses our annoyance with the habit. We can do the same with *would*.

She **will** go to bed late and then moan about being tired.

Past and present continuous

We can use the past and present continuous to talk about past and present habits. The meaning is usually one of annoyance. We often use these tenses with adverbs of frequency, e.g. *always*, *often*, *frequently*, *constantly*.

They **were constantly competing** against each other.

She**'s always calling** me.

tend to/have a tendency to

We use *tend to* (+ infinitive) and *have/have got a tendency to* (+ infinitive) to describe present and past habits.

Jess **tends to** be quite quiet in the mornings.

He**'s got a tendency to** stay out quite late in the evenings.

We **had a tendency to** fight about the silliest of things.

keep on/kept on

We use *keep (on)* (+ *-ing* form) to describe present habits and *kept (on)* (+ *-ing* form) to describe past habits. These forms often describe annoyance.

You **keep on** calling me by my sister's name!

We **kept on** making the same mistakes over and over again!

Other phrases

We use *be prone to* (+ *-ing* form) and *be inclined to* (+ infinitive) to describe likely negative past or present behaviour.

I **was prone to** accidents when I was a kid.

He**'s inclined to** act now and think later.

We use *As a rule* or *Nine times out of ten* with the past or present simple to describe past or present typical behaviour.

As a rule, I don't socialise much during the week.

Nine times out of ten, we lost our matches.

PRACTICE

1 Complete the sentences with *would* where possible. Use *used to* if not.

1 I .... have lots of friends but not these days.
2 When I was young, my aunt .... bring me a gift every time she visited.
3 I .... live in a flat up the road, but I moved here last year.
4 Every day after school, my friends and I .... cycle to the park.
5 Zach .... be a real party animal, but not now he's got kids.
6 My friend Toluwani and I .... meet up once a week when we lived near each other.

2 Choose the correct words to complete the sentences. Which sentences express annoyance?

1 When my parents were out, I **'d** / **'ll** put on some music and dance around the house.
2 Erik **will** / **would** stare at his phone instead of talking to me these days!
3 At primary school, I **'d** / **'ll** call my teacher 'mum' by mistake! Embarrassing!
4 My friend Jen **will** / **would** often complain about her job when we're together.
5 I **'d** / **'ll** sometimes think of things to get from the supermarket but forget them again two minutes later.
6 My parents **will** / **would** always come into my room without knocking and it drove me mad!

3 Use the prompts to write sentences using either the present continuous or the past continuous.

1 Anna / always / forget / my birthday / these days
2 One of my friends / always / get / into trouble / when / younger
3 I / always / get told off / for talking / when / I / at school
4 My little brother / always / steal / my stuff / when / we / kids
5 I / always / leave / my phone / in strange places
6 My friends and I / always / struggling / think of things to do

4 Match the sentence beginnings (1–6) with the endings (a–f).

1 We're all prone
2 I'm inclined
3 I have a tendency to
4 Nine times out of ten,
5 Annoyingly, I keep on
6 My family and I tend not

a dropping my phone and breaking it.
b to do my homework in the mornings.
c bite my bottom lip when I'm stressed.
d I sleep through my alarm.
e to losing things in our house.
f to speak much during the week.

1B reduced relative clauses

REFERENCE ◀◀ page 12

We can 'reduce' relative clauses by using present and past participles (participle clauses) instead of a relative pronoun and a full verb form.

The people **living** in the slums were offered new flats.

(The people **who were living** in the slums …)

Some of the houses **built** near the river were prone to flooding.

(Some of the houses **which were built** near the river …)

Present participles (-*ing* forms)

We use a present participle in the reduced relative clause when the verb in the original clause has an active meaning and the noun before the participle is the subject of the verb.

I recognised the man **sitting** in the café.

(… the man **who was sitting** in the café.)

The present participle can refer to the present, past or future.

There is plenty of information for people **intending** to buy one of the new flats.

(… for people **who are intending** …)

People **studying** at university in the past didn't have to pay such high fees.

(People **who studied** …)

Students **taking** their exams next year will notice some changes to the exam papers.

(Students **who will take** …)

We can use the present participle for a state as well as an action.

People **wanting** to buy one of the new flats must pay a deposit in advance.

(People **who want** …)

Past participles (-*ed* forms)

We use a past participle in the reduced relative clause when the verb in the original clause has a passive meaning and the noun before the participle is the object of the verb.

The buildings **destroyed** in the fire will be rebuilt.

(The buildings **which were destroyed** …)

The past participle can refer to the present, past or future.

She lives in an apartment **owned** by her parents.

(… an apartment **which is owned** …)

The programme, **broadcast** last week, showed the impact that climate change is having.

(The programme, **which was broadcast** last week, …)

Any applications **received** after the deadline will not be considered.

(Any applications **which are received** …)

PRACTICE

1 Choose the correct participle to complete the sentences with reduced relative clauses.

1 They are creating a new area **designed / designing** to encourage people to socialise.

2 The streets **led / leading** up to the square have lots of small shops and cafés.

3 The materials **used / using** to build the new school are all environmentally friendly.

4 People **employed / employing** by the company often live some distance away.

5 Candidates **applied / applying** for the job must have suitable qualifications.

6 The guests **stayed / staying** at the resort all made positive comments about the food.

2 Complete the sentences with the correct present or past participle form of the verbs in the box.

> attract   contact   destroy   live   use   work

1 People .... in this style of office are usually more productive.

2 It's a career which appeals to people .... by high salaries and lots of travel.

3 Residents .... close to the factory often complain about the noise.

4 Some of the buildings .... by the fire were over 200 years old.

5 The witnesses .... by the police were all able to provide useful information.

6 The app is perfect for people .... public transport in the city.

3 Complete the second sentence so it means the same as the first sentence. Use a reduced relative clause.

1 There are plenty of active edges. These are designed to slow people down as they walk past.

There are plenty of .... slow people down as they walk past.

2 People live in the slums. They suffer from mental and physical health problems.

People .... mental and physical health problems.

3 Some of the rooms were modernised last year. We stayed in one of them.

We stayed in one of the .... last year.

4 Some people want to buy their tickets in advance. They can do this online.

People .... in advance can do so online.

5 A building company will restore the old theatre. They will try to keep its original features.

The building company .... to keep its original features.

6 The local authority has proposed a new public space. It will include a fountain.

The new public space .... include a fountain.

1C How to ... talk about hypothetical preferences

REFERENCE ◀◀ page 15

We can use a range of different expressions to talk about things we would or wouldn't like to do.

Expressing a preference between two or more options

Given the choice, I'd ...
If it was up to me, I'd ...
I'd rather ...
I'd sooner ...
I'd go for ... (noun or -*ing* form)

Talking about things you are very keen to do

I'd jump at the chance to ...
I'd give my right arm for a chance to ...

Talking about things you aren't keen to do

I'd probably give ... (noun or -*ing* form) **a miss.**
I wouldn't choose to ...

Expressing a strong feeling of not wanting to do something

No way would I ever ...
I'd run a mile at the thought of ... (-*ing* form)
You wouldn't catch me ... (-*ing* form)
Nothing would make me ... (infinitive without *to*)

PRACTICE

1 **Choose the correct phrases to complete the conversations.**

1 A: Shall we cook something this evening or do you want to go out to eat?

B: **I'd sooner** / **I wouldn't choose to** eat out, to be honest. I don't really feel like cooking.

2 A: I've put my name down for an obstacle race in June. Do you fancy doing it with me?

B: You're joking! **Nothing would make me** / **I'd jump at the chance to** crawl through mud and climb over stupid obstacles!

3 A: We could watch a crime drama if you want. Or there are plenty of comedy shows.

B: **Given the choice, I'd** / **No way would I ever** watch the comedy. I could do with cheering up.

4 A: Have you heard? Jake's gone on a rock-climbing holiday.

B: I know, I can't believe it! **You wouldn't catch me** / **I'd go for** doing something dangerous like that!

5 A: I'm going to New York in the summer.

B: You're so lucky! **I'd run a mile at the thought of** / **I'd give my right arm for a chance to** go there!

2 **Complete the sentences with the words in the box. There are two words you do not need.**

arm   catch   choice   make   miss   rather   up   way

1 I don't mind going to a karaoke bar to listen to the rest of you, but I'll probably give the singing a .... !

2 If it was .... to me, I'd go to a live concert rather than watch one on TV.

3 No .... would I ever go swimming with sharks!

4 I'd give my right .... for a chance to play tennis at Wimbledon!

5 Given the .... , I'd go to India – it's such an interesting country.

6 You wouldn't .... me performing on a stage!

3 **Rewrite the sentences using the words in brackets.**

1 I hate the idea of climbing Mount Everest!   (catch)

....

2 I would really love to go to Mexico.   (jump)

....

3 I would prefer to stay in this evening.   (up to)

....

4 I don't think I would choose the sightseeing tour.   (miss)

....

5 I would love the chance to be in a reality TV show.   (arm)

....

6 If I could choose, I'd buy a sports car.   (choice)

....

GRAMMAR BANK

2A cleft sentences

REFERENCE ◀◀ page 21

We use cleft sentences to emphasise particular information in a sentence. We use the cleft structure at the beginning of the sentence to emphasise the information that comes after it.

The players slow the game down to waste time. (a 'normal' sentence, with no added emphasis)

What the players do is slow the game down to waste time. (a cleft sentence, which emphasises the information after the cleft structure)

To make a cleft structure, we can use *What* + subject + verb + *be*.

They want to win the competition. → **What they want is** to win the competition.

We enjoy competing against other teams. → **What we enjoy is** competing against other teams.

We can use a cleft structure to emphasise the object of a verb.

He faked an injury. → **What he faked was** an injury.

I'll send you the link for the website. → **What I'll send you is** the link for the website.

They changed their kit. → **What they changed was** their kit.

If we want to emphasise the whole action (verb and object), we can add the correct form of the auxiliary verb *do*.

He faked an injury. → **What he did was** fake an injury.

I'll send you the link for the website. → **What I'll do is** send you the link for the website.

They changed their kit. → **What they did was** change their kit.

Notice that in structures with the auxiliary verb *do*, the auxiliary verb is in the same tense as the main verb in the normal sentence. The main verb in the cleft sentence is in the infinitive form.

She **dived** in the penalty area. → What she **did** was **dive** in the penalty area.

We**'ll watch** them carefully to see if they are cheating. → What we**'ll do** is **watch** them carefully to see if they are cheating.

When the main verb in the normal sentence is in a continuous form, the form of the auxiliary *do* and main verb in the cleft sentence become an *-ing* form.

They **are playing** for time. → What they **are doing** is **playing** for time.

She **was pretending** to be injured. → What she **was doing** was **pretending** to be injured.

We don't use *do* with verbs that describe feelings or states.

I love competitive games. → What **I love** is competitive games. (a feeling) NOT ~~What I do is love competitive games.~~

She has a lot of talent. → What **she has** is a lot of talent. (a state) NOT ~~What she does is have a lot of talent.~~

PRACTICE

1 Complete the cleft sentences by adding one word.

1 He enjoys playing football with his friends.
What he enjoys .... playing football with his friends.

2 They complained to the referee.
What they .... was complain to the referee.

3 He borrowed my phone.
What he .... was my phone.

4 He faked an injury.
What he did was .... an injury.

5 She pretends to be injured.
What she .... is pretend to be injured.

6 We noticed someone cheating.
What we noticed .... someone cheating.

2 Read the pairs of cleft sentences. What is emphasised in each one – the object of the verb (O) or the whole action (A)?

1 She broke her ankle.
  a What she broke was her ankle.
  b What she did was break her ankle.

2 They won the tennis tournament.
  a What they won was the tennis tournament.
  b What they did was win the tennis tournament.

3 I'll make a chocolate cake.
  a What I'll do is make a chocolate cake.
  b What I'll make is a chocolate cake.

4 He stole some jewellery.
  a What he did was steal some jewellery.
  b What he stole was some jewellery.

3 Complete the cleft sentences. Emphasise the bold part of the normal sentence.

1 He lied about **his qualifications**.
What .... his qualifications.

2 They **robbed** a supermarket.
What .... a supermarket.

3 She planted **an apple tree**.
What .... an apple tree.

4 They watched **a horror movie**.
What .... a horror movie.

5 She **threatened to tell the police**.
What .... the police.

6 I love **swimming in the sea**.
What .... in the sea.

2B ellipsis and substitution

REFERENCE ◀◀ page 24

Ellipsis

Ellipsis means omitting words. We often omit words, especially in informal English, because the listener or reader can still understand what we mean from context. We tend to omit subjects (sometimes with *a/an*), auxiliary verbs and modal verbs.

We identified a potential partner and (**we**) contacted them. (subject)

We've been researching and (**we've been**) developing this product for some time. (subject + auxiliary verb)

We should form an alliance and (**we should**) combine our resources. (subject + modal verb)

We sometimes omit verb phrases to avoid repeating them. When we do this, we include an auxiliary verb.

Not many people have one, but I **do** (have one).

We haven't got the technology, but they **have** (got the technology).

They were hoping to complete it by today, but they **haven't** (completed it).

Ellipsis is particularly common in conversational English, whether it's spoken or written (e.g. in social media messages).

(**That's**) Interesting!

(**That's a**) Good idea!

(**It's**) Nice to meet you.

(**That's**) Not true.

(**That**) Sounds good to me.

(**Did you have a**) Fun day?

(**It's**) Nice weather today.

Substitution

We sometimes replace a word or phrase with another word or phrase in order to avoid repetition. We tend to use *one*, *do/did*, *so*, *do so*, *not*, *the same* and determiners (e.g. *some*, *many*) for this.

I didn't have a job last year, but I've got **one** (a job) now.

My brother went into the car industry and so I **did the same** (went into the car industry).

There are a few people here but **not many** (people are here).

A: Do you think it'll happen?

B: I expect **so** (it will happen).

C: I hope **not** (it won't happen).

Notice that we use a form of *do* + *so* in place of a verb phrase we omit to avoid repetition. It means 'do it'. It tends to sound more formal.

We were asked to partner with the company and we **did so** (partnered with the company).

He says he'll leave, but we don't think he'll **do so** (leave).

PRACTICE

1 Decide which words have been omitted or substituted.

1 Ready yet?
2 Should we stay or go?
3 I've never tried this product, but I'd like to do so.
4 Do you like this brand or do you prefer that one?
5 Sounds like a good plan.
6 Sorry I'm late.
7 A: Do you think it'll all go to plan?
   B: I hope so!
8 I didn't like it very much, but everyone else did.

2 Cross out the words you can omit from the sentences.

1 We can give up or we can try once more.
2 Did you have a good weekend?
3 I called the company and I complained.
4 They hadn't been here before yesterday, but I had been here before.
5 We'll invite you to our house and we'll cook for you.
6 Dani called and she said she'll be late.

3 Substitute the words in bold to avoid repetition.

1 I don't have that exact jacket, but I have a similar **jacket**.
2 We haven't achieved our goal yet, but we hope to **reach our goal** soon.
3 It's predicted that it'll rain during the day, but I hope **it won't rain during the day**.
4 I didn't send the gift. Melanie **sent the gift**.
5 A: Do you think you'll be there tonight?
   B: I expect **I'll be there tonight**.
6 My brother climbed over the wall, so I **climbed over the wall**, too.

2C How to ... compare and evaluate ideas

REFERENCE ◀◀ page 27

We can use a number of different phrases to compare and evaluate. When comparing, we may want to describe a big difference, a small difference or no difference.

Comparing	Evaluating
A big difference	**Effective**
Informal	be valuable to (someone)
way/miles/loads more ... than ...	be invaluable to/for (someone)
Neutral	be effective for (someone)
much/a lot/far (more) ... than	be useful for (someone)
nowhere near as ... as	be effective in (doing something)
nothing like as ... as	be useful in (doing something)
Semi-formal/formal	
considerably/significantly/infinitely (more) ... than ...	
A small difference	**Not effective**
Neutral	be useless for (someone)
a little/slightly/a bit (more) ... than	be useless at (doing something)
almost as ... as	be a waste of time/energy (for someone)
Semi-formal/formal	be ineffective for (someone)
marginally (more) ... than	be ineffective in (doing something)
	be unhelpful for (someone)
No difference	
just as ... (as)	
every bit as ... (as)	
equally ... (as)	

Comparing

It's **much easier** to give a bonus **than** create a whole new pay system.

A minimum salary scheme would take **way** longer to set up.

I think option 1 is **marginally more** interesting than option 2.

A four-day week is **infinitely** better than a five-day week.

This computer seems to be **every bit as** useless **as** the last one!

Evaluating

The mentor programme is **invaluable for** people who need some support.

It would be **effective in** helping junior members of staff.

It'll be **useful in** making people feel appreciated.

It's **a waste of time** and effort **for** the company.

The scheme would be **ineffective in** achieving what it wants to achieve.

PRACTICE

1 Put the words into the correct order to complete the sentences.

1 than / more effective / a free lunch / Being thanked / miles / is / by your boss

2 equally / beneficial / is / as / working in an office / as / Working from home

3 nowhere / as / Wearing a suit / comfortable / wearing jeans / near / as / is

4 way / expensive / taking the bus / than / Driving to work / more / is

5 waste / is / Going home for lunch / energy / a / of

6 Non-financial incentives / every bit / important / as / are / financial incentives / as

2 Use the prompts to write sentences.

1 Jobs with promotional opportunities / far / motivating / those without

2 Great colleagues / just / important / a great salary

3 Financial incentives / effective / rewarding hard work

4 My bonus this year is / nowhere / much as my bonus last year

5 Free childcare / useless / staff without children

6 There are / loads / people in your department than mine

7 My salary is / marginally / lower / your salary

8 Free gym memberships / useful / sporty people

3 Complete the conversation with the phrases (a–f).

A: What do you think of the new pension scheme?

B: It's ¹_____ as the old one.

A: I know. The company contributes ²_____ it used to. A whole five percent! It'll be ³_____ persuading people to save.

B: I agree. But then again, our annual bonus has increased by a lot, so we'll be getting ⁴_____ money at the end of the year, which is great.

A: True. I guess when you look at it like that, overall we'll end up with only ⁵_____ than we did before.

B: Yes, we'll have ⁶_____ much, but not quite.

a loads more
b nowhere near as good
c useless at
d almost as
e far less than
f marginally less

3A *as if/as though*

REFERENCE ◀ page 34

We use *as if* and *as though* after verbs such as *act, be, feel, look, seem, sound* and *taste* and to make a comparison and say how something appears, feels, seems, etc. They are followed by a clause. Although *as if* and *as though* have the same meaning, *as if* is more commonly used.

It's **as though** he's not really here.

You look **as if** you're really stressed.

I felt **as if** I hadn't eaten for a week!

We can use the simple present tense after *as if* or *as though*. This means that the comparison is real or probable.

She acts **as if** she **is** very important. (She probably is important.)

He talks **as if** he **knows** which way to go. (He probably does know which way to go.)

They behaved **as though** they **like** the hotel. (They do like the hotel.)

We can use the simple past tense after *as if* or *as though*. This means the comparison is unreal or improbable.

She acts **as if** she **was/were*** so important. (She is not important.)

He talks **as if** he **knew** which way to go. (He probably doesn't know which way to go, or we don't know whether he knows or not.)

They behaved **as though** they **liked** the hotel. (But they do not.)

*We can use *I/he/she/it* with *was* or *were* when describing something unreal or improbable. *Were* is more common in written English.

We can use the past perfect after *as if* or *as though* for comparisons in the past. This means the comparison is real or imaginary. The verb before *as if/as though* can be in the present simple or the past simple with no difference in meaning.

It sounds **as though** you'd really **hurt** yourself./It sounded **as though** you'd really **hurt** yourself. (You had hurt yourself.)

She talks about the competition **as if** she'**d won**./She talked about the competition **as if** she'**d won**. (She didn't win the competition.)

I feel **as if** I'**d heard** the story before./I felt **as if** I'**d heard** the story before. (I probably had heard the story before.)

It seems **as if** he'**d had** a shock./It seemed **as if** he'**d had** a shock. (He probably had had a shock.)

We might follow *as if* and *as though* with an infinitive or prepositional phrase.

Tom moved his lips slightly **as if to smile**.

I screamed **as if in pain**, but really I was just frustrated.

In informal communication, we sometimes use *like* instead of *as if/as though*. This is particularly common in British English.

You look **like** you'**ve been swimming**. Why are you wet?

They seem **like** they'**re** a nice family.

PRACTICE

1 Choose the correct options to complete the sentences.

   1 Look at this mess! It looks as if nobody ever **cleans** / **will clean** in here.

   2 When I saw Jack yesterday, he looked as if he **is** / **was** really stressed.

   3 It seems as though nothing **opening** / **opens** before 8 a.m.

   4 You act as if you '**d been** / **were** in charge, but you aren't!

   5 It seemed as though everyone **already heard** / **had already heard** about the news except me.

   6 I felt as if I '**ve** / '**d** been dragged through a hedge backwards!

2 Complete the sentences using the prompts in brackets.

   1 ...., doesn't he? (He / always / look / as if / he / be / down in the dumps)

   2 They seemed .... a lot of experience, but in fact they didn't. (though / have)

   3 When he turned away, ... (it appear / as if / he / not hear / me)

   4 .... with her sister at the moment. (She / feel / as if / something / be / not right)

   5 It looked .... a hundred times before. (if / he / make / the cake)

   6 ...., but there's a big problem. (Right now / you / act / as though / nothing / be / wrong)

3 Complete the second sentence with *as if/as though* so it means the same as the first sentence.

   1 It looked cold outside. It wasn't.
   It looked .... outside, but it wasn't.

   2 He looked at me. He hadn't noticed me before.
   He looked at me .... for the first time.

   3 She looks worried. Maybe she's worried about the exam.
   She looks .... about the exam.

   4 They spoke like experts on the subject. They weren't.
   They talked .... on the subject.

   5 We felt that we weren't seeing this film for the first time.
   It felt .... this film before.

3B *no matter*

REFERENCE ◀◀ page 37

We use *no matter* + a relative pronoun + clause to say that something is true whatever the situation is. It means the same as *It doesn't matter*, but it gives more emphasis to the idea that the information is true.

It doesn't matter when we leave. It'll be fine.

No matter when we leave, it'll be fine.

We use relative pronouns *who, whose, what, which, where, when, why* and *how*.

No matter whose pen I steal, I quickly lose it again!

No matter what time it is, we'll eat something when we arrive.

No matter how tired I am, I always manage to do some exercise after work.

We use a present tense after *no matter* whether it refers to general habits or the future. When it refers to the future, the other clause will use a future form.

No matter where you live, I come and visit you. (general habit)

No matter where you live, I'll come and visit you. (future promise)

Notice that when we use *no matter*, it has two clauses. The clauses can be reversed. When we use *it doesn't matter*, we use one clause.

No matter which dessert you pick, I'll want some!

I'll want some of your dessert, **no matter** which one you pick!

It **doesn't matter** which dessert you pick. I'll want some!

We can also use *no matter* with *that* to say something is not important and won't affect a situation.

No matter that you can't come tomorrow. I'll see you next week.

No matter that we've got no food in the house. We'll order a takeaway.

We sometimes use *no matter what* at the end of a sentence.

I'll always support you, **no matter what**.

I will definitely leave work by 6 p.m. and meet you tonight, **no matter what**.

PRACTICE

1 Put the words in the correct order to complete the sentences.

1 where / I am / No matter / stay / in the world, / in touch / we'll

2 you are, / still be / No matter / you can / how old / adventurous

3 times / forgot / she still / how many / reminded her, / No matter / I

4 learn from / how / We can / mistakes, / small / no matter / all

5 the washing-up / how / I'll do / I am, / No matter / tired

6 no matter / drive me / They / they do / up the wall, / what

7 I expect / team / No matter / we'll win / we play, / which

8 to go inside / you chose / I refuse / No matter / this restaurant, / why

2 Complete the sentences with the correct form of the verbs in brackets.

1 No matter who he _____ (ask), no one seems to know the answer.

2 No matter how I _____ (feel) later, I _____ (give) you a call.

3 I promise that we _____ (not / give up), no matter how difficult it _____ (get).

4 I _____ (buy) this dress, no matter how much it _____ (cost).

5 No matter how often we _____ (tidy) this room, it _____ (be) messy again in just a few minutes.

6 Becky _____ (do) the wrong thing yesterday, no matter what her intention _____ (be).

7 No matter how late you _____ (get) home, I _____ (make) dinner for you.

8 No matter what the weather _____ (be) like, I _____ (go) for a walk every day.

3 Complete the second sentence so it has a similar meaning to the first.

1 He calls me by the wrong name, but I know who he means.

No matter _____ by the wrong name, I know who he means.

2 Rafael will help tonight, even if he's really tired.

Rafael will help tonight, no matter how _____ .

3 We try hard, but our team never wins.

No matter _____ , our team never wins.

4 I love a good story. The genre doesn't matter to me.

I love a good story, no matter _____ .

5 I'll always cycle everywhere, even when I'm old.

No matter _____ .

6 I try hard to remember people's names. I always forget their names.

_____ no matter _____ .

3C How to ... engage with other people's views

REFERENCE ◀◀ page 39

Engaging with someone else's view

During a discussion, we often disagree with other people's views. It is still important to engage with their views to show that we are listening to their ideas, even though we may not agree.

That's a (very) good point.

That makes sense.

I can see where you're coming from.

I can see the logic in that.

I can see why you're suggesting ...

That's quite a neat idea.

That's a really good/neat idea.

Making a countersuggestion

When we have engaged with the other person's view, we often go on to express our own opinion, for example by making a countersuggestion.

On the other hand, ...

But on a practical level, ...

It might be more effective to ...

One disadvantage of that would be ...

Alternatively, what about ... ?

Engaging and making a countersuggestion

A: Personally, I think we should hand out big fines to people who drop litter.

B: **I can see where you're coming from, but on a practical level**, it might be difficult to force people to pay.

A: I think we should put up our prices.

B: **I can see the logic in that, but one disadvantage of that would be** that we may lose some of our customers.

PRACTICE

1 Match the opinions (1–5) with the responses (a–e).

1 I think we should add tips to the bill automatically, so people can't avoid giving one.

2 I think the library should definitely fine people who return books late.

3 If we want to discourage car use, we could offer incentives like free coffee to students to come to college by public transport.

4 Why don't we offer free meals to kids, as a way of encouraging families into the restaurant?

5 I think if we see people dropping litter on the beach, we should ban them from going there.

a I can see where you're coming from. But it might be more effective to offer an incentive if they return them on time.

b I can see why you're suggesting that. On the other hand, customers might resent being forced to be generous.

c I can see the logic in that. But on a practical level, it would be quite hard to catch people in the act.

d That's quite a neat idea. Alternatively, we could simply close the car parks, which would force them to find other forms of transport.

e That's a really good idea. But one disadvantage of that would be that not charging them would clearly be expensive for us.

2 Complete the conversations with one word in each gap.

1 A: I think we should ban phones in all school classes. They're just a distraction!

   B: I can see where you're _____ from. But on a _____ level, it would be quite hard to stop kids smuggling their phones in.

2 A: I suggest we reduce the price of healthy meals in the cafeteria, to encourage people to eat them.

   B: I can see the _____ in that. But one _____ of that would be that it would reduce our profits.

3 A: We could simply ban all dogs from the park. That would solve the problem.

   B: I can see why you're _____ that. On the other _____, some people need their dogs, for example if they have a disability.

4 A: Why don't we all sit down together once a month and work out which bills are due and how much we each need to pay?

   B: That makes _____ . _____ , what about paying a fixed amount of money each month into an account? Then one person could just pay the bills as they come in.

3 Work in pairs. Engage with the opinions and make a countersuggestion.

1 We should stop using any plastic in the cafeteria.

2 I think all cars should be banned from the city centre.

3 Students who hand work in late should have marks taken off.

4 Supermarkets shouldn't be allowed to sell unhealthy snacks.

5 People who behave in an aggressive way online should be banned from the internet.

6 Drivers who break the speed limit should have their licence taken away.

4A uses of *should*

REFERENCE ◀◀ page 44

We use *should* in a variety of ways. There are different forms.

	Active	Passive
Present/Future	*should(n't)* + infinitive without *to*	*should(n't) be* + past participle
At this time	*should(n't) be* + *-ing* form	–
Past	*should(n't) have* + past participle	*should(n't) have been* + past participle

We use *should* to give advice and suggestions.

You **should take** a photo of us all.

They **shouldn't take** photos in here.

We use *should* to say what is ideal or desired, or to express obligation. Notice that sometimes 'they' is the subject. 'They' often refers to 'people in charge'.

They **should give** us a day off.

You **should put** your seat belt on.

We use *should* + infinitive without *to* to talk about likelihood/possibility.

I've changed the settings. It **should work** better now.

We **should see** you all later.

We use *should have* + past participle to talk about regrets.

I **shouldn't have said** that.

We **should have done** more to help.

We use *shouldn't* to criticise.

She **shouldn't be** working so hard.

You **shouldn't have put** that photo online.

In formal contexts, we can use *should* after *if* in conditional sentences to talk about possible and hypothetical (unlikely) situations in the present or future, i.e. in first and second conditional sentences.

If someone should see me take a photograph here, I could be in trouble.

If is sometimes omitted in conditional sentences, and *should* is inverted, i.e. *Should* + subject + infinitive without *to*. This is very formal in tone.

If you need further information, call this number. → **Should you need** further information, call this number.

If you take a photo in here, you'll be arrested. → **Should you take** a photo in here, you'll be arrested.

PRACTICE

1 Match the first lines (1–6) to the second lines (a–f).

1 You should have tried harder.

2 The rain should clear up later.

3 If the team should lose, they would not continue in the tournament.

4 I shouldn't have sent Donal that message.

5 You should all get outside for some fresh air.

6 They should provide free lunches for us.

a I really regret it now.

b That's my advice for you anyway.

c Sorry to criticise, but it's how I feel.

d It would be impossible.

e That would be ideal for everyone.

f That's what's predicted.

2 Complete the sentences with the correct form of the verbs in brackets.

1 We shouldn't .... (talk) about this right now.

2 We should .... (leave) home earlier this morning. We're going to be late.

3 You should .... (see) the look on your face. It's so funny!

4 The plane should .... (take off) around now.

5 This awful photo of me should never .... (share) with anyone now or in the future!

6 Should you .... (experience) any problems, please contact us immediately.

7 We should .... (give) a pay rise last month, but weren't.

8 If our situation should .... (improve), we shall amend our plans.

3 Complete the second sentence so it means the same as the first. Use *should* or *shouldn't*.

1 We're watching a film instead of studying. It's not ideal.

We .... instead of watching a film.

2 You sometimes ride your bike without a helmet.

You .... when you ride your bike.

3 It's possible that you will have doubts. In this situation, contact us.

If you .... , please contact us.

4 We were given a really hard essay to write.

We .... such a hard essay to write.

5 The decision was made too fast.

The decision .... so fast.

6 If the door is locked, guests must call reception.

.... , guests must call reception.

4B the continuous aspect

REFERENCE ◀◀ page 48

There are three aspects of verb forms: simple, perfect and continuous.

The simple aspect in the past emphasises that an action is complete, e.g. We **visited** Dublin last week.

The perfect aspect in the past emphasises that an action is completed before another action, e.g. Tom **had** already **left**.

The continuous aspect focuses on the action and its duration, rather than the completion of the action and its result.

We can use the continuous aspect to talk about actions in the past, present and future. All the continuous forms use the appropriate form of *be* and the *-ing* form of the verb.

Verb form	Examples
Present continuous	**I'm working** at the moment. Where **are** you **living** now?
Past continuous	It **was raining** hard. What **were** they **doing**?
Present perfect continuous	He**'s been sitting** there all afternoon. **Have** you **been waiting** long?
Past perfect continuous	I could see that she **had been crying**. We **hadn't been expecting** any visitors.
Future continuous	**I'll be seeing** Jack tomorrow. Where **will** you **be staying**?
Future perfect continuous	By next month, I**'ll have been working** here for three years.
Continuous infinitive	My phone seems **to be working** now.

We can use the continuous aspect to talk about:

- actions in progress at a particular time.
  She**'s working** at the moment.
  He **was watching** TV when we arrived.

- temporary situations.
  I**'m staying** with friends at the moment.
  We **were living** in Rome at that time.

- situations that are changing.
  My French **is getting** better.
  The weather **was getting** colder.

- actions that continue over a period of time.
  I**'ve been studying** all afternoon.

In contrast to the continuous aspect, we use the simple tenses to talk about facts, permanent situations, finished actions and habits.
I **visited** my brother in New York last year. He **works** for a bank and **goes** to the gym every day.

Remember that some verbs are state verbs and we don't use them in continuous forms.
I **don't understand** what you're saying.
I**'ve** always **loved** this restaurant!

PRACTICE

1 Choose the correct verb forms to complete the text. Sometimes both are possible.

Green branding

Not all towns and cities [1]**have / are having** beautiful buildings or historic monuments to help them create a powerful brand. However, in recent years, interest [2]**has grown / has been growing** in branding cities as sustainable or green. Nowadays, people [3]**become / are becoming** more and more committed to the idea of fighting climate change, so an increasing number of cities [4]**begin / are beginning** to sell themselves as environmentally friendly. Twenty years ago, Hamburg, in northern Germany, [5]**had / was having** a reputation as an industrial centre. Pollution in the city [6]**was increasing / increased** at this time and the local authorities realised that they [7]**had been focusing / had focused** too much on jobs and industry and not enough on the environment. The local government [8]**introduced / was introducing** a series of green initiatives to focus on making the city greener and their initiatives [9]**have transformed / have been transforming** the city into one of the greenest cities in Germany. A green roofs policy was introduced in 2015, which means that soon some of the early roofs [10]**will have been growing / will have grown** for ten years, keeping the air clean and reducing pollution. Waste heat from copper production is now being used to supply energy for the city and it is hoped that in the future such schemes [11]**will be providing / will provide** even more of the city's energy needs.

2 Complete the questions with the correct continuous form of the verbs in brackets.

1 Where do you think you _____ (work) in five years' time?
2 Do you like the place where you live? How long _____ (you / live) there?
3 What _____ (you / do) last Saturday at midday?
4 What book _____ (you / read) at the moment?
5 By next summer, how long _____ (you / learn) English?

3 Work in pairs. Ask and answer the questions in Ex 2.

4C How to ... steer a conversation towards a topic

REFERENCE ◀◀ page 50

Giving yourself time to think

During an interview, we may be asked a difficult question that we don't really want to answer because the answer might not give a good impression. We can use a phrase to give us time to think of what we can say.

That's a good question.

That's an interesting question.

I've thought about this quite a lot.

This is something I feel quite strongly about.

That's quite a broad topic.

Steering the conversation

Instead of answering the difficult question directly, we can change direction in the interview and steer the conversation to a topic which we want to talk about because it gives a good impression of us.

The most important point here is ...

What I can say is ...

Perhaps I could just talk about ...

Can I just say that ... ?

Maybe I can give you an example of ...

Giving yourself time to think and steering the conversation

We can use these two groups of phrases individually or we can use them together, giving ourselves time to think first and then changing direction and steering the conversation.

A: What qualities are important when you have to deal with an emergency situation?

B: **That's an interesting question. Maybe I can give you an example of** a time when I was in an emergency situation. It happened about six months ago and ...

A: Do you find it difficult to accept negative feedback?

B: **That's quite a broad topic. Perhaps I could just talk about** my last job and the kinds of feedback I had from my manager. In general, the feedback was very positive, but on a few occasions, ...

PRACTICE

1 Complete the conversations with one word in each gap.

1 A: How important do you think ongoing training is in a job?

B: This is something I feel quite _____ about. The most important _____ here is that I'm always looking for opportunities to improve my skills and learn new ones, so that I can perform well at work.

2 A: Do you think you have the qualities you need to be a travel representative?

B: I've _____ about this quite a lot. What I _____ say is that I've always been praised for my people skills and my colleagues have always found me very easy to work with.

3 A: How important was good communication in your last job?

B: That's quite a(n) _____ topic. Perhaps I could _____ talk about one particular incident where communication was especially important and I was able to demonstrate my good communication skills.

4 A: What's the best way to deal with a conflict situation?

B: That's a(n) _____ question. Maybe I can just give you a(n) _____ of a time when a conflict arose and I managed to deal with it successfully.

2 Work in pairs. Take turns to ask and answer the questions (1–4). When you answer, give yourself time to think, then steer the conversation to focus on the information in brackets.

1 A: How important is it to keep learning new skills in a job?

B: (Focus on a particular skill you learnt during your last job.)

2 A: What qualities do you think you need to be a successful team worker?

B: (Focus on a time when you worked successfully in a team.)

3 A: You don't have any formal management qualifications. Do you think this will be an issue for you?

B: (Focus on an example of when you were in charge at work.)

4 A: What's the best way to deal with customers who are dissatisfied?

B: (Focus on a situation in which you successfully dealt with someone who was angry.)

5A mixed conditionals

REFERENCE ◀◀ page 58

We use a mixed conditional when we want to talk about a hypothetical (imaginary) situation in the past and a hypothetical present result of that situation.

If we'**d chosen** to travel by train rather than by car, we'**d be** there by now.

You **wouldn't feel** so sick if you **hadn't decided** to eat all that cheese.

The verb in the *if* clause is in the past perfect form (as it would be in a third conditional) and *would(n't)/might (not)/may (not)* + *infinitive* without *to* or *be + -ing* form features in the other clause (as it would in the second conditional).

If I'**d gone** to university, my life **might be** very different to now.

Deli **would still not be talking** to me if I **hadn't apologised**.

Rather than a present result, the result might be in the future. Here, we might use *would(n't) be + -ing* form.

If you **hadn't told** me about the concert, I **wouldn't be going**.

Penny **would be starting** her new job on Monday if she **hadn't rejected** the offer.

We can also use a mixed conditional when we want to talk about the hypothetical past result of a hypothetical present situation or state.

If I **weren't** so afraid of planes, I'**d have flown** with you to Brazil.

If flats **weren't** so expensive to buy around here, we'**d have bought** something ages ago.

The verb in the *if* clause is in the past simple form (as it would be in a second conditional) and *would(n't)/might (not)/may (not) have* + past participle features in the other clause (as it would in the third conditional).

If I **weren't** so indecisive, this whole situation **would have ended** weeks ago.

I **wouldn't have called** you if it **wasn't** so important.

PRACTICE

1 Match the sentence beginnings (1–6) with the endings (a–f) to form mixed conditionals.

1 If you weren't my best friend,
2 You might not be so tired if
3 If I didn't love food so much,
4 If she'd explained it more clearly,
5 She'd be eating with us now if
6 I wouldn't be where I am today if

a I would have only had a starter.
b I'd understand what to do better.
c I would've been offended by your comment!
d I hadn't worked really hard.
e you hadn't stayed up watching films all night.
f her train hadn't been delayed.

2 Complete the sentences with the correct form of the verbs in brackets to make mixed conditional sentences.

1 If I hadn't had a pay rise, I .... (not / be) able to afford this holiday.
2 If Matt .... (spend) less time on social media every day, he'd have found a job by now.
3 You .... (not / fall) over this morning if you didn't look at your phone all the time!
4 You wouldn't need me to pay for lunch if you .... (not / buy) me flowers earlier.
5 If I hadn't used all my holiday up, I .... (go) with you to Portugal next week.
6 I'd have told you if you .... (can / keep) a secret, but you can't!

3 Rewrite the sentences as one sentence, using mixed conditionals.

1 You're so stubborn. We didn't come to an agreement for a long time.
   If .... to an agreement ages ago.
2 I didn't listen to your advice. I regret my decision.
   If .... my decision.
3 I didn't charge my phone battery. I've got no battery left.
   If .... some battery left.
4 I get seasick. I didn't go on a cruise with my friend last year.
   If .... on a cruise with my friend last year.
5 I'm not good with my hands. I didn't make you a gift.
   If .... you a gift myself.
6 I got up early. I'm tired now.
   If .... tired now.
7 I didn't study medicine. I'm not a doctor.
   If .... a doctor right now.
8 I didn't know you were such a good cook. I'm cooking dinner right now.
   If I .... dinner right now.

5B the perfect aspect

REFERENCE ◀◀ page 61

The perfect aspect looks back from one time to another and emphasises that an action is completed before another time. In some cases, the exact time may be unimportant/unknown. Sometimes the action is incomplete, started in the past and is still relevant now.

Verb form	Active	Passive
Present perfect	The animals **have learnt** to change their behaviour.	The project **has been praised** by environmentalists.
Past perfect	She **had studied** the animals for years before the trip.	In the past, a lot of animals **had been killed** by poachers.
Future perfect	By next year, they **will have trained** the animals to behave in a different way.	If we don't act now, the ecosystem **will have been destroyed** by 2050.
Perfect infinitive	The project didn't appear **to have caused** any problems.	The cameras seemed **to have been accepted** by the animals.

Present perfect

We use the present perfect for an action that was completed in the past when we don't know or don't say exactly when. We often use it to talk about our experiences.

I**'ve seen** gorillas in the wild. I **haven't been** to New York.

Compare this to the past simple, where we usually state the time the action took place.

I **saw** gorillas in the wild **last year**.

We also use the present perfect with *for* or *since* for an action that started in the past and still continues, or has a present result.

I**'ve lived** here **for** two years. (I still live here.)

I**'ve known** Ali **since** we were at school. (I still know him.)

Bats **have been protected** for many years. (They still are.)

I can't play tennis because I**'ve hurt** my arm. (a past action with a consequence in the present)

Past perfect

We use the past perfect to look back from a time in the past to a time before that.

I couldn't call you because my phone **had been stolen**.

Future perfect

We use the future perfect to look back from a time in the future to a time before that.

In ten years' time, we **will have saved** these animals.

In six months, we hope the animals **will have been trained**.

Perfect infinitive

We use the perfect infinitive after verbs like *seem* and *appear* and modals like *need* and *ought* to look back to a previous period.

He appeared **to have forgotten** us.

Some of the elephants seem **to have been killed**.

PRACTICE

1 Choose the correct words to complete the sentences.

1 How many animals have **killed / been killed** this year?

2 We hope **we arrested / to have arrested** the poachers before long.

3 We're pleased because we **had reduced / have reduced** the number of bear attacks.

4 The project failed because it **hadn't been planned / hadn't planned** carefully enough.

5 A lot of their natural habitat seems **it was destroyed / to have been destroyed**.

2 Complete the sentences and questions with the correct active or passive perfect form of the verbs in brackets.

1 They used methods which they _____ a few years earlier. (develop)

2 Don't worry – I _____ the flat before you get home. (clean)

3 Where's my tablet? It seems _____ ! (disappear)

4 We walked past the old school which _____ by fire a few years before. (destroy)

5 I don't think there will be much cake left – I'm guessing it _____ by now! (all / eat)

6 The elephants appeared _____ by poachers. (shoot)

3 Choose the correct options (A–C) to complete the text.

Biologists ¹_____ nudging techniques to help protect grizzly bears in a national park in Canada. They were concerned that a large number of the animals ²_____ by trains. They installed a system of flashing lights and alarm bells which were triggered by an approaching train and acted as an early warning. The project seems ³_____ a success. Scientists found that the warning system ⁴_____ the grizzlies to move off the tracks before the trains arrived. Other animals seem ⁵_____ by the warnings, too, as scientists found that the number of deaths of elks, wolves and small mammals ⁶_____ . The project ⁷_____ interest from other countries. Supporters of a similar scheme in India hope that in a few years' time it ⁸_____ the number of deaths caused by collisions between elephants and trains.

		A	B	C
1	A	have used	B have been used	C had used
2	A	will have been hit	B have hit	C had been hit
3	A	has been	B to have been	C had been
4	A	had prompted	B will have prompted	C seems it has prompted
5	A	to have influenced	B have influenced	C to have been influenced
6	A	had fallen	B had been fallen	C seems to fall
7	A	has attracted	B had attracted	C had been
8	A	has reduced	B will have reduced	C will have been reduced

5C How to ... summarise

REFERENCE ◀◀ page 63

We summarise when we want to check we've understood what a speaker said or inferred, or when we just want to give the key points of something, e.g. a concept or what has been discussed previously. When we summarise, we paraphrase what has been said before.

So, what you mean is that you tried it before and it worked to a degree. (check understanding)

So what you're saying is that you don't think this idea will work. (check inference)

Basically, a petition involves getting people's signatures. (summarise a concept)

In a nutshell, we've got two very different ideas to choose between. (summarise discussions)

Checking understanding of what a speaker said or inferred

So what you're saying is (that) ...

So what you mean is (that) ...

To put it another way, ...

In other words, ...

Summarising key points

In brief, ...

In a nutshell, ...

Basically, ...

To recap, ...

So to summarise, ...

So what we're saying is (that) ...

Notice that *to recap* and *to summarise* are slightly more formal than the other phrases.

Notice that in spoken English, a speaker may begin with *to put it another way, in other words, in a nutshell, basically,* but they may also end with these words/phrases.

Basically, it's something you use to filter unclean water.

It's something you use to filter unclean water, **basically**.

To put it another way, it's not something you want to use.

It's not something you want to use, **to put it another way**.

PRACTICE

1 Match the sentence beginnings (1–5) with the endings (a–e). Which sentences are checking understanding? Which summarise key concepts?

1 So what you're

2 OK, so in a

3 In other

4 Well, to put it

5 So to

a another way, you think we need to do more.

b saying is that you don't think it'll work.

c words, you support it.

d summarise, we all like the idea but it's time-consuming.

e nutshell, it's a quick, easy and cheap solution.

2 Add a necessary word to each sentence.

1 So what you mean a petition is more likely to gain interest online than offline.

2 So what you saying is that we need to get the support of a non-profit organisation.

3 In nutshell, it's a way of gaining support from the public while also raising money.

4 To put another way, it's not good to irritate the people whose support you need.

5 Brief, the problem is getting worse and we need to do something about it.

6 So summarise, the majority of us support the proposal.

3 Read the quotes and then write a summary using the word in brackets.

1 'We don't really want celebrities turning this event into a demonstration about social issues, but at the same time, outfits which highlight these issues do get attention from the press, which we do want. We just don't want it to take away from the art, which should be the real focus of the event.'

.... (saying)

2 'I'm not convinced by protests about climate change. We see them all the time, but nothing seems to change except people's perceptions towards the protestors when they disrupt people's journeys to work and so on. That can't be what the demonstrators really want.'

.... (nutshell)

3 'It's all very well people doing silly things to get attention for some kind of issue, but all it does is get people's attention for a few days. As soon as the interest dies down, people forget about it. I'm just not sure it's worth the effort.'

.... (words)

4 'It's hard to raise people's awareness of an issue when there are so many problems for us to worry about. I think sometimes the number of issues is so overwhelming and the thought of us solving them seems so difficult that it's easier just to pretend none of them exist. But we have to keep going with this. We can't give up.'

.... (put)

6A inversion

REFERENCE ◀◀ page 70

When we use some negative adverbials at the beginning of a sentence, we change the order of the subject and auxiliary verb. This is called inversion. We use these structures in more formal language, to emphasise the point we are making.

I have never seen such a wonderful sight! ('normal' word order)

Never **have I seen** such a wonderful sight! (inversion)

We use inversion with these adverbials:

Never (before)

Under no circumstances

Not only … , but also …

Only + time expression

In no way

I had never been so scared before. → **Never before had I been** so scared!

You should not give your bank details to anyone under any circumstances. → **Under no circumstances should you give** your bank details to anyone.

He was not only handsome, but also rich. → **Not only** was he handsome, **but** he was **also** rich.

It was only clear to me later that he had been lying. → **Only later was it clear** to me that he had been lying.

I was not happy with the decision in any way. → **In no way was I happy** with the decision.

We can invert the auxiliary verbs *have* and *will*, and also modal verbs such as *can* and *should*.

I will never go there again. → **Never will I go** there again!

She can't complain about the decision in any way. → **In no way can she complain** about the decision.

You shouldn't lie to the police under any circumstances. → **Under no circumstances should you lie** to the police.

Where the normal affirmative sentence has no auxiliary verb, we use *do* or *did* in the sentence with inversion.

They only **met** the landlord three months later. → Only three months later **did they meet** the landlord.

She not only plays the piano, but she also sings. → Not only **does she play** the piano, but she also sings.

PRACTICE

1 Put the words in the correct order to make sentences with inversion.

1 no / circumstances / I / agree / will / to this deal / under

   Under no circumstances will I agree to this deal.

2 never / had to process / before / we / so much information / have

3 not only / the decision / quick / was / but / also / was / it / correct

4 later / learn / I / only / the truth / did

5 acceptable / is / in / way / no / this behaviour

2 Choose the correct words to complete the sentences with inversion.

1 Not only **I have forgotten** / **have I forgotten** his address, but I've also forgotten his name!

2 In no way **should she be** / **she should be** in charge of this project!

3 Only when he had left **realised I** / **did I realise** that he had been telling the truth.

4 Under no circumstances **they must be** / **must they be** allowed into the venue.

5 Never **have I seen** / **saw I** such a mess!

3 Complete the second sentence so it means the same as the first sentence. Use inversion.

1 I have never had such amazing food before!
   Never .... amazing food!

2 This doesn't change my opinion in any way.
   In .... my opinion.

3 I only began to feel ill after the meal.
   Only .... to feel ill.

4 He was not only arrogant, but also rude.
   Not .... , but he was also rude.

5 You should not tell anyone about this research under any circumstances.
   Under .... about this research.

6 I will never forget their kindness.
   Never .... their kindness.

6B passive structures

REFERENCE ◀◀ page 72

We use the passive form when we want to focus on the action, not on the person who does the action (the agent). This may be because:

• we do not know who the agent is.

It **was delivered** yesterday.

• it's clear who the agent is to both speaker and listener from the context or a previous mention of the agent.

The man **was arrested** yesterday.

• it's 'people in general'.

English **is spoken** around the world.

• we want to maintain the same subject and this forces the use of the passive.

They ordered six chairs but they **were sent** only five.

• we want to avoid blaming someone or admitting our own wrongdoing.

He broke a glass. → A glass **was broken**.

The passive is used in all contexts, but is often a key feature of formal English as it helps to maintain objectivity.

Passive and perfect infinitive

We use a passive infinitive form after modal verbs and verbs that are followed by the infinitive (e.g. *need, want, hope*). We might also use it as the subject of a sentence. It is formed with *to be* + infinitive, although *to* is omitted after modal verbs such as *may, might, will*.

You **could be given** a promotion if you keep doing what you're doing.

I **want** the meeting **to be finished** by 4 o'clock today so I can leave early.

To be sent shoes for a child when you ordered shoes for an adult is annoying!

When we want to refer to the past, or a completed action at a future time, we use a **perfect infinitive**. It is formed with *to have been* + past participle. The *to* is omitted after modal verbs such as *may, might, will*.

I might **have been sent** the wrong item.

My birthday seems **to have been forgotten** by my brother.

Passive and perfect *-ing* form

We use a passive *-ing* form (*being* + past participle) after verbs which are followed by a gerund (e.g. *avoid, keep, enjoy*), prepositions and as a subject of a sentence.

I avoid **being tagged** in photos by not being on social media!

I'm really looking forward to **being taken** on a tour of the city.

Being given an end-of-year bonus was unexpected but welcome.

When we want to refer to the past, we use a **perfect gerund**. It's formed with *having been* + past participle.

We don't mind **having been missed** off the list once, but twice is annoying.

I resent **having been ignored** for much of the meeting.

After **having been promised** a pay rise, I was disappointed when I didn't get one.

We can also use a perfect *-ing* form to form a participle clause when we want to refer to the past.

Having been awarded a prize for her work, Sally was delighted.

Having been born in Australia, I've got an Australian passport.

PRACTICE

1 Choose the correct verb forms to complete the sentences.

 1 We appear to **have misled / have been misled**.

 2 You may **be sent / to send** an interesting email later.

 3 I should **be given / have been given** an apology yesterday.

 4 I don't enjoy **being called / to call** in the middle of the night.

 5 I might **have told / have been told**. I don't remember.

 6 He denied **to be / having been** given the job by mistake.

2 Complete the sentences with the correct passive form of the verb in brackets.

 1 Ben hopes _____ (give) a pay rise by the end of the year.

 2 I appear _____ (send) the wrong documents.

 3 The cake needs _____ (cut) into eight pieces.

 4 We should _____ (warn) about this last week.

 5 I don't mind _____ (miss) the party last Friday, but I'm sad I didn't get to see Musa.

 6 I always avoid _____ (give) too much work to do by pretending to be very busy!

3 Rewrite the second sentence with a passive or perfect infinitive or *-ing* form, so it means the same as the first.

 1 The shirt I ordered didn't fit – it's possible I was sent the wrong one.

 I might _____ the wrong shirt, because it didn't fit.

 2 We won't need to do any more work on the project.

 No further work _____ on the project.

 3 It's possible for the customer to request a refund.

 A refund _____ by the customer.

 4 I possibly sent our client the wrong information.

 The wrong information may _____ to our client.

 5 I'd worked hard for weeks, so I was disappointed with my grade.

 I was disappointed with my grade, after _____ hard for weeks.

 6 I'm looking forward to the HR manager showing me around the building.

 I'm looking forward to _____ around the building by the HR manager.

6C How to ... negotiate in a dispute

REFERENCE ◀◀ page 75

We can use a number of different phrases when negotiating a dispute. We use phrases to complain about a situation, make an offer and accept the offer.

Complaining

When we complain about something, we usually add a reason for the complaint, e.g. we suggest that something is not reasonable or acceptable.

It isn't reasonable to expect me to (live without a washing machine).

I don't think it's fair that (I have to put up with noisy building works).

(There's still no hot water, and) **this isn't really acceptable**.

Making an offer

When we make an offer, we often use a phrase to emphasise that we are offering something.

What I can do is (reduce the rent for two months).

Maybe we could come to an arrangement about (the rent).

I can offer you (alternative accommodation while the building works take place).

Accepting the offer

When we accept an offer, we often add a phrase to confirm that it is acceptable, or to give a reason.

(Yes, a rent reduction of fifty percent is fine.) **That's acceptable to me.**

(I like the idea of alternative accommodation for a month.) **That sounds like a good compromise.**

(Yes, getting the flat redecorated would be good.) **I'd be happy with that.**

PRACTICE

1 Complete the sentences with one word in each gap.

1 Yes, that sounds .... a good compromise.

2 .... I can do is get an electrician in to look at the heating.

3 I don't think it's .... that you leave your bike next to the lift.

4 Maybe we could .... to an arrangement about the rubbish.

5 I'd be happy .... that.

6 I'm sorry, but this isn't really ....

2 Look at the sentences in Ex 1 again. Decide if each one is complaining (C), making an offer (M) or accepting an offer (A).

3 Choose the most suitable response to each sentence (a or b).

1 I can offer you a refund on your rent.
   a Yes, that's acceptable to me.
   b It isn't reasonable to expect me to pay that.

2 I don't think it's fair that you have a party every week!
   a I agree. That's acceptable to me.
   b What I can do is make sure the party always finishes at midnight.

3 What I can do is help you decorate your flat, to make up for the inconvenience.
   a I don't think it's fair that I have to do that!
   b I'd be happy with that.

4 It isn't really acceptable to leave your bike in the entrance hall.
   a Leaving it there sounds like a good compromise.
   b Maybe we could come to an arrangement about where I can leave it.

7A adverbials

REFERENCE ◀◀ page 81

Adverbials add extra information to a sentence about time, frequency, manner, etc. They can be a single word or a phrase.

Adverbials of manner

These describe how something happens. They usually come after the verb and object, but they can also come before the verb or at the beginning of a sentence, for emphasis. When they are used at the beginning of a sentence, they are followed by a comma.

Words can fall out of fashion **quickly**.

She usually drives **carefully**.

It's important to spend your money **in a sensible way**.

She **quietly** closed the door.

Carefully, she put the lid back on the box.

Time adverbials

These describe when something happens, or how long it happened for. They usually come after the verb and object, but can come at the beginning of a sentence, for emphasis. When they are used at the beginning of a sentence, they are followed by a comma.

I saw Sam **last week**.

We moved to London **in 2010**.

We sat outside in the garden **for a while**.

Two weeks ago, I saw him in the city centre.

Frequency adverbials

These describe how often something happens. Frequency adverbs usually come before the main verb, but after the verb *be*. Adverbial phrases of frequency usually come after the verb and object, but can come at the beginning of a sentence, for emphasis. When they are used at the beginning of a sentence, they are followed by a comma.

I **often** go shopping there.

She's **usually** at the gym in the morning.

I walk that way to work **pretty much every day**.

From time to time, I wonder how much I really enjoy my job.

Intensifying adverbs

These modify an adjective and make the meaning of the adjective stronger or weaker. They come before the adjective.

She looked **extremely** happy.

It was **quite** warm outside.

He was **incredibly** angry.

Sentence adverbials

These show the speaker's attitude and make a comment about the sentence. They usually come at the beginning of the sentence and are followed by a comma.

Surprisingly, there was no charge for the service.

Interestingly, there weren't many people there.

To my delight, I bumped into two of my friends in the restaurant.

PRACTICE

1 Underline the adverbials in the sentences.

1 We played computer games all afternoon.
2 Every once in a while, we meet up for a chat.
3 She looked at me in a suspicious manner.
4 Unfortunately, the restaurant had to close.
5 The city centre was incredibly busy.
6 To my astonishment, she announced that she had quit her job.
7 I still go to visit them on a fairly regular basis.
8 He was quietly reading his book.

2 Look at the adverbials in Ex 1 and decide what kind of adverbial each one is: manner, time, frequency, intensifying or sentence.

3 Choose the correct words to complete the sentences.

1 I opened **the door silently / silently the door**.
2 We **at the end of the day returned home / returned home at the end of the day**.
3 She was **every day / incredibly** interested in my work.
4 **In a disappointing way / Disappointingly,** they didn't make it to the final of the competition.
5 We should follow the map **carefully / always**.
6 She looked **slightly shocked / shocked slightly** when I told her what had happened.
7 **A few days ago / In a friendly way,** we met up for a coffee and a chat.
8 He is **unsurprisingly / usually** at his desk by eight o'clock in the morning.

7B fronting: reasons, causes and explanations

REFERENCE ◀◀ page 85

We can use *as/because/since*; *because of*; *seeing as*; *as a result of* + object; and *-ed* participle clauses to introduce the reason or cause of something.

As Italian cuisine is popular around the world, it's often people's favourite food.

As a result of globalisation, we can all buy the same type of coffee.

Impressed by the local cuisine, I tried my best to learn all about it.

As the most important information is often given in the second part of a sentence in English, we may introduce the reason or cause at the start of the sentence in order to focus on the result or effect at the end. We may also place it at the start in order to connect it to what came before.

Because you've never tried Ethiopian cuisine, I'm going to take you to an Ethiopian restaurant later. (focus on going to the restaurant)

You've never tried mocha coffee? Well, **because of** that, we're going to have a cup right now. (relates to information that came before).

as/because/since

We use *as/because/since* + clause, and *because of* + object, to introduce a reason or cause. A comma then separates it from the second clause which gives the result or effect. Note that the two clauses can change, with the reason or cause second.

Since you like Vietnamese food, I'm sure you'd enjoy Cambodian food.

I'm sure you'd enjoy Cambodian food, **since** you like Vietnamese food.

seeing as

We use *seeing as (how)* + clause in the same way we use *as/because/since*. Note that it tends to be used informally and is more common in British English than in other types of English.

Seeing as you've never tried Indonesian food, we should order some.

Seeing as how it's dinner time, we should eat.

as a result of + object

We use *as a result of* + object to introduce a reason or cause when we're being more formal. The object might be a noun or noun phrase. The noun phrase may be short or long.

As a result of the cultural exchange of foods, we learnt a lot about each other's culture.

As a result of visiting several countries in Southeast Asia, Tara developed a love of spicy dishes.

As a result of what can only be considered to be a terrible mistake by the manufacturer, a key ingredient of the dish was omitted.

-ed participle clauses

We can use an *-ed* participle clause to introduce a reason or cause.

Annoyed by the lack of salt in her soup, she complained to the waiter. (Because there was a lack of salt in her soup …)

Forced to eat the same food every day for a week, Laura was looking forward to trying something new. (Because Laura had been forced to eat the same food …)

in light of/in view of (the fact that)

We can use *in light/view of* + noun/noun phrase or *in light/view of the fact that* + clause to introduce a reason or cause. They mean 'considering'.

In light of concerns about the impact of almond milk on the environment, I've stopped drinking it.

In view of the fact that trends come and go, the restaurant menu changes twice a year.

PRACTICE

1 Find and correct one error in each sentence.

1 Because health issues, I decided to go vegetarian.

2 As result of seeing a recipe online, they decided to make *nasi goreng*.

3 Frustrating by the lack of choice, we went to a different restaurant.

4 Since that I don't eat meat, I can't have this dish.

5 As a result of burn the food, I decided not to make the recipe again.

6 Because of I'd never tried such an unusual dish, I ordered it immediately.

7 See as it's getting late, we should eat.

8 In the view of the fact that 3D printers can print food, we may all print our own dinner in the future.

2 Link the sentences together. Use the words in brackets.

1 I don't eat bread. I have a wheat allergy. (since)

2 We're interested in vegan food. We decided to try some. (interested)

3 The restaurant had robot servers. We decided to give it a try. (because)

4 The dessert menu looked impressive. Everyone ordered something. (by)

5 We were pleased that strawberries were in season. We bought some. (pleased)

6 We're not hungry. Let's miss lunch. (seeing)

7 The demand for local ingredients is growing. Farmers' markets are growing in popularity. (view)

8 People are consuming alternative types of milk. Cow's milk is losing popularity. (because of)

3 Complete the sentences with a reason or cause. Use your own ideas.

1 As I love _____ , I often eat _____ .

2 Because of a dislike for _____ , I tend not to eat _____ .

3 Curious about _____ food, I'd love to try _____ .

4 As a result of never eating out at a _____ restaurant, I'd like to visit one.

5 Seeing as I'm not keen on _____ food, I usually avoid _____ restaurants.

6 In view of the fact that _____ , I don't usually drink _____ .

7C How to... exaggerate

REFERENCE ◀ page 87

We sometimes exaggerate an action or state, the size or quantity of something, or make comparisons in order to emphasise a point and/or create a more dramatic effect. We tend to do this in more informal situations. Notice that when we make comparisons or describe likenesses, the comparison or likeness is exaggerated.

Exaggerated actions or states

My (feet) **are killing me.**

I'm starving. (I could eat a horse.)

I'd die of (embarrassment/shame).

I wouldn't be seen dead in (a pair of shoes like that).

Exaggerated size or quantity

You take/It takes (forever/hours) **to** (do it).

(I bet) **they cost a fortune.**

They're about ten sizes too small.

I've told you (a million) **times,** (I don't like denim jackets).

It looks like (it's been around for centuries).

Comparisons or likenesses

There's nothing better than (shopping at a vintage store).

It's like trying to find a needle in a haystack.

You'll (literally) **be green with envy.**

PRACTICE

1 Match the sentence beginnings (1–8) with the endings (a–h).

1 This jacket is ten times
2 I'd die of
3 These sunglasses cost
4 I wouldn't be seen
5 I've told you
6 My back is
7 My journey to work
8 There's nothing

a better than an old vintage bag.
b an absolute fortune.
c killing me.
d takes forever.
e embarrassment if I wore that.
f a million times before – no!
g dead in those trainers.
h smaller than it was. It's shrunk!

2 Complete the exaggerations with the words in the box.

> a hundred   centuries   hours   needle   shame   ton

1 At the end of a shopping trip, my bags weigh a ....
2 Trying to find my phone in this house is like trying to find a .... in a haystack.
3 This old T-shirt looks like it's been around for a few ....
4 I'd die of .... if that happened to me.
5 You've bought .... times more apples than we need.
6 Why does it take you .... to get ready?

3 Change a word or phrase in the sentences to exaggerate.

1 My knees are hurting me.
2 The taxi took a long time to arrive.
3 Those shoes look like they cost a bit.
4 I'd be embarrassed if I made that mistake.
5 Come on, it's easy. You've done it lots of times before.
6 Why does it always feel like the food takes a while to arrive?

8A concession

REFERENCE ◀◀ page 93

We use adverbials to admit that an opposing point of view has merit or is true.

Although utopias are idyllic, dystopian worlds provide more interesting stories.

Dystopian stories can be quite depressing, but **at the same time** the endings often give us hope.

These adverbials often form concession clauses, i.e. with *although*, *while* and *even though*.

While dystopian fiction is popular amongst all age groups, it's particularly popular amongst young adults.

Even though the world can be quite depressing at times, there is a lot to enjoy.

Concession clauses can come at the start or end of a sentence, but they usually come at the start of the sentence, as we want to admit that an opposing point of view is true, but then quickly move onto expressing a counterargument which expresses our true beliefs. Alternatively, the concession may refer to something another speaker said, so we refer to it first and then give our own view. Compare the impact of putting the concessive clause at the start and the end:

Although books encourage us to use our own imaginations, films are more visual and less time-consuming.

Films are more visual and less time-consuming, **although** books encourage us to use our own imaginations.

We can use *however*, *at the same time* and *that said* to show a contrasting point of view, but these phrases come before our own belief or our counterargument, and not the opposing point of view we are admitting is valid or true. Note that these start a new sentence.

Tales of struggle can be uplifting. **However**, utopias give us something to aspire to.

New stories are published every day. **At the same time**, they're all versions of stories from history.

E-books are convenient. **That said**, there's nothing better than a paper book.

We can use the adverbial phrase *admittedly … but* to introduce an opposing viewpoint.

Admittedly, there have been some excellent sci-fi stories, **but** I prefer romance.

Admittedly, what you said is true, **but** I don't believe it's always the case.

We also use *though* to provide an alternative viewpoint. In spoken or informal written communication, we often add it to the end of our point.

Though the ending was disappointing, I enjoyed the show.

The story was good, **though** the acting was pretty terrible.

The book was brilliant. The film was rubbish, **though**.

We can use the structure *adjective + though/as* to make a concession, e.g. *True though that is, True though that may be, Interesting as that seems, Clever though he may be, Horrible as that is, Brilliant as she may seem*.

True though that is, I would argue that it's different for everyone.

True though that may be, it's not the most interesting story.

Clever though he is, he's not always 100 percent correct about everything.

Interesting as that is, it doesn't support your argument.

PRACTICE

1 Put the words in the correct order to make sentences.

1 a long time. / it was fun. / It took / same time, / At the

2 useful. / see it's / I don't / While / I can / like it,

3 she is, / she / serious. / Funny / can be / though

4 it's easy. / hard though. / The last part / Most of / is

5 better resources. / Although / there are / helpful, / it's

6 I don't / True / may be, / agree. / that / though

2 Link the sentences together using the word in brackets and correct punctuation. The first sentence is the concession. More than one answer might be possible.

1 The characters are strong. The story line is weak. (while)

2 I don't appreciate your tone of voice. I understand your point. (at the same time)

3 I'm strong. It's too heavy for me to lift. (though)

4 It wasn't their best match. They're still the best in the world. (admittedly)

5 She's generally happy. She has some challenges in her life. (that said)

6 You said it's expensive. It tastes delicious. (true)

3 Complete the sentences with an opposing viewpoint. Compare your ideas with a partner.

1 Although ...., it's very popular.

2 It's not easy to .... At the same time, it's not impossible.

3 Depressing as dystopian stories are, ...

4 Admittedly, ..., but I think it's great!

5 .... You can't get much better though.

6 While ...., there are better places to visit.

8B future forms

REFERENCE ◀ page 96

will

We use *will* to make general predictions about the future.

This technology **will become** much more widely used in the future.

I don't think the product **will succeed**.

be going to

We use *be going to* to express a plan or intention.

The company **is going to try** to improve the device.

Researchers **are going to explore** the possibility of creating energy from clouds.

We also use *be going to* for predictions based on evidence in the present.

Look at the sky. It**'s going to rain**!

She can't carry all those drinks. She**'s going to drop** them!

Future continuous

We use the future continuous to talk about an action that will be in progress in the future.

In ten years' time, we**'ll be using** a lot more renewable energy.

I probably **won't be living** here in five years.

Future perfect

We use the future perfect to talk about an action that will be finished at a particular time in the future.

In ten years' time, researchers **will have found** a solution to this problem.

There's no point calling him at midnight – he**'ll have gone** to bed!

We can also use the future perfect in the passive form.

The project **will have been completed** by next year.

Do you think the problem of climate change **will have been solved** by 2050?

Future perfect continuous

We use the future perfect continuous to talk about the length of an action as seen from a particular time in the future.

Next year, I**'ll have been studying** English for ten years.

By 2050, people **will have been using** electric vehicles for ages!

Modal verbs

We can use *might*, *may* and *could* instead of *will* in future forms to show that we feel less certain about a future event.

I think the lecture **might** be interesting.

I **may** be working in Paris next year.

Experts **could** have found a solution to the energy crisis by next year.

Some of these problems **may** have been solved in a few years' time.

1 Read the sentences. Match the verb forms in bold with the descriptions (a–e).

1 I think our diet **will be** healthier in future.
2 I can't come for lunch tomorrow – I**'ll be travelling** to London then.
3 Don't worry. The party **will have finished** by midnight.
4 Next summer, I **will have been working** here for three years.
5 It **might rain** tomorrow.

a an action in progress in the future
b an action that will have continued for a particular amount of time, at a point in the future
c an action that will be finished at a particular time
d a general prediction about the future
e a prediction that is less certain

2 Choose the correct verb forms to complete the sentences.

1 Do you think their meeting will **finish / have finished** by now?
2 I'm so excited – this time tomorrow, we'll **be flying / have been flying** to Florida!
3 I'm picking my car up at four this afternoon. Hopefully, it will **have repaired / have been repaired** by then.
4 I'll call you at eight if I'm free, but I **may still work / may still be working**.
5 Next March, we **'ve been living / will have been living** here for ten years!
6 Why don't you phone the lost property office again tomorrow? Your bags **might have found / might have been found** by then.

3 Complete the second sentence with the correct future form of the verb in brackets so it means the same as the first sentence.

1 The train leaves at 10.30.
The train .... (leave) by 11.00.
2 We're going to watch a film this evening. It starts at 7.30 and finishes at 10.00.
At 8.30, we .... (watch) a film.
3 They're delivering the parcel at 11.00.
The parcel .... (deliver) by lunchtime.
4 It's possible that I will have a job in Spain next year.
I .... (work) in Spain next year.
5 I started waiting in this queue forty-five minutes ago!
In fifteen minutes I .... (wait) for an hour!
6 We will inform you of our decision on Monday morning.
By Monday afternoon, you .... (inform) of our decision.

8C How to ... maintain and end a discussion

REFERENCE ◀◀ page 99

We can use a number of different phrases in order to maintain a discussion or bring it to an end. When we want to maintain a discussion, we use phrases to agree or disagree with what other people have said. When we want to end a discussion, we often use a phrase to summarise the discussion.

Expressing an opinion

We can use different phrases to express opinions in slightly different ways.

Frankly, I think the idea of never going on holiday is crazy! (This is a strong and definite opinion.)

As I see it, the time to enjoy yourself is when you're young. (This is my personal opinion, but I understand that others might not agree.)

I dare say I could save a small amount of money each month. (I accept that this is true, but it is not a strong opinion.)

It seems to me that it's more important to use the money you earn to have fun. (This is my personal opinion, based on my experience.)

Agreeing

We can use different phrases to express agreement in slightly different ways.

'I'm hopeless at saving money.' '**That makes two of us.**' (Exactly the same is true for me.)

I can definitely **see what** Mia **is saying**. She's got a good point. (I can understand Mia's point of view, although I don't necessarily agree with it strongly.)

Yes, **I can see what you're saying**. That makes sense. (I can understand your point of view, although I don't necessarily agree with it strongly.)

I'm with Tom **here**. You need to plan for the future. (I completely agree with Tom.)

Disagreeing

When we disagree with someone's opinion, we often express recognition of their opinion or point of view first, before we present a different opinion or point of view.

Yes, I probably waste quite a lot of money. **But the other side of the coin is** that I work hard and don't want to spend all my free time worrying about money!

I guess that's one way of looking at it, but on the other hand, you might actually enjoy travelling more when you're a bit older.

Yes, we all want to have fun. **But another way of looking at things is that** you can actually have more fun, and for longer, if you save money when you're young.

Summarising and ending a discussion

We often summarise at the end of a discussion, and comment on how much we have enjoyed the discussion, and how similar or different our opinions are.

Well, **it's been great talking to you** about this.

It's surprising. **We seem to have quite similar ideas.**

I don't think we'll ever agree. But **I guess we're all different.**

PRACTICE

1 Complete the sentences with one word in each gap.

1 Yes, that makes two .... us!

2 I guess that's one .... of looking at it, but …

3 I .... say I could be a bit more careful with my money!

4 As I .... it, the more money people have, the more they want!

5 I'm .... Jack on this point. I completely agree with him.

6 I don't think we'll ever agree, but I .... we're all different.

2 Complete the conversations with the correct phrases in the boxes.

> I guess that's one way of looking at it, but
> As I see it   I dare say   I'm with

1 Ada: What do you think of the idea of becoming as rich as you can, so you can give most of your money away?

Max: I think it's a crazy idea! You could end up doing a job you absolutely hate! [1] .... , you should do what you can to help others, but you shouldn't ruin your own life in the process! [2] .... I could probably give more to charity than I do, but I also think it's fine to just enjoy the money you have.

Ada: [3] .... don't you admire wealthy people who use their wealth to help others?

Zoe: [4] .... Max here. I think it's fine to just earn money and spend it on yourself!

> But another way of looking at things is
> Frankly, I think   I guess we're all different
> That makes two of us

2 Casper: I read an article the other day arguing that all jobs in a company should be paid the same salary. What do you think of that idea?

Joe: [5] .... it's ridiculous! I mean, some jobs are clearly more challenging than others, so they should definitely be paid more.

Casper: [6] .... that if everyone works the same number of hours, they're all making the same effort, so they should get equal reward. I definitely think that there shouldn't be such a big gap between the best-paid and worst-paid jobs.

Eva: [7] .... We should definitely aim for a more equal society.

Joe: Well, I don't see it that way, but [8] ....

VOCABULARY BANK

1A phrasal verbs: friendships

« page 9

1 A Read about a friendship. Match the phrasal verbs in bold with the meanings (1–9). Two of the phrasal verbs have the same meaning.

> Claire and I didn't **take to** each other at first. We were only eleven when we met. I was new at the school and got on well with her best friend, so I suppose I **came between** them and their friendship. However, over time, we **warmed to** each other and by the time we started secondary school, we were really close. I **hung around** with her all the time and we only ever **fell out** once over something really silly. We **made up** after just a day of not talking to each other. Unfortunately, life took us in different directions after school and we **drifted apart**. We still see each other occasionally. I **invite** her **along** to my birthday celebrations every year and she **stops by** my flat if she's passing. We **bump into** each other in the supermarket, too. So, we're still friends, just not as close as we once were.

1 ask someone to go with you somewhere
2 gradually stop being friends
3 spend a lot of time with
4 have an argument
5 meet someone when not expecting to
6 make a short visit to a person or place
7 start to like
8 become friends again after an argument
9 cause trouble between people

B Which of the phrasal verbs in Ex 1A refer to relationships with friends? Which refer to socialising with friends?

2 A Complete the questions with the correct form of the phrasal verbs in Ex 1A.

1 Who did you .... with most at school?
2 Are you still friends with this person or have you slowly .... over the years?
3 Have you ever .... with a friend and stopped speaking? Did you make up again?
4 Did you .... your closest friend instantly when you first met, or did it take time to .... them?
5 Where was the last place a friend .... you .... to?
6 Who was the last friend you .... in a shop?
7 Whose home do you .... to say hello if you're in the area?
8 What kinds of things tend to .... people who are friends?

B Work in pairs. Take turns to ask and answer the questions in Ex 2A.

1B urban spaces

« page 13

1 Read the sentences about some places in a city. Match the words in bold with the meanings (a–j).

1 The factory is located on a small **industrial estate** on the **outskirts** of the city.
2 A lot of old **slums** have been demolished in **inner-city** areas and replaced with modern apartment blocks.
3 Their apartment building is in a **residential** area of the city and is a beautiful example of eighteenth-century **architecture**.
4 We moved out of a **built-up** area in the city centre to a leafy **suburban** street.
5 This house is a beautiful new **residence**, built using modern **construction** methods.

a describing part of a city where there are houses rather than factories or shops
b a general word for the style of buildings
c the parts of a city around the edge, away from the centre
d poor-quality homes that are not in good condition
e a house or flat that people live in
f an area where there are a lot of factories
g describing an area that is close to the centre of a city
h the act of building something
i describing an area in a city where there are a lot of buildings and not much green space
j describing an area on the edge of a city where a lot of people live

2 A Choose the correct words to complete the sentences.

1 I prefer modern **outskirts / architecture** to historic styles of building.
2 I wouldn't like to live in **a suburban / an inner-city** area because I'd have to travel into the centre every day for work.
3 I would hate to live close to **an industrial estate / a residential area** because of the noise and pollution.
4 I think it's disgraceful that there are still **residences / slums** in my city – everyone deserves a decent home to live in.
5 I think the **residential / construction** industry should do more to combat climate change.
6 I think governments should do more to create green spaces in **built-up / outskirts** areas.

B Work in pairs. Which of the sentences in Ex 2A do you agree with?

2A winning and losing

◀◀ page 20

1 Read the extracts from news reports (1–6) about winning, losing and cheating. Then answer the questions (a–d).

1 Sasha Brown is very inexperienced, so she**'s the underdog** in this game. Her opponent **is** definitely **the favourite** and should win comfortably.

2 Was he really tripped, or did he **dive** to try and get a penalty?

3 I don't believe she's really injured. I think she**'s playing for time** because the game's nearly over.

4 All this messing around by his opponent has definitely **put** him **off** and caused him to make mistakes. This kind of behaviour isn't against the rules, but it's definitely **bending the rules**.

5 Manchester United are having a great season – they**'re unbeaten** in nine games now.

6 He can't win the game now, so he may choose to **concede**.

a Which phrases refer to different ways of cheating or not playing fair?

b Which phrases refer to how likely someone is to win or lose?

c Which phrase describes someone who hasn't lost before, or for a long time?

d Which verb means to admit that you have lost?

2 A Complete the opinions with the correct form of the words and phrases from Ex 1.

1 I don't believe that anyone plays fair 100 percent of the time. Everyone .... a little bit to gain an advantage.

2 I hate it when tennis players shout when they play a shot. I'm sure they only do it to .... their opponent ....

3 It really annoys me when footballers .... in the penalty area or slow things down and .... at the end of a game. It really spoils the game for me!

4 In a sports competition, I'd rather .... and be expected to lose than .... and be expected to do well.

5 I think there must be a lot of pressure on sportspeople when they .... for a long time, and they know that everyone else wants to defeat them.

6 I hate it when sports games are very uneven and one player or team is winning too easily. The losing player or team should be allowed to .... before the end.

B Work in pairs. Which of the opinions in Ex 2A do you agree with?

2C work benefits

◀◀ page 26

1 A Read about the benefits a company offers its staff. Find definitions in the text of the phrases in bold.

When you join our company, you'll receive a number of **job perks** in addition to the usual employee benefits of a regular salary (note that we offer **equal pay** for all staff so everyone who does the same job is paid the same) and paid holiday. We offer excellent **health insurance** which will cover the costs of all your medical needs, and our **pension scheme** will help provide you with a good standard of living when you retire. We offer new mothers and fathers the opportunity to take a month's extra **maternity/paternity leave** on top of the national requirement for time off to spend time with their babies and we also have **on-site childcare** so parents can leave their children close by, in a safe environment, while at work. There are further **financial incentives** as we know that a bit of extra money can be both useful and motivating. There's our end-of-year **bonus scheme** where all staff receive a sum equal to a maximum of five percent of their annual salary, depending on the profitability of the company that year. We offer **tuition assistance** to help anyone wanting to take a formal course related to their work. Finally, there's a **mentor programme** for new members of staff. We pair you with a more experienced employee to help you during your first year at the company.

B Complete the sentences with the correct form of the phrases in bold from Ex 1A.

1 Joan had her baby last week. She's on .... for six months.

2 Dental care isn't included in our .... so we have to pay for it.

3 If the bosses want us to work more hours, they need to offer us some kind of .... so we can earn more.

4 My company offers ...., which is paying for my course.

5 I'm helping one of the new staff as part of the company's ....

6 Companies are required by law to offer .... to men and women doing the same jobs.

7 My company doesn't have any .... so I take my daughter to a local kindergarten.

8 All the staff are going to get an extra €250 this year, as part of the company ....

2 Work in pairs. Which of the benefits in Ex 1A do most companies offer their employees in your country? Of the others, which do you think they should offer?

3B idiomatic phrases: emotions

« page 35

1 A Replace the phrases in bold with the phrases in the box.

> bursting with pride
> down in the dumps   made my day
> on cloud nine   pumped about
> scared stiff   shaken up
> sick to death of

1 I'm **really excited about** the concert that's coming up in.
2 When Declan walked up on stage to get his prize, I was **feeling very proud**.
3 We were all **shocked and upset** after seeing the news report.
4 You've looked **fed up** for a few days now. Is there anything wrong?
5 I was **really happy** while we were winning. I'm not now that we're losing!
6 I'm **fed up with** listening to you complain all day every day. Give it a rest!
7 It was midnight and I was on my own, so I was **very frightened** when someone knocked on the door.
8 Hearing I'd got the maximum score possible in my test **made me very happy**.

B Match the idiomatic phrases in Ex 1A with the emotions 1–5.

1 happiness
2 excitement
3 feeling fed up/sadness
4 pride
5 fear

2 What might someone in these situations say? Use the idiomatic phrases in Ex 1A.

1 You've found out you're getting a promotion at work.
2 A fire broke out in a house just a few doors away. You had to help the family get to safety.
3 Someone keeps sending you loads of messages every day when you're busy.
4 You've been invited to a really cool party.
5 You hate flying, but you have to fly somewhere.
6 A member of your family just won an award for their charitable work.

3C persuading and motivating

« page 38

1 A Complete the table with the correct verbs related to the nouns. Use the verbs on page 38 to help you.

Verb	Noun	Verb	Noun
1	persuasion	4	pressure
2	motivation	5	coaxing
3	manipulation	6	drive

B Choose the correct nouns to complete the sentences.

1 I hate it when friends put **pressure** / **coaxing** on me to go out.
2 I think it's always better to use gentle **drive** / **persuasion** rather than get angry with people.
3 I've got tremendous **drive** / **pressure** and enthusiasm for my work.
4 No amount of **motivation** / **coaxing** from my friends would persuade me to sing in public!
5 I would never use **manipulation** / **drive** to get someone to do something they don't want to do.
6 I don't have the **persuasion** / **motivation** to exercise every day.

2 Work in pairs. Which of the sentences in Ex 1B are true for you?

4A photography

« page 46

1 A Read the tips on taking a great portrait. Which do you find helpful? What other tips could you suggest?

Top tips for portrait photos

1 Avoid holding your camera in your hand so you get photos that are **in focus** and not **blurred**.
2 Ask the person to stand in natural light and **pose** naturally.
3 Don't just focus on the person while taking the photo. Look at the whole **composition**. Make sure things in the background don't take attention away from the person in **the foreground**.
4 Take more than one **shot** to see what works best. **Zoom in** to get a nice **close-up** of the person's face and **zoom out** to get their whole body.
5 **Frame** your photo so the subject is in the centre, or a little to the left or right of centre. Don't cut off half their head!

B Complete the definitions with the words in bold in Ex 1A.

1 If a photo is _____, things in it are unclear in shape.
2 If a photo is _____, everything in it is very clear.
3 The part of a photo closest to you is _____ .
4 If you want to make the subject of a photo seem bigger, you _____ .
5 If you want to make the subject of a photo seem smaller, you _____ .
6 The way in which a photo is made up is its _____ .
7 When you _____ a subject in a photo, you put a border around them.
8 An informal word for a photo is a _____ .
9 A _____ is a photo which is very close to the subject.
10 When you _____ for a photo, you sit or stand in a particular position.

2 Tell a partner about a portrait photo you have taken recently. What techniques did you use? Use the vocabulary from Ex 1A.

4C skills, abilities and experience

1 A Complete the table with the words in the box.

> competence   experience   experienced
> incompetent   proficiency   skill
> skilled   untrained

Positive adjective	Negative adjective	Noun
1	inexperienced	2 ....
competent	3	4 ....
5	unskilled	6 ....
trained	7	training
proficient		8 ....

B Choose the correct words to complete the questions.

1 How long do you think it takes to achieve **proficiency / proficient** in a language?

2 Would you apply for a senior job even if you weren't very **experienced / unskilled**?

3 Do you know anyone who often makes mistakes because they are **incompetent / trained**?

4 Which **skilled / skill** would you most like to learn?

5 Do you think someone should be paid less for doing a job if they are **competent / inexperienced**?

6 Should medical staff be allowed to treat people before they are fully **trained / training**?

C Work in pairs. Ask and answer the questions in Ex 1B.

2 A Work in pairs. Write a questionnaire using the words in Ex 1A.

B Ask and answer questionnaires with another pair. What's the most interesting answer you heard?

5B the natural world

1 A Complete the table with the words in the box.

> breed   conserve   conservation   instinctive   environment
> environmental   migrate   migratory   poach   poacher
> prey on   predatory   reproduce   reproductive

Verb	Noun (an activity or quality)	Adjective	Noun (a person or animal)
1	poaching		2 ....
3	reproduction	4	
5	migration	6	migrant, immigrant
7	breeding		breeder
8	9		conservationist
	10	11	environmentalist
	instinct	12	
13		14	predator, prey

B Complete the sentences with the correct form of the words in brackets.

1 Plastics should be banned because they cause a lot of .... damage. (environment)

2 To protect animals, it is important to understand their .... habits. (reproduce)

3 Climate change is making it difficult for some animals to .... (migration)

4 Some animals seem to have an .... fear of water. (instinct)

5 Farmers sometimes kill animals or birds that .... young farm animals. (predator)

6 Some endangered animals can be .... in captivity and then returned to the wild. (breeding)

7 .... of endangered animals should be punished severely. (poach)

8 Humans have a duty to .... the natural world around them. (conservation)

2 Work in pairs. Discuss the sentences in Ex 1B. Can you think of examples to support or contradict each one?

5C social and environmental issues

◀◀ page 62

1 A Match the news stories (1–3) with the topics below.

- climate change
- homelessness
- inequality

1 Local governments are working to ensure that there are **equal opportunities** for everyone who applies to work there, so that minority groups are not **neglected** and there is **diversity** within every department. This will ensure people from a variety of backgrounds are in charge of decision-making.

2 Activists are campaigning for the end of **deforestation** and the reduction of **fossil fuel** use in favour of renewable energy such as wind. They are also concerned about the amount of recyclable material ending up in **landfill sites** around the world.

3 A new charity has been set up to look after the **welfare** of people suffering financial **hardship** in order to stop them losing their homes. Local charities that fund **shelters** for people who end up **sleeping rough** on the streets have welcomed this new charity, hoping that it will reduce the number of people they have to help.

B Match the words and phrases in bold in Ex 1A with the meanings (1–10).

1 the cutting or burning of all trees in an area
2 a person's health and happiness
3 not looked after or paid enough attention
4 places where rubbish is buried under the ground
5 sleep outside because you have no home
6 a range of different people
7 something that makes your life difficult, e.g. lack of money
8 the same chances for everyone in employment
9 coal and gas, for example
10 places that provide safety and somewhere to sleep

2 Work in pairs. Are the issues in bold in Ex 1A issues in your area? Which are you concerned about? Why?

6B phrases with *right* and *wrong*

◀◀ page 71

1 A Choose the correct options to complete the sentences.

1 I was sure I was in the **right / wrong** and everyone else was incorrect.
2 I can't stand this presenter. The way she says things really rubs me up the **right / wrong** way.
3 This knowledge is dangerous and must never get into the **right / wrong** hands.
4 Things are going well with the project. We're on the **right / wrong** track so far.
5 We were supposed to meet at the cinema, but Jane got the **right / wrong** end of the stick and waited for me at the bus stop.
6 The wedding was planned really carefully so that nothing would go **right / wrong** and everything would go **right / wrong**.
7 Once we know what mistake we made, we can put it **right / wrong**.
8 Tom believed that he was in charge, but I soon put him **right / wrong**!

B Match the highlighted phrases in Ex 1A with the meanings (a–i).

a likely to lead to a correct or successful result
b annoy somebody without intending to
c succeed or happen correctly
d misunderstand a situation
e be discovered by someone who may want to cause harm
f make someone understand the correct facts of a situation
g have the best reasons/arguments in a disagreement
h make a situation better
i not succeed or happen incorrectly

C Work in pairs. Talk about at least five of these things.

1 A time you were in the wrong, but thought you were in the right.
2 Somebody or something that rubs you up the wrong way.
3 Something that shouldn't get into the wrong hands.
4 A time when something went wrong before it went right.
5 A time you had to put something right.
6 A time you had to put someone right about something.
7 Something in your life that you think is on the right track.
8 A time you got hold of the wrong end of the stick.

6C buildings and homes

1 A Read three bad reviews of holiday flats. Which one sounds the worst? Why?

Ellen S
14 hrs ago

The apartment block was really **run-down**, with paint peeling off the walls and one or two broken windows. Inside, the flat was really **cramped** – there was hardly room to move around, and nowhere to store our bags!

Date of stay: August 2022 ♡ Like ◌ Comments

947MaryJane
9 hrs ago

We were expecting a modern block of flats, but in fact the building was old and **crumbling** – I was worried it might collapse on us! Inside, the flat was dark and **dim**, even during the day – really depressing.

Date of stay: August 2022 ♡ Like ◌ Comments

59DolphinD
9 hrs ago

A dreadful flat! It obviously hadn't been cleaned because the floors were muddy and the bathroom was **filthy**! The heating wasn't working, so it was quite **chilly**, too.

Date of stay: August 2022 ♡ Like ◌ Comments

B Complete the sentences with the correct words in bold in Ex 1A.

1 I like a lot of space, so I'd hate to live in a small, ... flat.
2 I can't stand being cold, so I wouldn't put up with a .... flat.
3 A building must be solid – no one wants to live in an old building that's .... !
4 I always keep my flat clean. I don't know how people can live in .... conditions.
5 A flat needs to have big windows, so it's nice and bright, not .... and gloomy.
6 I don't mind if a building looks a bit .... on the outside, as long as it's bright and modern on the inside.

2 Work in pairs. Discuss the questions.

1 Which of the sentences in Ex 1B do you agree with most strongly?
2 What else is important for you in a house or flat?

7B food and drink

1 A Complete the blog post extracts with the words in the boxes.

| diet   vegans   vegetarians |

@Dingam | 57 mins   comment | share

As well as [1] .... who don't eat meat, and [2] .... who avoid any animal-related products, there are also pescatarians. Pescatarians have a [3] .... that includes fish, but no meat.

| calories   cholesterol   nutrients |

@Sandman2 | 51 mins   comment | share

A healthy diet isn't just about keeping the number of [4] .... we eat at a sensible level, it's about consuming a variety of food types to get the [5] .... we need to be healthy and making sure we don't eat too many of the types of food that can cause [6] .... to build up in our blood.

| binge on   grab a snack   junk food |

@GailP | 30 mins   comment | share

I love to [7] .... unhealthy foods on the odd occasion, but most of the time I eat healthily. I plan my meals, take lunch with me to avoid buying [8] .... like burgers and chips and I don't bring unhealthy food into the house. That way, when I go to [9] .... , I'm forced to have an apple rather than biscuits.

| in season   organic   out of season |

@SheenaR | 17 mins   comment | share

When buying fruit and veg, I try to buy things that are [10] .... rather than [11] .... and from abroad. That way, I know I'll be buying things that haven't travelled far to get to me. If I can afford it, I go for [12] .... alternatives as I know they're natural and no chemicals have been used to grow them.

B Work in pairs. Tell your partner about these things. Use as many vocabulary items from Ex 1A as possible.

- an alternative diet that you've tried, would like to try or would never try
- what you consider when buying food
- healthy eating habits and less healthy eating habits you have

7C describing clothes

1 Match the items in the pictures (1–8) with the adjectives describing them (a–h).

a matching
b chic
c dull
d striped
e scruffy
f waterproof
g loud
h baggy

2A Read the questions and make notes on your answers. Use adjectives from Ex 1 where possible.

1 How would you describe the clothes you wear on a regular basis?

2 How would you describe clothes you might wear for special occasions?

3 Are there any types of clothes you never, or would never, wear? Why?

B Work in pairs. Take turns to ask and answer the questions in Ex 2A.

8B science and technology

page 95

1 Read extracts from six product reviews. Then match the adjectives in bold with the meanings (a–f).

1 I love my new muscle massager. This **hand-held** device is great for massaging tired muscles and helping my body to relax.

2 This microwave is really **user-friendly**. You don't need to read the instruction book at all.

3 This is an extremely **energy-efficient** heater, so it will save you lots of money.

4 The health tracker uses **state-of-the-art** technology to monitor a range of different aspects of your health.

5 One of the best things about this device is that it's completely **recyclable**, so there's no waste.

6 Unlike a lot of cleaning products, this one contains no **hazardous** chemicals, so it's definitely environmentally friendly.

a able to be used again or be converted into new products
b simple to understand and use
c able to be operated by holding it in your hands as you move around
d dangerous
e not using very much energy
f very modern

2 Work in pairs. Talk about:

1 a hand-held device that you have bought recently.
2 something you buy regularly that is recyclable.
3 a new device you would like to buy that uses state-of-the-art technology.
4 something you avoid buying because it contains hazardous materials.
5 a machine or device that you think should be more energy-efficient.
6 something you use regularly which isn't very user-friendly.

8C money

page 98

1 Read what six people say about saving money. Then answer the questions (a–c) about the adjectives in bold.

1 I avoid buying designer brands because I think they're **overpriced** and not worth the money.

2 I drive a small car which is very **economical** on fuel.

3 My flatmates and I do our food shopping together because we find it's **cost-effective** to do it that way.

4 I never eat out in **pricey** restaurants.

5 I always keep an eye out for **complimentary** tickets to shows.

6 I tend to shop online and try to find things that are **discounted**, for example in the sales.

a Which two adjectives mean that something is expensive?
b Which three adjectives suggest that something is cheap, or cheaper than usual?
c Which adjective means that something is free?

2 Work in pairs. Which of the sentences in Ex 1 are true for you?

COMMUNICATION BANK

4A Ex 8A Student A

Prepare to put forward the proposal below and persuade others to agree with it. Think of your reasons and consider how to present them in a persuasive way.

Post-photo editing should be prohibited in advertising.

6D Ex 6A

Bixham's is a small company which makes garden furniture. It has been operating for almost forty years and of the twenty staff members, almost all have been working at the company for at least fifteen years. The new company director is concerned about the company's profitability and competitiveness and wants to introduce more up-to-date technology into their systems. Currently, orders are taken over the phone and input manually into a spreadsheet. The order is printed out and delivered by hand from the office to the factory floor, a stage often slowed down when the printer jams. Communication between teams is usually done face-to-face. The director knows from trying to make other changes that staff members have the attitude of 'If it ain't broke, don't fix it'.

1C Ex 5A Group B

Work in pairs. Complete the survey below with your own *Would you rather ... ?* questions.

WOULD YOU RATHER ...

1 cook for your housemates or do their laundry?
2 spend a week visiting a city or visiting the mountains?
3 ....
4 ....
5 ....
6 ....

6B Ex 7 Student A

1 **Read the first sentence aloud to your partner. Your partner will say the same idea in a more formal way. Listen and check it's appropriate. Help where necessary. Repeat with the other sentences.**
   1 I accidentally ordered the wrong stuff.
   2 I messed up. I sent the wrong document.
   3 I hate it when they give me a low score.

2 **Listen to each sentence your partner reads aloud. Say the same idea in a more formal way, using the prompts to help you.**
   1 I appear to have ....
   2 The filter might ....
   3 I'm delighted at ....

5A Ex 2A

Results

Count up your points. Never = 0, Hardly ever = 1, Sometimes = 2, Often = 3, Almost always = 4

0–8: You're so indecisive, you often end up not making a decision at all.

9–16: You are good at making decisions, but spend a lot of time worrying you've made the wrong choice.

17–24: You're fairly decisive, but self-doubt can sometimes slow you down.

25–32: You have the confidence and strategies to be decisive, and rarely doubt yourself.

6A Ex 6A Student B

You will argue against the algorithm. Read the ideas below and add some more ideas of your own.

Ideas against:

Algorithms:
- are not capable of being 'emotionally intelligent'; will never understand individual humans and their needs.
- will always be influenced by the prejudices of programmers.
- may make mistakes that go undetected or unchallenged because of trust in machines.
- ....
- ....

Humans:
- are more 'agile' at decision-making; can respond differently in different situations.
- can weigh up practical, logical and emotional factors at the same time.
- can be challenged and persuaded to see another point of view.
- ....
- ....

2C Ex 2C

However, this has not been the case so far. The company has continued to grow in terms of custom and profits. At least one senior member of staff joined the company because of its philosophy, despite having to take a huge pay cut, and Price says that staff continue to be motivated, although now they can worry less about money and focus more on other things such as health and family. Ten percent have managed to purchase their own home and many are able to pay into a pension scheme. Prior to the minimum wage, no more than two babies were born each year to employees. In the four and a half years since the wage rise, this has risen to over forty overall – something Price is proud of.

6B Ex 8A Student A

You accidentally submitted an early draft of an assignment to your teacher rather than the final draft. You didn't realise until you received your grade back from the teacher, with a much lower mark than expected. Prepare to tell this story, how you feel about it and what you'd like to happen. Tell your story to:

- a friend.
- your teacher.

Think about what you will say and how you will change from giving an informal account to a more formal account.

6C Ex 5A Student A

Read the instructions in 1, then role play the scenario with Student B. When you have finished, read the information in 2 and swap roles.

1 You are a tenant and have just moved into a new flat. Think of three complaints about your flat. Use the ideas below or your own ideas. Plan how you can express your complaints and think about what you want from your landlord. Then negotiate with your landlord.
   - The central heating is not working, so the flat is very chilly.
   - The cooker is not working.
   - There is mould in the bathroom.
   - The flat overlooks a very noisy street (you weren't warned about the noise).
   - The rooms are dark and dim, even with the lights on.

2 You are a landlord of a student flat. A new tenant has just moved in and wants to talk to you about some complaints. Think about what your tenant might complain about and plan what solutions you can offer. Use the ideas below or your own ideas. Then negotiate with your tenant.
   - rent reduction
   - one-off compensation payment
   - make improvements to the flat, e.g. redecoration

7C Ex 6B Student B

5B Ex 8C

The project is still underway. Ken Ramirez and his team have made it difficult for the elephants to use their traditional migration route by blocking the way with fallen trees. They have encouraged the elephants to use a new, safer route by adding watering holes along the route. The animals seem to be learning to use the new route.

8A Ex 6B

Wherever we go, whatever we do online, we're watched, just like in the novel *Nineteen Eighty-Four*. That was written in 1949 about a dystopian future. That future is now.

Technology isn't something new. It's been around for millennia, making people's lives easier, better, more comfortable and safer. Today, it brings people around the world closer together. That's not a dystopian world, it's much closer to a utopian world.

Social media is damaging our relationships. It creates loneliness, greed, paranoia, and highlights a deep divide between people in beliefs and attitudes. The result is an increasing lack of trust of others.

Today's use of technology puts great power in the hands of a few very large and very influential companies rather than in the hands of the people who use it.

Today, technology allows for medical advances, global communication, productivity and access to knowledge which are greater than ever before. When technology is used for the good of everyone, it has the potential to create a utopian world.

4A Ex 8A Student B

Prepare to put forward the proposal below and persuade others to agree with it. Think of your reasons and consider how to present them in a persuasive way.

People should not be allowed to take photos of famous people in public places.

4C Ex 6B

A Receptionist
1 What do you think are the most important qualities for a receptionist?
2 What experience do you have of customer service?
3 To what extent are you a team player?
4 What is the best way to deal with difficult customers?

B Summer camp assistant
1 What experience do you have of working with children?
2 What experience do you have of working outdoors?
3 What skills do you have (music, art, etc.)?
4 How do you think your previous work experience will help with this role?

C Project manager
1 In what ways are your academic qualifications relevant to the role?
2 What experience do you have of management?
3 What experience do you have of working to tight deadlines?
4 How competent are you at other languages?

1C Ex 5A Group C

Work in pairs. Complete the survey below with your own *Would you rather ... ?* questions.

WOULD YOU RATHER ...

1 spend a day with no phone or spend a day with no people?
2 give up sweet foods or savoury foods?
3 ....
4 ....
5 ....
6 ....

6B Ex 7 Student B

1 Listen to each sentence your partner reads aloud. Say the same idea in a more formal way, using the prompts to help you.

1 The incorrect item appears ....
2 The wrong document was ....
3 I'm not keen on being ....

2 Read the first sentence aloud to your partner. Your partner will say the same idea in a more formal way. Listen and check it's appropriate. Help where necessary. Repeat with the other sentences.

1 I've received the wrong thing.
2 I might have turned the filter on by mistake.
3 They offered me the job. I'm over the moon.

1B Ex 6A

6B Ex 8A Student B

You attended a remote meeting with a client using a video conferencing tool. Unfortunately, you had a filter on and you appeared as a cat throughout the meeting. Due to your settings, you didn't find out until you replayed the recording. Prepare to tell this story, how you feel about it and what you hope the outcome will NOT be. Tell your story to:

• a friend.
• your manager.

Think about what you will say and how you will change from giving an informal account to a more formal account.

6C Ex 5A Student B

Read the instructions in 1, then role play the scenario with Student A. When you have finished, read the information in 2 and swap roles.

1 You are a landlord with several flats. A new tenant has just moved into one of your flats and wants to talk to you about some complaints. Think about what your tenant might complain about and plan what solutions you can offer. Use the ideas below or your own ideas. Then negotiate with your tenant.

• alternative accommodation in one of your other flats
• one-off compensation payment
• make improvements to the flat, e.g. new appliances

2 You are a student and have just moved into a new student flat. Think of three complaints about your flat. Use the ideas below or your own ideas. Plan how you can express your complaints and think about what you want from your landlord. Then negotiate with your landlord.

• There is no hot water.
• The fridge is not working.
• The bathroom was filthy when you moved in.
• The windows won't open and the wood is rotten.
• There are cracks in some of the walls.

7C Ex 6B Student A

6B Ex 8A Student C

You ordered a new bed for your new home, but you've found out too late that it's actually a bed for a small child. You haven't received it yet but it's too late to cancel the order, according to the company's policy. Prepare to tell this story, how you feel about it and what you'd like to happen. Tell your story to:

• a friend.
• the customer service operator of the company.

Think about what you will say and how you will change from giving an informal account to a more formal account.

4A Ex 8A Student C

Prepare to put forward the proposal below and persuade others to agree with it. Think of your reasons and consider how to present them in a persuasive way.

Schools should teach young people about issues related to taking selfies.

1C App instructions

WRITING OUTPUT | a set of instructions
GOAL | simplify a source text
MEDIATION SKILL | writing for your audience

How to open an account

WARM-UP

1 Work in pairs. Discuss the questions.

1 What apps do you use the most? Why?

2 What app would you recommend? Why?

3 What makes a good app? Why?

PREPARE

2 A Read the email in the Scenario. What does Angelo want you to do?

B Read the instructions *How to open an account*. What in particular do you think makes these instructions hard for a lower-level English speaker to understand? Think about these things.

| length density of information |
| organisation grammar vocabulary |

SCENARIO

From: Angelo
To: You

Hi! I'm Angelo, your aunt Marisol's friend. I'm here in Dublin now. My new home is nice, but I don't know any friends. I don't use social media or any apps. I download a friendship app, but I don't understand the instructions. My English is not good. Please help! Please reply with simple instructions – thank you!

Angelo

Download the app, open it and then create an account. You'll be asked to select the relevant Frendz mode. The Frendz app has been designed with friends and colleagues in mind. There are therefore two modes: social and business. If you're looking to make friends, choose the former. If you're after work connections, choose the latter. Simply tap on the mode you want and then scroll down to complete your profile with your name and other details. For the social mode, make sure you type in your location so the app can match you with people in the vicinity. When you have finished adding your information, tap on 'Save'. You can change the mode any time by clicking on 'Mode' in the top right of the screen. Choose 'Social' or 'Business'. You will need to make a different profile.

Creating your profile might take a bit of time, but it's well worth it. The photos you choose will show others the kind of person you are, so choose wisely. Make sure at least two include a clear image of your face. You should try to look open and friendly whether you're in Social or Business mode, but your social images are more likely to be of free-time activities. In the Business mode, you only need to upload one photo of yourself. Write a short biography – maybe ask a friend to help you with this for your Social profile. Get a colleague to do it for your Business mode. They can often identify things you didn't think to include. You can connect your profile to other social media pages you have if you like. Simply select the social media in the list and type in your username.

You now need to verify your profile. You do this by tapping on 'Verify' and following the instructions. Basically, you'll be asked to choose a pose and take a photo of yourself in that pose. The images you uploaded on your profile and the photo you took of yourself will be examined by a human rather than a computer. The person will then confirm you're the same person. To edit your profile in the future, click on your profile image at the top right of the screen and choose 'Edit'.

Once your profile has been created, you can start to look for possible friends on the app. Tap on the three dots in the top left of the screen and select 'MyFrendz'. Profiles of people you might have something in common with appear on your screen. Swipe left if you don't feel you want to talk to them. Swipe right if you do. If that person swipes right on your profile, you'll be able to talk to each other. Tap on 'Talk' (bottom right) to see all of your chats with people. It's a good idea to delete chats that have ended so your box isn't too full. We'd recommend doing this once or twice a month.

3 Read the Mediation Skill box. What is the main information that Angelo wants to know about opening an account?

MEDIATION SKILL
Writing for your audience

When writing any text, it's important to consider the audience. Think about their purpose for reading the text, their existing knowledge of the topic and the context (e.g. blog post, journal). Use this information to decide these things:

- the main point of the text (the main message the reader wants/needs to know).
- the text structure (length, sections, subheadings).
- what information to include (information related to the main idea, examples that help understanding).
- what information to leave out (information not related to the main point, unnecessary details, additional examples not needed for understanding).
- what grammar to use (short, simple sentences with an active voice).
- what vocabulary to use (simple, common vocabulary and no unknown abbreviations).
- what terms to explain (repeated terms, terms vital for meaning).
- what terms to omit (those which appear only once and aren't vital for understanding).

4 A These are two possible headings for the simplified instructions for Angelo. Add a third idea of your own. Then, choose the best one.
   1 Instructions for the Frendz app
   2 A 'how-to' guide on using Frendz
   3 ....

B Complete the subheadings for the instructions with your own ideas.
   1 Choose 'Social' or 'Business'
   2 ....
   3 ....
   4 ....

C Which is the most appropriate structure for Angelo's instructions. Why?
   1 Subheading + short paragraph (x4)
   2 Subheading + numbered points (x4)

D Tick the information which is NOT relevant to Angelo's instructions. Think about his specific needs.
   1 which mode to select and how
   2 how to move between modes
   3 how to create a Social profile
   4 how to create a Business profile
   5 connecting your profile to your social media
   6 how to link your social media to your profile
   7 how to verify your profile
   8 how to edit your profile in the future
   9 how to find friends
   10 how to find and delete conversations

5 A Look at texts A and B and answer the questions.

> **A** Your feed can be filtered so that only those people who live within your vicinity can be seen. You can do this by tapping on 'Options' and selecting the relevant areas for you. Once done, save your choices.

> **B** To see people who live in your vicinity (i.e. area), click on 'Options'. Tick (✓) the areas near you. Click on 'Save'.

   1 Which instructions are for high-level speakers of English? Which are for lower-level speakers of English? How do you know?
   2 How has the writer simplified the language in the instructions for lower-level speakers of English?

B Rewrite this section of the instructions in Ex 2B for Angelo, simplifying the content and language.

> The Frendz app has been designed with friends and colleagues in mind. There are therefore two modes: social and business. If you're looking to make friends, choose the former. If you're after work connections, choose the latter.

C Match the terms (1–8) with the definitions (a–h). Look at the instructions in Ex 2B to help you.

   1 profile
   2 social mode
   3 tap on
   4 verify your profile
   5 pose
   6 edit
   7 three dots
   8 swipe left/right

   a show your profile is real
   b put your finger on the screen and move it left/right
   c information about who you are
   d (…)
   e system for finding friends
   f sit/stand in a particular position
   g make changes to
   h touch the screen with your finger

D Work in pairs. Which terms in Ex 5C can you leave out of Angelo's instructions and explain using simpler words? Which should you keep and explain?

MEDIATE

6 A Write a set of instructions for Angelo, simplifying the instructions in the source text in Ex 2B and taking his level of English and technical knowledge into account.

B Swap your instructions with another student and discuss the questions.
   1 Do the instructions achieve their purpose?
   2 Are they structured appropriately? How/Why not?
   3 Is the information included appropriate for the audience? Is there anything missing/unnecessary?
   4 Is the language appropriate for the audience? How/Why not?

C Redraft your instructions where appropriate, taking any feedback from your partner into account.

2C Unlimited holiday

SPEAKING OUTPUT | a discussion
GOAL | evaluate problems, challenges and proposals
MEDIATION SKILL | evaluating

WARM-UP

1 Work in pairs. How much paid holiday do employees typically have in your country? Do you think this is enough, not enough or more than enough? Why?

PREPARE

2 Read the Scenario. What does Vikram need to do?

SCENARIO

Vikram receives this message.

Company messaging board

@Vikram As you know, three years ago we decided to change the way we dealt with paid holiday at this company. Rather than employees getting a set number of days off, we get unlimited paid leave each year. We also provide staff with a £1,000 voucher towards a holiday. Today, we've published an internal report on the effect of both schemes. Staff productivity and job satisfaction increased in year one, but in year two they fell slightly and in year three, they've fallen fairly significantly. Staff take fewer days off. We're deciding whether to continue both schemes, go back to the old scheme of having a set number of days and no holiday voucher, or do something new. It'd be great if you could share your thoughts on this with us.

3 A ◆) **MB2.01 |** Listen to Vikram and his HR colleagues discussing the £1,000 holiday voucher scheme. What course of action do they decide to take?

B ◆) **MB2.01 |** Read the Mediation Skill box. Listen to the conversation again. Tick the phrases you hear.

MEDIATION SKILL
Evaluating

When deciding on a course of action, it's important to evaluate the current situation to understand the benefits, problems and their causes. Use phrases like the ones below to help you think of, and evaluate, possible actions.

Evaluating the current situation
One thing that's worked/working (well) is …
There's clearly a problem with …

Understand the cause of a problem
The (most likely) root of the problem is …
That/This/It could be because …
Maybe/Perhaps what's happening is (that) …

Coming up with possible actions
One way to tackle (this problem) might/would be to …
A good solution would be (to)… (because) …

Evaluating possible actions
The benefit (of this) is that …
One (unintended) consequence (of this) might be …

Selecting the best course of action
We should go with (this idea) because …
Are we all agreed that the best course of action is … ?

4 A ◆) **MB2.02 |** Listen to five employees giving their views about the unlimited paid holiday scheme to Vikram. Is each employee for (F) or against (A) the scheme?

B ◆) **MB2.02 |** Listen again and make notes on the reasons given for the employees' points of view.

C Work in pairs. Using the comments in Ex 4B to help you, note down the benefits and problems of the scheme in Ex 2, their possible causes and possible solutions.

MEDIATE

5 A Work in groups. You work in the HR department with Vikram. Evaluate the unlimited holiday scheme in Ex 2 and decide what the company should do. Use your notes in Ex 4B and 4C to help you.

B Share your decision with the class. Which group's idea do you think is the best?

3C Gamification

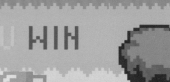

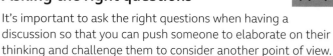

SPEAKING OUTPUT | a debate
GOAL | encourage others to elaborate
MEDIATION SKILL | asking the right questions

WARM-UP

1 Work in pairs and discuss the questions.

1 Why do we play games (e.g. board games, video games)?

2 What are typical features of video games (e.g. score, levels)?

3 What are some examples of video game features in everyday life?

PREPARE

2 Read the Scenario. What does your friend want you to do? Why?

SCENARIO

@mk25 We have to talk about this. I've got some strong views on it and no doubt you think the opposite!

To increase motivation among students and staff at our further education college, we have implemented a scoring system where:

• students collect points for effort, improvement and work quality.

• teachers collect points for their students' results.

• student scores are listed on a public leader board.

• teacher scores are listed on a public leader board.

• students and teachers receive gifts after collecting a certain number of points.

3 A 🔊 **MB3.01** | Listen to two students discussing the new scoring system. Do they support it? What are the reasons for and against it?

B 🔊 **MB3.01** | Read the Mediation Skill box. Then listen to the conversation again. Tick the phrases you hear. What effect do they have on the discussion?

MEDIATION SKILL
Asking the right questions

It's important to ask the right questions when having a discussion so that you can push someone to elaborate on their thinking and challenge them to consider another point of view.

Getting someone to elaborate
What (exactly) do you mean by that?
What makes you say that?
Why do you think (this is true)?
How would/does (it) work?
How will it (do that)?
What do you think the effects of (it) will be (on …)?
How do you think people might respond to (this)?
Does that mean you think … ?
What are your thoughts?

Challenging someone's point of view
But don't you think that … ?
But isn't it true/the case that … ?
What about … ?
Might it have a negative effect (on …)?
Might there be a better alternative?
But what if … ?
Do you think everyone would agree with you?
What do you mean by that?

4 Look at the statement below. How could you get the speaker to elaborate? What could you ask to challenge their point of view? Make a list.

'I think competition should be banned in educational contexts.'

5 Work in pairs. Prepare to argue for or against the points in Ex 2. Note down your reasons.

MEDIATE

6 A Work with a pair from the other half of the class. Debate the points in Ex 2. Give your opinions and ask questions to encourage elaboration and challenge each other's point of view.

B Decide which pair's argument was the most convincing and why. Do you feel you asked the right questions? Why/Why not?

4C Your personal brand

WRITING OUTPUT | an email
GOAL | relay information in a professional journal
MEDIATION SKILL | taking notes on a written text

WARM-UP

1 Work in pairs and discuss the questions.

   1 Do you think we present ourselves in the same way or in a different way to different people? Why? Give examples.

   2 Should we always be ourselves with other people? Why/Why not?

PREPARE

2 A Read the Scenario. What does your friend want you to do? Why?

SCENARIO

From: aniaania@mail.uk **To:** messageme@mail.uk

Hi! I passed my professional exams! Great, right? This is the start of hopefully a very successful career! But I need your help. I need to make sure I create a really positive professional image online. You said you read something recently about how to do this in a business journal. Can you share the tips with me? Thanks!

Ania x

B Work in pairs. What advice would you give Ania? Why?

3 A Work in pairs and discuss the questions.

   1 When might you have to take notes on a written text? Why?

   2 If you took notes on a text, what process would you follow?

   3 What kind of information would your notes contain and how would you lay them out?

B Read the Mediation Skill box. Which of these tips would you like to try? Why?

MEDIATION SKILL
Taking notes on a written text

Taking notes when reading can help us to read with focus, process what we read better, identify the main points, think more critically about the text and have a record for future reference. To achieve these benefits, we can follow these tips.

1 Highlight key terms and points when reading.

2 Put notes into our own words.

3 Organise notes according to text type and our preference, e.g. linear notes (subheadings, numbering, etc.), or visual notes (mind map, timeline, diagram, etc.).

4 Keep the notes brief with main points only.

5 Note down our own thoughts, questions and conclusions.

6 Develop a system of abbreviations and symbols for note-taking.

4 A Read text extracts 1 and 2 and match them with notes A and B. What effective features can you see in both notes? Which style of notes do you prefer? Why?

> **1** Your personal brand is the way that you present yourself to others in a professional context. This brand can grow organically, as a result of you demonstrating the skills and expertise which people come to recognise you by. Or, you can work hard to build your brand so that you have control over how others perceive you and you can differentiate yourself from others in your field.

> **2** Have you ever put your name into a search engine to see what comes up? It's the first step in seeing how people who come across your name online perceive you. In a favourable light? In a less than favourable light? It might be excruciatingly embarrassing, but searching for yourself online (or 'ego surfing' as it's called) is the first step in knowing exactly what changes you need to make to your social media to ensure you're perceived in the way you want.

A Search yourself online ('ego surfing')
– See how you're perceived
– Make appropriate changes to your social media (How?)

B
Personal brand (PB) = way u present yourself in prof. context

grow organically (demonstrate skills/expertise)

build it yourself (more control, can differentiate yourself)

B Reorganise notes A into a mind map like notes B, or reorganise notes B into an outline like notes A.

5 A Read the article and take notes so that you can send the information to Ania. Follow the tips in the Mediation Skill box.

B Compare your notes with a partner's. How are they similar or different? Is there anything in the content or layout of your partner's notes you would like to include in your own?

C Plan your email to Ania. Decide how you'll start, what tips you'll include and how you'll finish. Consider the tone you'll use.

MEDIATE

6 A Reply to Ania's email, relaying the information from the article in Ex 5A. Use your own words. Use your notes in Ex 5A and ideas from your partner's notes in Ex 5B to help you.

B Swap emails with a partner. Does your partner relay the main tips from the article effectively? How?/Why not?

Building your personal brand on social media

We all have a personal brand – the perceptions that others have about our professionalism, our expertise and our competencies. If we want to be successful in our careers, we need to ensure our brand fits us and fits our work context. Probably the best place to build our personal brand is via social media.

Start by identifying your audience and thinking about which platforms will reach them best. Then, focus on those platforms. You can cross-post (i.e. write one post and have it appear on different platforms) using online tools to save time. After you've identified your audience and platform(s), you can set goals, i.e. what you want to achieve and by when. For example, do you want to increase your number of followers, increase your post rate or raise your share rate? Create realistic short-term goals to keep yourself on track towards your long-term goal.

Once you have your goals in mind, you can start to plan your content. Firstly, think about the type of content you want to put out. What area of expertise do you want to be known for? If you're working in marketing, perhaps you want to focus on digital marketing. If you're in sales, maybe you want to focus on the psychology behind buying and selling. Avoid selecting too narrow a field so that you can appeal to a sufficiently wide audience.

Now you know what you want to post about, you can start posting. So, the first question is, how often? Too many posts, and people might get fed up with you. Too few, and they might not notice you. It depends on your audience, but experts suggest three to four posts a week with the rest of the time filled with comments on other people's posts. The next question is, what to post? Do you create your own posts or share others'? Well, it's a happy medium of the two. You need to demonstrate the ability to create your own content,

to show others who you are, what you know and how you think, but you can also show that you're paying attention to others by sharing and commenting on their content, too.

The final question to ask when it comes to posting is how personal to get. Do you have one account for friends, family and work? Or do you have two accounts to keep friends and family separate from your working life? There are, as is usual, pros and cons to each option. If you have one account, you can bring in aspects of your personal life to show people who you really are as a person. Don't feel you need to always present yourself as living a perfect life, either. People appreciate hearing that others face challenges, too. Present your imperfections, but remain positive where possible.

Of course, if you're concerned that posts related to family and friends or your thoughts about the world might interfere with your professional brand, (or friends and family may post things you don't want professional peers to see), then keep a separate account for just your loved ones. You can still post some personal content on professional accounts.

Finally, despite mentioning *followers* above, it's best if you think of followers as relationships. You don't want to increase your number of followers, you want to deepen your relationships with people who have similar work interests as you. That way, you'll build a brand that shows you're a person who cares about, and is interested in, the views and expertise of others.

5C Buying local

SPEAKING OUTPUT | a presentation
GOAL | simplify a complicated argument
MEDIATION SKILL | presenting the components of an argument

WARM-UP

1 Work in pairs. Discuss the questions.

1 Where do you tend to do most of your shopping? Why?
2 What items do you prefer to buy locally as opposed to online? Why?
3 What is the impact of people buying online rather than buying locally?

PREPARE

2 Read the Scenario. What does the organisation want volunteers to do?

SCENARIO

You see this post on social media.

@ShopLocalCampaign

Our town centre is dying. People are choosing to buy online rather than buy local and as a result, a quarter of shops in the town are currently empty. This weekend, we need volunteers to hand out flyers and explain clearly and patiently to local people why buying local is so vital. If you can help, DM me.

3A 🔊 **MB5.01** | Listen to three volunteers presenting an argument. Which one do you think is the clearest and most effective? Why?

B Read the Mediation Skill box and think about the presentations given by Volunteer 1 and Volunteer 3.

1 What is the main argument of each one?
2 What do you think of their arguments?

MEDIATION SKILL
Presenting the components of an argument

When presenting a complicated argument, it helps to break it down into component parts. It is important to organise points logically and avoid overly complex language.

1 State the claim.
Shopping locally is better for us than shopping online.

2 Give your reason(s).
When we shop in store, we connect to people locally.

3 Provide clear evidence.
• Avoid complex or technical terminology.
personal connections NOT ~~emotional, social and cognitive connectedness~~
• Use language that is easy to process. Keep sentences short.
They help to keep our immune systems strong. NOT ~~They enhance our body's ability to recognise foreign substances and produce antibodies.~~
• Omit statistics which are overwhelming, but keep those that are simple to process.
A quarter of shops are empty. NOT ~~Visitors to the area have fallen incrementally to around 76.5 percent of what they were a decade ago.~~

4 Address the opposing viewpoint to gain trust from listeners.
• Admit it has some merit.
• Dismiss it with an alternative point of view.

5 Summarise the key points to conclude.

4A 🔊 **MB5.02** | Listen to Volunteers 1 and 3 again. Take notes on the detailed information the volunteers give.

B Work in pairs. Prepare to simplify one of the arguments in Ex 4A and present it to a member of the public. Use the steps in the Mediation Skill box to help you.

Student A: Look at your notes for Volunteer 1. Argue that people should shop local as it is more environmentally friendly.

Student B: Look at your notes for Volunteer 3. Argue that people should shop local as it is beneficial to the local economy.

MEDIATE

5A Work with your partner. Take turns to present your argument in a clear and simple way.

B Did both presentations make the issue and argument easier to understand? Why/Why not?

6C Mediating disputes

WRITING OUTPUT | a summary
GOAL | accurately report the outcomes of a meeting
MEDIATION SKILL | summarising agreements and expectations

WARM-UP

1 Work in pairs. Why might two colleagues fall out with each other? What should their manager(s) do in this situation?

PREPARE

2 Read the Scenario. What is the problem? What do you need to do?

SCENARIO

From: generalmanager@mail.uk
To: hrofficer@mail.uk

Please can you attend a meeting in my office at 2 p.m. today to take notes and send follow-up admin? Two members of Naomi's team are unhappy about working together on their current project.

3 🔊 **MB6.01** | Listen to the meeting. Take notes on these things.

- what the exact problems are
- what action each employee agrees to
- how the employees agree to communicate in the future

4 Read the Mediation Skill box. Why do you think it's important to set out agreements and expectations in writing?

MEDIATION SKILL
Summarising agreements and expectations

After meetings that involve mediation or negotiations, agreements and expectations are normally set out in writing. The summary focuses on the outcome of the meeting, not the history of the dispute.

Acceptances regarding the issue(s)
(Syed) accepted/recognised (that) …
(Both Syed and Grace) acknowledge (that) …

Details of actions agreed to
(Both Syed and Grace) agreed to …
(Grace) undertakes to/will endeavour to …

Expectations regarding future communications
From now on, both parties will (actively) (talk/discuss/communicate) …
If (Syed fails to) … , it is agreed that (Grace) will (remind him) …
(Grace) will address concerns to …

5 A Read the mediation summary and answer the questions (1–3).

1 What is the dispute about?
2 What's been agreed by Mr Cahill and Mr and Mrs Hamilton?
3 What do you notice about the layout (the way the information is organised)?

Meeting regarding the position of a fence – 24 April

Dispute: Mr Cahill believes Mr and Mrs Hamilton took some of his land when erecting a new fence between their properties.

1. Acceptances

a. Mr Cahill recognised that Mr and Mrs Hamilton have not deliberately tried to take extra land.

2. Actions agreed

a. Mr Cahill and Mr and Mrs Hamilton agreed to allow a surveyor to inspect the position of the fence and will endeavour to follow the surveyor's decision.

b. Mr and Mrs Hamilton agreed to reposition the fence if necessary.

c. All parties will communicate through their chosen legal representatives until the issue has been resolved.

B Plan to write a summary of the agreements and expectations decided on in Ex 3. Decide what information to include using the organisation in Ex 5A.

MEDIATE

6 A Write a summary of the agreements and expectations from the meeting in Ex 3.

B Swap summaries with a partner. Is the summary accurate and clearly set out?

C Redraft your summary where appropriate, taking any feedback from your partner into account.

7C Fast fashion

WRITING OUTPUT | a summary paragraph
GOAL | compare, contrast and synthesise information in texts
MEDIATION SKILL | synthesising information

WARM-UP

1 **Work in pairs and discuss the questions.**

1 How often do you buy new clothes?
2 What happens to your old clothes?
3 Do you ever repair clothes when they tear or come apart? Why/Why not?

PREPARE

2 **Read the Scenario. Who is writing to you? What do they want you to do?**

SCENARIO

From: Professor Newley
To: You

Thank you for agreeing to assist some of our first-year fashion students this term. As a PhD student specialising in this area, I think you'll enjoy it. Please find attached extracts from three articles on the topic of fast fashion. I'd like you to write a paragraph on one of the main points raised in the extracts, comparing and contrasting viewpoints. Please send it to the students to read before our next lesson, when they'll discuss it. I'll leave which point you focus on up to you!

3 **Read the three extracts (A–C). What points do they make about these themes? Make notes.**

1 fast fashion and the environment
2 fashion accessible to everyone
3 the lifespan of clothes

A The term 'fast fashion' immediately brings to mind polluted waters, huge piles of unwanted clothes and the estimated eight to ten percent of global carbon emissions it produces, but there's a reason it contributes billions of dollars globally – it democratises fashion. By that, I mean that it allows people from all economic backgrounds to purchase and wear fashion that in the past would not have been possible due to high costs. This is why it's been so successful over the last two decades.

B Fast fashion most definitely needs to slow its growth. Its impact on the environment has been well documented, with toxic chemicals from factory waste water and micro plastics from material, and over half of unwanted clothes ending up in landfill sites as people get bored with them. But it's the viewpoint that fast fashion allows everyone to participate in fashion that I want to oppose here. Yes, fast fashion allows people of all incomes to look fashionable, but fashion retailers also rely on those people not having income to purchase higher-quality goods to make their money. And while retailers and brands become financially successful, those making the clothes are not always paid a fair wage.

C Fashion may well have been costly for many people in the past, but clothes were at least well made and designed to last. These days, fashion is accessible to more people, but many of the items we buy are cheap for a reason – they're not designed to last more than a season. People used to adopt a 'make do and mend' approach, i.e. they repaired clothes to make them last longer rather than replaced them. In recent generations these skills have been lost, but they appear to be making a comeback with younger people learning to make their own clothes, or upcycle the ones they have to make them last longer. This is in part to reduce waste caused by fast fashion, and in part the desire to make clothes unique through design. At least one fashion retailer is supporting this trend, offering tips on their websites.

4 A Read the Mediation Skill box. When might synthesising information be necessary?

MEDIATION SKILL
Synthesising information

Information from multiple sources

Synthesising information means taking similar and/or different information from multiple sources. For example:

Source 1: The squares of old material used in *boro* give strength to clothes.

Source 2: *Boro* is the 18th-century Japanese tradition of mending clothes using old material.

Source 3: *Boroboro* is often shortened to *boro*.

Source 4: *Boro*'s popularity on social media is increasing.

The information is brought together in a text to create one cohesive idea. For example:

The use of *boro* (short for *boroboro*) appears to be a growing trend.

This centuries-old Japanese skill of repairing and strengthening clothes with old material is becoming popular on social media.

How to synthesise information

1 Read information from a variety of sources.
2 Look for similarities and differences between the main points.
3 Decide on the main point of your text.
4 Decide how to organise the information in your text logically.
5 Write your text. Put the ideas into your own words and cite sources where appropriate.

B Synthesise the information from each set of sources (1–3) in one or two sentences.

1 **Source 1:** Retailers can offer up to 20,000 different items at one time.
Source 2: Fashion is described as 'fast' when brands design and produce clothes quickly.
Source 3: Fast fashion allows brands and retailers to quickly react to changing trends.
Synthesised information: ....

2 **Source 1:** Slow fashion is gaining interest in a bid to reduce fashion's impact on the environment.
Source 2: The term 'slow fashion' was first used in 2007 by journalist Kate Fletcher.
Source 3: Slow fashion is similar in nature to ethical, sustainable fashion.
Synthesised information: ....

3 **Source 1:** Social media makes learning how to sew easy.
Source 2: Home sewing is one of many crafts that has gained popularity in recent years.
Source 3: The sale of sewing machines has increased by thirty percent in recent years.
Synthesised information: ....

5 A Choose one of the themes from Ex 3. Read your notes and identify the similarities and differences between the points made in the extracts.

B Decide on the main point you want to make in your paragraph. Write a sentence outlining this main point.

C Make a note of the supporting information and contrasting viewpoints.

MEDIATE

6 A Write a paragraph synthesising the similar and different main points from the article extracts in Ex 3. Use your notes from Ex 5A–C to help you.

B Swap paragraphs with a partner and discuss these questions.

1 Do your paragraphs say similar or different things?
2 Do the paragraphs fairly represent the original source material?
3 Is the information brought together logically in both paragraphs?
4 Is the information put into your own words in both paragraphs?

C Revise your paragraph where necessary, using your partner's feedback.

8C Saving schemes

SPEAKING OUTPUT | a discussion
GOAL | contribute to collaborative decision-making
MEDIATION SKILL | co-developing ideas

WARM-UP

1 Work in pairs. What are some ways that you've tried to save money? Were they successful? Why/Why not?

PREPARE

2 Read the Scenario. What do you need to do? Why?

SCENARIO

If we're going to book a holiday for the end of next summer, we need to start saving now. We've got about a year and none of us have much spare cash. Let's put our heads together and try to come up with some saving schemes so we all have enough by next summer.

3 A 🔊 **MB8.01** | Listen to three friends planning how to save money. What two ideas do they agree on?

B Work in pairs and discuss the questions.

1 What do you think of the ideas suggested in Ex 3A? Why?

2 Do you think you could ever adopt these savings techniques? Why/Why not?

4 A 🔊 **MB8.01** | Read the Mediation Skill box. Then listen to the conversation again and tick the phrases you hear.

MEDIATION SKILL
Co-developing ideas

When discussing ideas, speakers often build on each other's suggestions before the right one is decided or agreed upon. Phrases such as these are often used.

Adding ideas to suggestions
We could also …   As well as that, how about … ?

Suggesting ways of achieving an idea
One way we could do that is to …   If we … , it/that would be even (better).
It would/might work if …

Pointing out possible drawbacks/problems
It might be difficult to …   I'm not sure that works (because …)

Suggesting alternatives
That gives me an idea.   Rather than … , we could …
We could substitute … with … .   How about we change it to … ?

B Complete the conversation with phrases a–h.

A: ¹............ save money by having fewer takeaways.

B: If we could cook together more, ²............ better. We wouldn't waste food.

C: Good point. ³............ doing that, ⁴............ reducing the number of takeaway coffees we buy?

A: Oh, that ⁵............ an idea. We could buy those travel coffee cups and put coffee in them when we leave home in the mornings.

B: Good idea! And ⁶............ buying lunch out, we can make sandwiches.

A: Bit boring but yeah, it'll be cheaper.

C: I'm not sure that ⁷............ me. We have pretty cheap food in our restaurant at work. I think it'll be just as cheap for me to eat there.

B: That's fine. You can just stick to what you usually do, then.

A: ⁸............ difficult for me to keep my sandwiches cold all day when I'm out of the office.

B: You can buy a cool bag and put them in there. I know it sounds like we're spending money, but it'll save us money in the long run!

a As well as   **c** it'd be even   **e** We could   **g** rather than
b works for   **d** gives me   **f** It might be   **h** how about

Tips for saving money

If you want to spend less and save more, follow these handy money-saving tips.

Water and energy bills
✔ Turn your heating down by 1°.
✔ Check that you're getting the best deal possible from your providers.
✔ ....

Shopping
✔ Write a shopping list and stick to it at the supermarket!
✔ Always wait a week before you buy something that is not vital.
✔ ....

Transport
✔ Cut fuel costs by checking the tyre pressure on your car and taking out extra weight.
✔ Share car rides with family, friends, colleagues and classmates when you can.
✔ ....

Food/Eating out
✔ Look for coupons and discounts online.
✔ Cook several meals from your ingredients and freeze them.
✔ ....

Social events
✔ Don't go out. Invite people to your home.
✔ Look for free events like free concerts and festivals.
✔ ....

Other
✔ Have a 'No spend' weekend once a month.
✔ Try the 50/30/20 approach to spending: 50 percent of your income on bills, 30 percent on fun and 20 percent on savings.
✔ ....

5 A Read the tips for saving money. Have you ever tried any of these? Tell a partner.

B Add one money-saving tip of your own under each subheading in Ex 5A.

C Work in pairs. Share your ideas in Ex 5B. What other money-saving ideas can you think of? Write down as many as possible.

MEDIATE

6 A Work with another pair. Have the conversation described in Ex 2.
- Make a plan to save money using at least five effective money-saving techniques.
- Make sure these techniques suit everyone in the group.
- Record your ideas.

B Prepare to share your money-saving plans with the class and explain your choices.

C Present your plan to the class. Listen to all the plans. Which group's plan, other than your own, do you think is the best? Why? Tell your group.

UNIT 1

Audio 1.01

P = Presenter   A = Addy

P: Making new friends when you're an adult can feel like an impossible task, especially now that so many of us work and study from home. Which is probably one explanation for the rise in popularity of friendship apps, where people go to find like-minded people to hang out with. Addy, you've given these apps a go. What prompted you to do that?

A: Well, last year I relocated for work to a completely new city and, other than my work colleagues, I didn't know anyone. My colleagues are nice and all that, but they're at least a decade older than me and most are married – just what you want as a twenty-two-year-old single person! Obviously, I wanted people my own age to socialise with. You know, people I can hang out with during the day and party with at night.

P: Why not join a club or something?

A: Yeah, people suggested that, but I like a bit more flexibility. I'm not keen on having to commit to meeting up at the same time every week and I'm not that into sports or anything. Anyway, I kept coming across this ad online for a friendship app which piqued my interest and eventually I bit the bullet and clicked on it to find out more. I found out there wasn't just one of these apps. There are dozens of them.

P: Really? Are they all more or less the same or are they different in some way?

A: Um … they're all fairly similar in terms of features, but they're different in how they go about matching people. There's one that tries to match you according to your personality, which I'm not really a fan of. I mean, I want to hang out with people that are on the same wavelength, yes, but not exact copies of me! The apps that match you according to your interests make more sense – to me anyway – and there are loads.

P: Really?

A: Yeah, some cater for all interests and some actually specialise in just one, like the one for book lovers for example, or the one for animal lovers. There are apps that connect you in other ways, too. There's one that sets you up with friends in countries you intend to travel to – that one's quite cool because you can speak in your mother tongue and the app translates what you say so you understand each other.

P: Wow! I had no idea there was such a range of these.

A: Yeah! There's even an app where they match you to sports partners based on your fitness level! Perfect for a, you know, a super-fit sportsperson like me!

P: Gosh. So, which one did you go for?

A: Well, I wanted to be sure that I could meet people locally because I don't just want online friends, so I signed up for two that let me search for people by location.

P: And were you successful?

A: Yes and no. The first app felt more like a community page on social media than a friendship app, but I was able to click with a few people my age on there. We chatted for a while and I even discovered one guy that I have a mutual friend with, which was great. Someone I went to uni with. Anyway, we started talking about meeting up and that's when I discovered they lived in a neighbourhood with the same name as mine, but in a different city. I'd clicked on the wrong location! So that was time well spent. I tried again though and met up with people who did actually live near me.

P: And how was that?

A: It was good. I liked them. I'm not sure how they felt about me at first though. I was thirty minutes late – a wonderful way to start a friendship. Then at the end of the evening, I discovered I'd left my wallet at home, so couldn't pay for my part of the bill. I'm sure they were just thrilled about that. But I've seen them a couple of times since and made it up to them.

P: I'm sure they understood.

A: Hopefully! Actually, it was the other app that worked for me. It connects people interested in local events, so you don't have to go to them on your own. Not that I really mind that, but I started chatting to people who were interested in a local music festival. And four of us bonded over our love of one of the bands. We met up at the festival and that was that – we're friends for life now. We laugh a lot, which is brilliant. I know I can confide in them, too. And they've introduced me to some brilliant other local bands. They even play themselves, but as I'm not particularly musical myself, I just watch and admire.

P: That's just brilliant. So, you'd recommend the app then.

A: If you find yourself in a situation like mine, definitely. Just don't expect to find the right app and the right friends at the first attempt. Try, try and try again and eventually, you'll hit it off with someone.

P: Good.

A: Just remember to select the right location!

Audio 1.02

My colleagues are nice and all that, but they're at least a decade older than me and most are married – just what you want as a twenty-two-year-old single person!

Audio 1.03

1 There's even an app where they match you to sports partners based on your fitness level! Perfect for a, you know, a super-fit sportsperson like me!

2 We chatted for a while and I even discovered one guy that I have a mutual friend with, which was great. Someone I went to uni with.

3 Anyway, we started talking about meeting up and that's when I discovered they lived in a neighbourhood with the same name as mine, but in a different city. I'd clicked on the wrong location! So that was time well spent.

4 I'm not sure how they felt about me at first though. I was thirty minutes late – a wonderful way to start a friendship.

5 Then at the end of the evening, I discovered I'd left my wallet at home so couldn't pay for my part of the bill. I'm sure they were just thrilled about that.

6 We met up at the festival and that was that – we're friends for life now. We laugh a lot, which is brilliant.

Audio 1.04

1 Obviously, I wanted people my own age to socialise with.

2 You know, people I can hang out with during the day and party with at night.

3 I mean, I want to hang out with people that are on the same wavelength, yes, but not exact copies of me!

4 I was able to click with a few people my age on there.

5 I even discovered one guy and I have a mutual friend, which was great.

6 And four of us bonded over our love of a particular band.

7 I know I can confide in them, too.

8 Try, try and try again and eventually, you'll hit it off with someone.

Audio 1.05

P = Presenter   A = Addy

P: You said earlier that you were looking to find friends that were on the same wavelength as you, but not people who have exactly the same character traits. Is that what you'd suggest people do when using a friendship app? Look for people with similar interests?

A: Hmm … well, I definitely stand by my view on character. It'd be boring if we all had the same personality. One of my new friends, Jak, she's a lot louder than me. She's always shouting even though we're standing right next to her. And she'll voice her opinions very strongly – she's so confident. I'm pretty quiet. I tend to listen rather than speak, but being with Jak is fun because she brings me out of myself.

P: So, we should look for people with similar interests?

A: Well, that is what I was looking for and it's what I got to some degree. I mean, music is clearly a mutual interest and we love going out and doing stuff together – but we have lots of different interests, too. I told you I'm not a big sports fan, but Dan and Nicole love sports. I'm really into cooking and healthy eating and so is Nicole, but Jak and Dan aren't. When we first started hanging out, they were always trying to make us go to fast-food places. I used to sit and watch them eat because I just couldn't bring myself to order anything. I kept trying to get them to order the salad, but they'd order extra chips just to annoy me! Over time though, they've come to like some of the healthier food places I like and they'll even have some salad with their order. They've eaten meals I've made for them, too! In return, I'll have the occasional burger.

So, going back to your question, no, I don't think you should only look for people with similar interests. It might work as a starting point, but we need to be open to a variety of types of people or we might miss out on some brilliant friendships.

Audio 1.06

1 She'll voice her opinions very strongly.

2 She'd order extra chips just to annoy me.

Audio 1.07

1 We'd meet up on Fridays and play squash.

2 Jon'll call me at all hours of the night just for a chat!

3 I'll message Alex on a Monday and not get a reply until Thursday!

4 They'd all come round to my house before we went out.

5 Sam'd spend more time at our flat than his own!

6 She'll borrow something and forget to give it back.

Audio 1.08

1 This building definitely needs to be modernised.

2 It's a great idea to merge the city with the countryside more.

3 There's a plan to refurbish the old cinema.

Audio 1.09

A: Oh, look at these 'Would you rather … ?' questions. I love this kind of thing – it's fun. Want to do them?

B: Er, … well, I know you love this kind of thing, so go on then.

A: First one: Would you rather do a deep-sea dive or do a bungee jump?

B: Oh, I've always wanted to do a deep-sea dive, so, yeah, that one for me. There's an incredibly amazing world down there – the kind of wildlife you don't normally see.

A: But wouldn't you be scared? I mean, I'd be worried about running out of air.

B: Yeah, but it would be supervised, so it would be super-safe. It would be so cool – I'd jump at the chance to do it – it would be a once-in-a-lifetime experience!

A: Wouldn't you like to try a bungee jump, though?

B: Oh no. I'm just awful with heights. I don't even feel comfortable being at the top of a tall building, so no way would I ever jump off a cliff or a bridge! I can't even bear to think about it!

A: Really? I'm the opposite. I don't even enjoy swimming in the sea, so I'd run a mile at the thought of deep-sea diving. I'd hate being so far under water. Given the choice, I'd choose the bungee jump any day. You'd get such an amazing adrenalin rush!

B: No, I can't imagine ever enjoying that!

A: Anyway, second question: Would you rather appear in a reality TV show or act or sing on stage?

B: Oh, I'd go for being in a reality TV show every time. I think it would be such fun to take part in a TV programme and see how it's made first-hand, and meet the presenters, too, of course. And I love being the centre of attention, so I'd have the time of my life!

A: Wouldn't you be worried about all the social media reactions? People don't always come across well on these shows.

B: Oh, I wouldn't mind that – it's all part of the fun. But singing's a different thing altogether. I really can't sing at all, so you would never catch me singing anywhere in public – it would be a disaster!

A: I'm with you there. Nothing would make me get up on a stage and sing! But then I'm not a big fan of reality TV shows either. Acting, though, that wouldn't be too bad. Yes, I'd sooner act on stage than sing on one. Anyway, final question. Would you rather binge watch a TV show all day or read a book all day?

B: Oh, this is easy. If it was up to me, I'd read a book all day. I can really lose myself in a good book. I completely lose track of time, especially if it's an exciting story.

A: Really? I'm not that into books, so I'd probably give reading a miss. I'd definitely choose the TV show though – I'd never say no to spending a whole day watching my favourite show, especially on a cold, rainy day.

Audio 1.10

1 Would you rather appear in a reality TV show or sing on stage?

2 I'd sooner act on stage.

3 I'd go for being in a reality TV show every time!

Audio 1.11

1 The culture of every family is different, so comfort foods are different from family to family, not just culture to culture.

2 The idea that comfort food is always bad for you is a myth.

3 There's no real evidence that comfort food actually comforts us. Because it can be bad for us, we need to deal with our emotions differently.

Audio 1.12

A: So why is it that comfort food is always bad for us?

B: I don't think it is. I think that's a bit of a myth.

A: Is it? I mean, what's your comfort food? Mine's a chip butty.

C: A chip what now?

A: A chip butty. You know, chips between bread.

C: So, a French fry sandwich?

A: I guess that's what you'd call it. Chips are crisps in the USA, right?

C: Right, and 'butty' means nothing to me. I mean, it does now you've explained, but it didn't before. It sounds, er … heavy.

B: It's really tasty – you should try one. But going back to the point about comfort food being bad for us, well …

A: Oh yeah, you said it was a myth.

B: Yeah.

A: But why?

B: You might like chip butties and I might love cold mashed potato for breakfast, but …

C: What? For breakfast? That's gross!

B: So, cold mashed potato is OK, but not for breakfast.

C: No! They're both gross!

B: Anyway, back to the myth idea – while we might like rubbish food when we're feeling fed up, for others it might be healthy, like chicken soup.

C: Oh yeah, I love chicken soup when I'm feeling ill. It's what my mom would give me when I was young.

B: Exactly, I think comfort food often reminds us of positive feelings when we were younger and that might be a treat like a chip butty or something to help us feel less ill like chicken soup.

UNIT 2

Audio 2.01

A: Hi, Maddie, how are you?

B: Oh, hey Jake. Yeah, I'm OK. I'm a bit tired, actually. I was up quite late last night working on my psychology project.

A: Oh, the one on cheating?

B: Yeah, it's due next Friday. Have you started yours yet?

A: No. There's a podcast to listen to, isn't there? I don't think I made a note of the link.

B: I can send it to you. And it's actually quite interesting. It's mainly about **why** we cheat.

A: Oh good, that's the bit that I found interesting in the lecture last week. It reminded me of this time when I was younger and watching my little sister Rona in a race at school. She won the race and of course she was delighted with herself. But the thing is, I could see that she didn't win fairly. There was another girl who was probably a bit faster than her and what Rona did was bump into her, to make her fall over. Of course, everyone else thought it was an accident and I could see that she was going to get away with it.

B: And did you do anything about it?

A: Yeah, I decided I had to say something. So, I told my mum and she talked to Rona, and Rona eventually admitted it was deliberate, so mum made her go and tell her teachers.

B: Ouch! I bet she hated that!

A: She did. She wasn't happy at all that she had to give back the medal! But you have to teach kids to play fair, don't you?

B: Yeah. It's a tough lesson, but you're right.

A: The thing is, I kind of get it that Rona was tempted to cheat. She was young and she just wanted to win. What I don't understand is why adults cheat, like footballers who dive in the penalty area or try to get other players sent off, or tennis players who play for time when they're losing. I mean, how can they hold their heads up?

B: Well, the podcast actually goes into this in some detail. There's a thing known as the 'cheater's high' and one study found that people who break the rules and get away with it don't usually feel ashamed, but actually feel pretty good about themselves.

A: Really?

B: Yeah. What they feel is that they're smarter than everyone else, so they deserve to win.

A: I find that really surprising. I think I'd feel incredibly guilty if I won something by cheating. I mean, it just isn't fair on everyone else!

B: Well, they were also saying that people only feel guilty when they realise the direct results of their behaviour – so maybe they see that their opponent is really disappointed, for example. If the situation feels anonymous though, and they can't see that anyone's suffering as a result of what they've done, they feel they've somehow 'beaten the system' and come out on top.

A: That's interesting. I also get that some people just want to win at all costs, so they might end up cheating, but what happens then? I mean, once they're recognised as the best, do they then relax and play by the rules?

B: Well, supposedly the opposite is true. When some people become winners, they're actually more likely to cheat.

A: Oh?

B: Yeah. Winning makes them feel they're better than others – they feel they can do whatever they like, so cheating can become acceptable to them. Also, it's harder to accept losing once you see yourself as a winner, so if someone is unbeaten for a long time, they feel they've got expectations to live up to and they're under pressure not to lose.

A: Hmm. And does it just come down to personality? I mean, is it just the case that there are a few bad individuals?

B: No, it's not just individuals. It seems that cheating is 'catching'. So, students who see fellow students cheating in an exam are more likely to do it themselves. It becomes acceptable. And it's the same in sports. Players who see their own teammates cheating, like faking injuries, are more likely to try it themselves.

A: And I suppose if people see members of the opposing team cheating, then they feel they have to cheat as well, in order to win.

B: Well, you'd think so, but, interestingly, if they see members of the opposing team cheating, it tends to make them feel angry and think it's wrong – they kind of take the moral high ground. So, in that situation, they're more likely to play fair themselves.

A: That makes sense. It's fascinating, really, but also sad that cheating is so common.

B: Yeah. The fact is that cheating has become so accepted that a lot of sportspeople think it's fine. The only thing they worry about is getting caught.

A: Yeah, it's interesting.

B: Anyway, you should have a listen yourself. What I'll do is send you the link now. There.

A: Great, thanks. I'll listen tonight. And then I really need to get started on the project!

Audio 2.02

1 What Rona did was bump into her, to make her fall over.
2 What I don't understand is why adults cheat.
3 What they feel is that they're smarter than everyone else.
4 What I'll do is send you the link now.

Audio 2.03

1 form an alliance
2 gain a competitive edge
3 forge partnerships
4 push beyond their limits
5 fulfil their potential

Audio 2.04

J = Jack   L = Lily

J: Hey Lily, have you heard what senior management are thinking of doing?

L: No, what?

J: They're talking about giving us some kind of extra perk as a 'thank you' for hitting all our targets this year.

L: Great! What are they offering? A twenty percent pay rise this year and an equally high pay rise next year?

J: Wouldn't that be something! No, I think they're deciding between an extra few days' holiday this year or some kind of financial reward, like an end-of-year bonus or something.

L: Hmm. Well, that's easy. I know what I'd go for.

J: The bonus, for sure. Extra money's invaluable for someone like me who's paying high rent in the city. Every little bit helps. And it'd probably be worth way more than extra holiday leave.

L: True, if you're talking financial worth, but extra time off is just as valuable. To me, anyway. I'd love a few extra days to relax and hang out with my friends.

J: Really? I guess you're right – for some people at least, time to unwind is every bit as important as extra cash. Which one do you think they'll go with?

L: Hmm, probably the holiday. I'm guessing it'll cost them less and they won't want to affect profitability too much.

J: Yeah, probably not. There was also talk of 'Casual Friday', where we can all come into the office on Fridays in jeans and trainers or whatever.

L: What? That's nowhere near as appealing as the other two options. They're infinitely more motivating!

J: Yep. It wouldn't be very effective in inspiring us to work harder either. Most of us just wear jeans and T-shirts on the days we work from home anyway.

L: Or pyjamas!

Audio 2.05

1 A twenty percent pay rise this year and an equally high pay rise next year?
2 Extra money's invaluable for someone like me who's paying high rent in the city.
3 It'd probably be worth way more than extra holiday leave.
4 … but extra time off is just as valuable.
5 … time to unwind is every bit as important as extra cash.
6 That's nowhere near as appealing as the other two options.
7 They're infinitely more motivating!
8 It wouldn't be very effective in inspiring us to work harder either.

Audio 2.06

1 It's way better to pay everyone a fair salary than not.
2 A month's holiday is equally as appealing as a month's salary.
3 Working from home is infinitely better than working in an office.
4 The scheme is nowhere near as good as I thought it would be.

Audio 2.07

A: Healthy competition is the key to success as far as I'm concerned. When we compete with others, we strive to do better and that leads to development – development of ourselves and development of other things. The result is that we consistently push our limits as humans and improve our lives.

B: For me, competition is more about competing with yourself than with others. I mean, if you spend time and energy on trying to do better than you've done before, you win, but if you spend all your time and energy focusing on others, you end up losing. It's problematic because you lose sight of your own goals.

UNIT 2 REVIEW

Audio R2.01

Competing for the countryside

The Peak District, in the north of England, was first designated as a national park in 1951, making it the first national park in the UK. Millions of visitors have enjoyed its beautiful scenery over the years and they continue to do so now. What most visitors are attracted to is the mountains and open countryside, far from urban areas, and many hotels and campsites thrive on this kind of tourism. However, there are competing views on how far the area should be developed. Owners of some local businesses would like to attract more visitors, to increase their profitability. This might involve companies providing more popular attractions such as theme parks, to gain a competitive edge over their rivals. On the other hand, environmentalists argue that such attractions are completely out of place in this rural area. They believe that developers should not be allowed to get away with spoiling the natural beauty and peace, but instead the focus should be on initiatives to improve the environment. The arguments continue, with few signs of cooperation between the different groups. It is unclear which side is going to come out on top.

UNIT 2 MEDIATION BANK

Audio MB2.01

A: OK, so let's discuss the holiday voucher scheme we introduced last year. We need to decide whether to continue it or not, and if we continue it, whether we need to change it in any way.

B: Well, we've done our research and it seems that giving every staff member £1,000 towards a holiday each year has had mixed reviews, so there's clearly a problem with it.

A: OK, but it sounds like it's not all bad.

B: No. One thing that's working is the extra money. Everyone said they appreciated it and that the amount of money was substantial and therefore motivating.

C: OK, that's good. So, what's the issue with it then?

B: Some staff members said they didn't appreciate the fact that it came in vouchers that they could only spend on travel.

A: Interesting. It could be because those staff members aren't interested in travelling. Not everyone is.

C: And perhaps some can't travel because they have commitments here, like looking after elderly parents.

B: Yes. So, the root of the problem is choice. Staff want the money but they want the choice of how to spend it.

A: Yes. So, how do we move forward then? Do we get rid of the scheme?

C: I don't think so. It sounds like there's enough positivity towards it to keep it.

B: Agreed.

A: OK, so how do we solve the issue with the dissatisfaction then?

B: I guess one way to tackle it would be to offer everyone cash instead of travel vouchers.

A: We don't really want to do that. There's already a bonus scheme in place. The purpose of this money and our unlimited holiday scheme is to make sure staff take the holiday they need to stay as stress-free and healthy as possible, so they can stay productive when they are at work.

C: OK, well, a good solution would be to offer more voucher options – so not just for travel, but for other free-time activities that people can enjoy locally.

B: That's a good idea. The benefit is that staff have greater choice over how they spend the money, but they still use it for the purpose it's intended for.

C: Yes.

A: Great! Are there any potential issues with this?

C: Hmm, I guess some staff members may have other financial priorities. They might feel that spending money on themselves is a luxury they can't afford when they're struggling in other ways.

A: It sounds like those people in particular need the chance to relax and spend time and money on themselves, so we want them to use the money for leisure and not on bills.

B: True.

C: I can't think of any potential problems, but one consequence might be that the money is spent on local businesses, helping the local economy. That's a good thing, so our marketing department might be able to use that in their promotion.

A: Good point! OK, so are we all agreed that the best course of action is to keep the scheme, but open out the choice to leisure and not just travel?

C: Yes.

B: Definitely.

A: Great, so the next thing then is to do some more research to find out if staff like this idea and to research possible voucher options …

Audio MB2.02

1 I think the scheme sounds great. I mean, who wouldn't want to pick and choose how much holiday they have and when?! But in my view, it's simply there as a means of attracting new employees to the company, because it doesn't motivate existing employees much anymore.

2 I'm happy with the scheme and I'd love to keep it. It's not perfect. I feel bad about taking time off when I know my colleagues have to cover me, but I like being in control of when and how much holiday I can take.

3 It sounds great in theory, but in practice it causes a lot of both guilt and anger among teams. It doesn't bring us together.

4 I preferred having a set number of days' holiday to be honest because I actually took them. Now, I'm so busy I end up taking fewer days and I'm more stressed and tired than ever!

5 Is there any way of adapting the scheme so we keep our freedom and feel able to take time off when we need it? Because if so, I vote to keep the scheme. If not, it might be better to go back to what we had before.

UNIT 3

Audio 3.01

Fandom's like being in a band where you don't just write but you write for others and they write for you; and you talk about stories and you kind of hang out. It's a social activity. But it's a social activity about words instead of about music.

From one definition you can claim the whole history of literature is the history of fanfiction. Arguably, *The Aeneid* is Homer fanfiction. You know, certainly the whole Arthurian universe is fanfiction. Right, Tom Stoppard's *Rosencrantz and Guildenstern* is Shakespeare fanfiction. But what people tend to mean when they talk about modern fanfiction is fanfiction written by amateurs about the mass media. And I would probably date it from Sherlock Holmes, who was a character who appeared in serialised mass media form, except the mass media was the magazine, and people almost immediately had a kind of modern fan-ish response about Sherlock Holmes and started writing stories about Sherlock Holmes. Not just the millions of professional stories and incarnations of Holmes, but a whole amateur world of Sherlock Holmes, where Sherlock Holmes becomes the site of a game that we're all playing. In fact, Holmesians call it The Great Game, of kind of, reading and writing Holmes in community.

Audio 3.02

Where the girl usually found soft, kind eyes, today, she saw eyes large and dark staring right at her. She gulped. Then took a breath and stared right back. To anyone else, she looked as if she was calm, but inside there was a big ball of terror. Eager not to appear afraid, she quietly spoke. 'You look different today, Grandma. Your eyes. I've never seen them so large. And your ears. They've grown.'

Her 'grandmother' licked her lips and almost smiled. 'All the better to see and hear you, my dear,' came the reply. The creature acted as though the disguise was convincing, but the girl wasn't fooled by its pathetic attempt to look and sound like an old woman. She kept up the pretence. 'Well, Grandma, you look as if you're a different person today. Are you sick? I've brought you something that might make you feel better, if so.' She watched as a long tongue appeared and swirled around large, brown lips. Her 'Grandma's' mouth opened to speak, but before that could happen, the girl reached into her basket and pulled out a violin. 'I want to play for you, Grandma,' she said. 'Your big ears will enjoy this.' The girl put the instrument to her shoulder and started playing. It was as if a thousand cats had entered the room all at once, each one screaming at the top of its voice for attention. The creature in the bed pulled back as far as it could go. It put its paws to its ears and wailed. The girl kept playing and playing, louder and worse than ever. Before long, the creature jumped up and ran for the door, a look of pain on its face as though it had been physically hurt. It threw open the door and ran into the night, glasses and nightdress falling to the floor.

The girl let out a breath and stopped playing. Silence hit the room. 'You can come out now, Grandma,' she said. A trap door in the floor opened and her grandmother climbed out. The feeling of relief was overwhelming and she ran to her and hugged her tight. It was as if she never wanted to let her grandmother go. 'It's OK, Grandma. You're safe now.' 'Thank you, my dear,' said her grandmother. 'That was very clever of you.' The girl smiled. 'I knew that awful instrument would come in handy one day,' she said.

Audio 3.03

1 The creature acted as though the disguise was convincing.

2 It was as if a thousand cats had entered the room all at once.

3 The creature jumped up as though it'd been physically hurt.

4 It was as if she never wanted to let her grandmother go.

Audio 3.04

1 It's as if the author's never read the original book.

2 It seemed as though the ending had improved.

3 You look as though you've seen a ghost.

4 I felt as if you were angry with me.

Audio 3.05 and 3.06

I = Imtiaz Dharker   P = Presenter

I: I eavesdrop all the time. I listen in shamelessly on conversations in cafés and in stations and on trains, and on the street.

P: Imtiaz Dharker is a poet, artist and film maker.

I: I think of it as part of my job to listen to what's going on around me in everyday life. Not just what people say, but how they say it. Their pauses and their hesitations. For me, that's like mining treasure, and some of it finds its way into the poems. There's eavesdropping at all kinds of levels. Listening to the human voices of course, but also listening in on the world; listening to nature and eavesdropping on the heart's secret, which poetry does all the time. I heard this woman speaking on the 106 bus. It's just a regular bus in Bombay – hot and stuffy. And she got on and I heard her saying this to a friend and I knew immediately that that could be a poem. I dived into my bag and got out a scrap of paper and put it down, and that was one of the best bits of eavesdropping I've ever had.

What she said: 'Never cook your anger with the food. It will cause indigestion and disturbance in your house.' What she said later: 'I cooked my anger with the food. They didn't notice. They ate it up and said it tasted good.'

Audio 3.07

1 It doesn't matter what I do or say, nothing is good enough for him. It drives me up the wall.

2 I always have butterflies in my stomach, but doing it last week, they felt like ducks flapping around. No idea why. Maybe it was something I ate!

3 He couldn't find it anywhere. We were all tearing our hair out. Then he realised it was in his pocket. I mean, why didn't he check there first?

4 There he was, covered in mud, looking at me with wide eyes. I nearly killed myself laughing.

5 I knew she'd lost her temper, but I didn't know it was because of jam. Who gets angry over jam?! She does, apparently.

6 I shouldn't have done it. I was on edge for the rest of the night and couldn't sleep at all.

7 I believed it and thought I was doing a good thing by spreading the word. Now I could kick myself.

8 It's a real pain that it stops you getting a good night's sleep. Maybe one of you can sleep outside?

Audio 3.08

No matter what I say, it's never right.
We always seem to end up in a fight.
No matter who I meet, there's always fright that you'll say
I said a thing that's not all right.

'Cos no matter how I feel, you always try your best
To cause me stress …
and put me right on edge.
No matter what I choose, all you want to do is shout
In a way that puts my choices all in doubt.
But no matter that your voice belongs to me,
And it never seems to want to let me be,
I try to never ever let myself agree.

Audio 3.09

1 No matter what I say, it's never right.
2 No matter who I meet, there's always fright …
3 'Cos no matter how I feel, you always try your best …
4 No matter what I choose, all you want to do is shout …
5 But no matter that your voice belongs to me …

Audio 3.10

No matter what they do, they drive me up the wall.

Audio 3.11

1 No matter where I am, you always seem to find me!
2 It doesn't matter that I'll miss the meeting.
3 I'm not sure I'm free tomorrow, but no matter.
4 No matter how hard I try, I can't seem to stop eating!
5 I know I'll get good service here, no matter who serves me.
6 I'll be there, no matter that it's far.

Audio 3.12

A: OK, so those are the film schedules for next week. Is there anything else we need to discuss?
B: Yes. Can we talk about the issue of people taking their own food into the cinema? I've noticed this seems to be happening more and more. It's bad for the cinema because it means they're not buying our snacks. Is there anything we can do to persuade people not to bring their own food to the cinema?
A: That's a very good point. Any ideas, anyone?
C: I think there needs to be a punishment of some kind. Personally, I think we should just ask people to leave if they do this, or fine them.
A: I can see where you're coming from, but on a practical level, we can't really start going in to ask people to leave halfway through a film. It would spoil it for everyone. Personally, I think the issue of people using their phones or talking during a film is much more problematic.
C: That's definitely an ongoing problem. Well, for now, getting back to the food issue, maybe we need to look at what we're charging for our own snacks? I mean, they are a bit on the pricey side. I think that's why they're taking in their own snacks in the first place.
A: I can see the logic in that, but on the other hand, we don't want to reduce prices too much, do we? How about we keep an eye out for people who are bringing in their own food and then don't allow them entry?
B: Hmm. I can see why you're suggesting a tough approach, Tali, but if they've already paid for their tickets, then it's potentially creating a bit of a conflict. It might be more effective to offer a reward rather than a punishment.
A: A carrot rather than a stick, you mean?
B: Well, yes. I mean, in my experience people respond better to coaxing, rather than being pressurised into doing something.
A: That makes sense. So, what kind of reward would you suggest?
B: Well, how about we offer a free snack included in the price of the ticket? Then people wouldn't feel the need to bring their own.
C: That's quite a neat idea. But one disadvantage of that would be that it would be quite expensive for the cinema. We wouldn't be able to add the full price of the snack to the ticket, so we'd lose out.
A: Yes, you're right. So, can we think of anything that wouldn't cost so much? Some kind of discount on their next ticket if they buy one of our snacks?
B: Yeah, the advantage of that would be that it would really motivate people to change their behaviour, as well as ensure they come back for another film.
C: Yes, it would certainly win the customers over. Alternatively, what about combining a carrot and a stick – a reward and a punishment? So, we keep an eye on the door and take away any of their own food that people are trying to take in – they can get it back after the film, of course. Then we offer them a discount on the ticket price for their next visit if they buy one of our snacks? That way, we encourage them to come back.
A: Yes, that's a really neat idea. Let's follow this up and look into the practicalities of implementing it.

Audio 3.13

1 I can see where you're coming from, but on a practical level, we can't really start going in to ask people to leave halfway through a film.
2 I can see the logic in that, but on the other hand, we don't want to reduce prices too much, do we?
3 I can see why you're suggesting a tough approach, Tali, but if they've already paid for their tickets, then it's potentially creating a bit of a conflict.

Audio 3.14

Someone that has influenced me greatly is a guy called Mike. When I was sixteen, I left school and got my first job. I was really young when I think back now, so it's not surprising that working full-time with all these grown men and women was a bit of a shock! I probably looked like a rabbit in the headlights! Anyway, Mike worked there. Some people might say he was an unofficial boss, but I saw him as more of a mentor. He wasn't loud, but he had this quiet confidence and people looked to him when they needed help. He was about my age now at that time, but he took me under his wing and looked out for me. He helped me to learn the skills I needed, but more than that, he helped me to become the man I am today. He taught me how to deal with conflict quickly, so problems were swiftly solved. He taught me the importance of honesty and loyalty, and how to take my time before making important decisions. He inspired me to work hard to be successful.

My dad hadn't really been in my life all that much up to then, so in many ways I'd describe Mike as a kind of father figure. His wife Sheena became like a second mum to me, too. Probably the main thing Mike taught me was how to be a father myself, how to guide my kids and be a role model for them. Mike retired a few years ago, but we're still in touch. My children call him and Sheena Gramps and Gran, which I love! He's now inspiring my kids.

UNIT 3 REVIEW

Audio R3.01
Extreme inspiration

A while ago, I started to feel that my life was dull and I was sick to death of the daily routines. I felt I needed to do something different – not necessarily something profound or life-changing, just something different. A friend suggested I have a go at one of his favourite extreme sports – street luge. The luge is basically a sledge on wheels that you lie on and use to ride downhill on steep roads. It took some coaxing, but eventually I agreed to give it a go. My friend provided some basic training, but even so, as the day approached, I had butterflies in my stomach day and night. No matter what I did, I couldn't relax. What if I was injured in a tragic accident? When the day came, excitement took over and I forgot my fears. The experience didn't disappoint – I felt as if I was flying as my luge sped down the deserted street. And how has it left me feeling? Definitely more confident and eager to try new things – and maybe inspire others to do the same!

UNIT 3 MEDIATION BANK

Audio MB3.01

A: Have you heard about this new points system the college have put into place?
B: Yeah, great!
A: What makes you say that?
B: Well, it'll motivate everyone.
A: How will it do that?
B: It'll add an element of competition.
A: Does that mean you think it'll be successful?
B: Sure, why not? I mean, it's kind of fun, isn't it? See if you can beat your friends! Or colleagues in the case of teachers. And who doesn't want to get free gifts?
A: That's true! What do you think the effects of competition will be on everyone?
B: I think it'll push people to work harder. We're all competitive, we all want to win, although I guess to different degrees.
A: Might it have a negative effect on some people?
B: It might, I suppose.
A: How?
B: It could create bad feelings among friends, I guess.
A: And what about teachers? How might they feel about being compared to their colleagues?
B: Well, it could motivate them, but I can see that it might be very stressful, too, and possibly very embarrassing. What are your thoughts?
A: Well, I think it has the potential to be a disaster.
B: What do you mean by that?
A: Well, you said that everyone's competitive to some degree but actually, I wouldn't say everyone is. I mean …

Audio 4.01

1 You should make sure you check first.
2 Everything should be OK.
3 Should anyone wish to take photos, they must seek permission.
4 If they should give us permission, we'll be happy.
5 You should post it online.
6 They shouldn't have posted it online.

Audio 4.02

P = Presenter   A = Anita   R = Rob

P: With me today to discuss unusual ideas for making the world a better place are Anita and Rob. Anita, you're up first. What's your proposal for improving the world?

A: Well, every second of every day, millions of images are uploaded to social media. I think it should be restricted to just one photo per person per day.

R: Really?

A: Yes. It sounds extreme, I know, but I really do think that being prohibited from uploading more than one photo a day would benefit us.

R: How?

A: Well, we spend too much time selecting and editing photos to share online and it's having a negative effect on our lives. If we were limited to one photo a day, we'd save valuable time and share photos of things that are really and truly what we care about. Not just random photos of our dinner, for example!

R: Maybe someone's dinner **is** important to them!

A: That's true. But I really do think that sharing just one image a day would cut time spent messing about on social media and it would eliminate those 'Oh no! I shouldn't have posted that photo!' thoughts we have in the middle of the night because we'd think more carefully about the one photo that we do upload.

P: Let me just pick up on that. If social media companies should limit us to one photo upload each day, might we not spend even longer on selecting and editing it because we feel it has to be absolutely perfect?

A: Hmm, possibly.

R: It's an interesting idea and I get where you're coming from, but I think this rule would be hard to implement. Firstly, I'm not sure social media companies would want to impose such a rule. And how would they regulate it? People would just have multiple accounts. I don't think it would deter everyone from posting more than one photo. And why one photo? If it's that big a problem, why not abolish sharing photos completely? That should achieve your goal of giving us more time to focus on more meaningful things.

A: Oh no, now that's a step too far!

Audio 4.03

Paris, New York – what comes to mind when you think about these cities? I bet if we compared our ideas, they'd all be pretty similar, not because we've all been to those places, but because we've been sold a brand. And that's what I'm going to be talking about today – place branding. We're all familiar with the idea that companies have to advertise and market their products in order to sell them. But cities and countries are increasingly finding themselves in a similar position. There are just under 200 countries in the world, and thousands of cities, and these places know that they are competing with each other for tourists, trade and investment from businesses, all of which can make a huge difference to their economy and the standard of living their people can enjoy. It's also easy for places to build up a negative image over time – perhaps a city has become associated with high levels of crime or a country is still remembered for a disaster that happened twenty years ago. Without branding and marketing, how can places compete and attract the tourists and investment they need?

Let's look at a well-known example from the past to see what difference an effective branding campaign can make. In the late 1970s, New York City was in trouble. It was experiencing financial problems and levels of crime in the city were sky high. In fact, there was so much crime in the city that for a while, unions had been running a campaign called 'Welcome to Fear City', which encouraged people to stay away from the city and advised them to never use the subway because it was so risky. It was clear that something needed to change. The city needed to find a way to change its image and bring in tourists and revenue. So, the New York Department of Commerce increased its tourism budget and invested in a bold rebranding campaign to make New York seem like an exciting, attractive place to visit. The result was the iconic phrase 'I love New York', with a heart instead of the word 'love', which can still be seen on T-shirts and other merchandise today. And the result of the campaign? The state's income from visitors tripled within a few years and New York became one of the world's go-to tourist destinations. It's strange to think that soon people will have been wearing those famous 'I love New York' T-shirts for over sixty years. Where would New York be now if that campaign hadn't happened?

So, how should places approach rebranding? The example of New York shows the power of a visual approach and a clear logo. Another example of this is Paris, where the branding uses an oversized 'A' in the city's name to represent its most famous monument, the Eiffel Tower. Again, this was a striking, visual image – who could fail to recognise it? It immediately advertised the Eiffel Tower and promoted the city as a tourist destination with interesting things to see and do. And the huge advantage of such a simple logo like this is that it can be used everywhere, from billboards on the walls of buildings to the sides of buses and information flyers for tourists. With any luck, images of the logo might also appear online and go viral, reaching an audience of millions.

But sometimes a more subtle approach is required. In 2005, Chile ran a campaign based around the slogan: 'Chile: All ways surprising'. Despite the hype of the campaign, it was not as successful as hoped and the country has now given up simple slogans and instead has been using a less direct and more long-term approach, encouraging businesses to all use a similar 'national' logo and message to promote themselves to customers abroad. The message focuses on what are seen as the country's main selling points: its range of natural attractions from deserts to glaciers, the stability of its government and the enterprising nature of the population. This approach of selling a common message seems to be working. Foreign investment in the country has increased in recent years and tourist numbers have hit record highs.

Another rule for place branding is to focus on the positive aspects of a place's individual heritage. There's no point in going for bland, generic tourist appeal, but instead places should think about what makes them unique and interesting. A good example of this is the campaign by the city of Barcelona to rebrand one of its districts, El Raval. The district was different to the standard tourist areas with their beautiful architecture and large stores, and it wasn't popular. So the city used the idea of the area being 'alternative' to create its modern image of being vibrant, diverse, creative and cool. As part of the campaign, they even invented a new verb: 'ravalejar', meaning to wander around El Raval and soak up the lively atmosphere.

My time's nearly up, but I just want to think about what happens once a campaign has run its course. Is the job done? Will the campaigns I've talked about still be running in twenty years' time? The answer is no. Let's go back to New York City. The initial rebranding of the 1970s created the image of a fun city for tourists to visit. But it focused mainly on Manhattan, with its well-known monuments and the big stores. In 2006 there was a push to promote other parts of the city and target a new generation of tourists. A new logo was developed which showed a kaleidoscope of different images of the city, to reflect the diversity of the different areas of the city. This created a new wave of tourism, not only to Manhattan but to Brooklyn and other boroughs. So, branding is an ongoing and creative process and places need to constantly be on their toes to remain competitive and popular. So, think about your town or city – could it benefit from new branding and what kind of image would you want to create for it? Thank you.

Audio 4.04

1 It's also easy for places to build up a negative image over time – perhaps a city has become associated with high levels of crime or a country is still remembered for a disaster that happened twenty years ago. Without branding and marketing, how can places compete and attract the tourists and investment they need?

2 It's strange to think that soon people will have been wearing those famous 'I love New York' T-shirts for over sixty years. Where would New York be now if that campaign hadn't happened?

3 Another example of this is Paris, where the branding uses an oversized 'A' in the city's name, to represent its most famous monument, the Eiffel Tower. Again, this was a striking, visual image – who could fail to recognise it?

Audio 4.05

1 Recently, they've been trying to attract more tourists to the city.
2 I think she'll have been working on this campaign.
3 Where were you? I've been calling you all afternoon!
4 I guess he'll have been watching the tennis.

Audio 4.06

1 We've been promoting this area of the city for over ten years.
2 Hopefully, they'll have been selling a lot of merchandise.
3 Soon, she'll have been living there for ten years!
4 We can ask them what they've been doing.

Audio 4.07

A: Hi, sorry I'm a bit late. I just bumped into Silvia.
B: No worries. Look, there's a table over there.
A: Great. Let's sit down.
B: So, how was Silvia?
A: Oh, she looked great! But actually, I'm feeling a bit annoyed with her.
B: Why?
A: Well, it sounds silly, but she was wearing some absolutely beautiful shoes – obviously new and obviously very expensive. But pretty much the first thing she said was, 'Oh, these new shoes are killing me! The leather is so stiff and the heels are too high! Yours look much more comfortable.' But I'm wearing a pair of scruffy old ones and I found it really annoying that she was getting me to look at her amazing new shoes by pretending there was something wrong with them.
B: Oh, yeah. She was, what's it called, 'humblebragging'.
A: What?
B: Oh, it was trending on Twitter recently. It's when someone complains about something, but what they're really doing is showing off. Some celebrity or other was 'complaining' about an award and started a Twitterstorm. There's even been a study to show that it's more annoying than just plain bragging.
A: Humblebragging? Never heard of it, but very interesting, and that's exactly what she was doing – complaining about how uncomfortable her shoes were to point out how amazing they looked!
B: My cousin does it all the time. He's a student and he always does really well in exams. But if you say 'Well done' to him, he pretends to be all humble and says something like, 'Oh, I can't understand it. I didn't do much revision at all. I don't know how I got ninety-eight percent' – so, pretending to be modest, but actually telling me how well he did!
A: It's so annoying!

Audio 4.08

1 I'm already proficient at computer programming, even though I've only been learning for six months. In fact, everyone comments on how good my programs are!
2 Last month, I was asked to be a real-time interpreter for a conference, translating from Portuguese into English. I'm quite inexperienced in Portuguese, so I was surprised, and it was really tough! But everyone seems to think I'm competent in translating and they said I did a decent job.
3 I'm a trained teacher, so I'm very confident about teaching colleagues new skills.
4 Yes, I'm quite handy with most tools, so I'm happy to work with unskilled assistants and train them on the job.

5 When I was offered my first promotion, I thought the new job would be beyond me. There were lots of people who were much more experienced than me, so I thought I'd be hopeless at it! But then I got promoted again six months later …
6 Oh, yes. I'm a master of spreadsheets! There's nothing I don't know about them and I'm really good at using them to create presentations, too!

Audio 4.09

1
A: So, a key part of this position is dealing with customers. Do you have experience of customer service?
B: Yes, it was part of my previous job, so I would say I'm very competent in dealing with customers. I get on well with them and build up good relationships. I'm also trained in managing disputes, so I can handle customers who are upset or angry.
A: That's great. And what do you think is the best way to handle difficult customers?
B: Er, that's quite a broad topic. Perhaps I could just talk about one incident that I dealt with recently. The customer was very upset because an order had been delayed. I spoke to the customer and reassured them we were doing everything we could to resolve the problem, and I offered them a discount, which they were quite pleased with. I feel I dealt with that situation very well.
A: OK. So, moving on to your qualifications. You have a degree in English?
B: Yes, that's right.
A: But, I can see that you don't have any formal qualifications in business. Do you think this would be an issue for you?
B: It's true that I don't have any formal qualifications. But the most important point here is that I'm committed to ongoing training. I feel it's important for me to keep studying and learning while I'm working, so I'm always looking for opportunities to gain new qualifications that are relevant for my job. I'm willing to work hard and learn, so I don't feel that having no formal qualifications would be a problem for me.

2
A: So, you're applying for a job in sales?
B: Yes, that's right.
A: And your previous job was as a receptionist in a hotel?
B: Yes, it was a busy hotel in the city centre.
A: OK. So, what skills from that job do you think are relevant to a job in sales?
B: That's an interesting question. What I can say is that in any customer-facing role, the relationship with the customer is the most important thing. And this is definitely one of my strengths. I'm passionate about building good relationships with customers. I've always had excellent feedback from guests at the hotel and from my manager, so I feel my ability to build relationships is extremely relevant and will be of great help to me in a sales role.
A: So, what did you enjoy about working in the hotel?
B: Oh, definitely the contact with the guests. I'm a real people person and I also enjoy working as part of a team.
A: Now, any sales job involves pressure to do well – pressure to make sales. And there

are demanding sales targets each month. How do you think you would cope with this pressure?
B: Well, I've thought about this quite a lot. Can I just say that I'm an extremely hard worker and I'm highly motivated to do well at my job, so I feel the challenge of meeting sales targets will actually push me to work even harder and perform even better than I have in previous jobs.

Audio 4.10

1 That's quite a broad topic.
2 Perhaps I could just talk about one incident that I dealt with recently.
3 The most important point here is that I'm committed to ongoing training.
4 That's an interesting question.
5 What I can say is that in any customer-facing role, the relationship with the customer is the most important thing.
6 I've thought about this quite a lot.
7 Can I just say that I'm an extremely hard worker and I'm highly motivated to do well at my job.

Audio 4.11

1 I have a lot of expertise in managing contracts, so I feel very confident in that role.
2 I'm proficient in Spanish, which is a very useful language in business.
3 I'm very competent in all aspects of design, so I can tackle any project that I'm given.

Audio 4.12

Good afternoon and welcome to our presentation of GlowVit, our brand-new daily vitamin tablet. We all know our bodies need vitamins, but in a busy life, it isn't always possible to eat the right foods. This revolutionary new product will help you both feel and look great! The special formula has been developed by scientists using the latest research techniques. One of its unique features is that the vitamins are slowly released into your body over a 24-hour period, which helps your body absorb more of them, so you can be sure you'll get all the benefits. GlowVit will appeal to customers as it's based on scientific research and we are confident it is a product that everyone can enjoy, not a luxury product, because we believe everyone should have the chance to feel and look amazing!

UNIT 5

Audio 5.01

1 You'd be more independent if you'd left home.
2 We'd be doing more sport if you hadn't taken up photography.
3 I'd have been bored if you weren't here.
4 She'd have called me if she had my number.

Audio 5.02

1 I'd be a pilot if I'd had the money for the training.
2 I'd have been a pilot if I had better eyesight.
3 We'd have recognised each other if we lived in the same street.
4 We'd recognise each other if we'd lived in the same street.

Audio 5.03

1 It is important to conserve this species, so more conservation measures need to be taken.

2 About eighteen percent of all birds migrate each year, but we don't know the details of all their migration patterns.

Audio 5.04

1 Some birds have an instinct to migrate each year, whereas others have an instinctive need to stay in the same territory.

2 Humans have caused a lot of environmental damage and environmentalists believe we must act quickly to repair it.

3 Some animals now struggle to reproduce in the wild because chemicals have interfered with their reproduction.

4 Poaching has a devastating impact on the number of elephants in the wild, so it is crucial the poachers are caught.

Audio 5.05 and 5.06

P = Presenter   D = Dan Everard

P: Hello, I'm Ellie Wood and welcome to this week's edition of *Nature First*. Now, in the past we've discussed lots of different conservation measures and today we're talking about a new and unusual way of keeping animals safe by 'nudging' them to change their own behaviour, so they in effect protect themselves.

With me is conservationist Dan Everard. Dan, first, what do you mean by 'nudging'?

D: Hi, Ellie. Yes, 'nudging' has been used on humans for some time now. It refers to techniques that are employed by organisations and governments to gently change our behaviour and encourage us to make different choices. For example, if a supermarket puts healthy snacks next to the checkout rather than chocolate bars, it's 'nudging' us to make healthier food choices – not telling us we have to, but encouraging us to change our behaviour.

P: And how can these techniques be applied to the natural world?

D: Well, some years ago a biologist and animal behaviourist called Ken Ramirez started getting involved in conservation projects. He had mainly worked with pets and domesticated animals before this, and he showed that you can train animals more effectively by using positive reinforcement – encouraging and rewarding them for 'good' behaviour, rather than punishing them for bad behaviour.

P: Ah, you mean nudging them?

D: Exactly.

P: OK. I can see that would work for training my dog to sit or lie down, but how does it relate to animals in the natural world? It surely can't work in the same way?

D: You're absolutely right. Training pet animals is all about building a relationship between the trainer and animal, but in the wild, it's essential that the trainer remains invisible. Yet the principles are the same – to discourage certain behaviours and provide rewards for the behaviours we want to encourage. But the discouragements and rewards need to be located in the environment around the animals, so they are reacting and making their own decisions and modifying their own behaviour.

Audio 5.05 and 5.07

P = Presenter   D = Dan Everard

P: It sounds fascinating. Can you give us some examples of how this kind of nudging has been used?

D: Yes, I can give you two examples, both based on work by Ramirez. The first is with chimpanzees in a national park in Sierra Leone, where poachers were killing them for their meat. The park rangers were actually situated quite close by, but as they didn't know exactly when the animals were in danger, they couldn't always get there in time to protect them. Now, chimpanzees post lookouts themselves around their group, and they start screaming when they see danger, to warn the others. But the sound created by only a few chimps unfortunately wasn't enough to alert the park rangers. So the strategy was to 'nudge' the chimps to all scream together when a human approached, to create a huge volume of noise so park rangers could get to the scene and catch the poachers.

P: Wow, so using the chimps' own instinctive behaviour, but modifying it.

D: Exactly.

P: And how did Ramirez and his team achieve this?

D: They installed a system of plastic pipes in the trees where the chimps were located and set up a remote camera to watch them. When a human approached, if a larger number of chimps screamed, the rangers would activate a mechanism so fruit and insects fell into the tree from the pipes – the chimps got a reward. And to get the reward, they needed to have screamed when humans were approaching, not just randomly.

P: And did it work?

D: It did. Once the chimps had been trained to change their behaviour, poaching in the area was reduced by eighty-six percent.

P: That's incredible. And what's the second example?

D: This one was in Alaska, where polar bears were going into villages in search of food. Clearly, these are huge, dangerous predators, so the inhabitants would shoot any bears that came too close. The strategy here was to educate the villagers on how to dispose of their rubbish so as not to attract the bears and also to encourage them to shoot in the general direction of any bears – not to kill them, just to scare them – and only if they touched bins or other human-made objects, so the bears would learn to avoid going near anything human. Secondly, they coaxed the bears to look for food elsewhere, by leaving trails of food towards areas further from the village, where the bears could find their own food naturally. Again, this project was extremely successful. In one village, it reduced the problem from 300 bear incidents per year to just three.

P: Wow – great result! And are there any downsides to this kind of nudging of animals in the wild?

D: That's a good question. Of course, there's the general moral issue of whether we, as humans, should interfere with animals in the wild. Conservationists also worry about unintended consequences – if we change animals' behaviour to solve one problem, will we have caused another problem in five years' time? We always need to think very carefully before we intervene.

P: That's fascinating. Thank you so much for …

Audio 5.08

1 A director of a recycling company has become the first person to travel coast to coast on a stand-up paddleboard. Jason Elliott set off from Liverpool on the west coast of England nine days ago, travelling along rivers and canals, and reached Goole on the east coast today. Jason, an experienced surfer and paddleboarder, wanted to raise awareness of the plastic pollution in our waterways caused by single-use plastic. In addition, he is raising money for a non-profit organisation that seeks to protect coastlines and waterways from the harmful effects of contaminated water. It's estimated that a million plastic bottles and two million plastic bags are sold every minute around the world, many of which end up in our inland waterways.

2 A computer game developed ten years ago is continuing to raise awareness of homelessness around the world. The game SPENT is designed to encourage people to become more sympathetic to the homeless by recognising the small decisions that can mean the difference between financial stability and poverty. In the game, players imagine they have become jobless and are down to their last $1,000. They have to negotiate a series of challenging financial decisions with the aim of reaching the end of the month still in credit. The game has been played more than sixteen million times by over seven million people around the world, with over $200,000 raised for food and shelter for the homeless. It has also been used as an educational tool by social workers, teachers and other professionals.

3 A group of protestors stopped traffic in the city centre this morning as part of a campaign to raise awareness of climate change. The group of around twenty activists sat in the street for two hours, causing traffic to be re-routed. The group are concerned about the increased number of lorries in the area which emit harmful greenhouse gases. These gases are a key factor in climate change which is predicted to have a significant effect on people around the world in the next few decades, causing environmental activism to increase.

4 The stars were out in force at last night's Met Gala in New York, with several using their outfits to promote social causes. The annual fundraiser, famous for its sometimes outrageous fashion, saw several outfits advocating social change – in particular addressing inequality experienced by the disadvantaged. The event gets the attention of press from around the world and is deemed to be the fashion event of the year.

Audio 5.09

1 In addition, he is raising money for a non-profit organisation that seeks to protect coastlines and waterways from the harmful effects of contaminated water.

2 A computer game developed ten years ago is continuing to raise awareness of homelessness around the world.

3 In the game, players imagine they have become jobless and are down to their last $1,000.

4 A group of protestors stopped traffic in the city centre this morning as part of a campaign to raise awareness of climate change.

5 The group are concerned about the increased number of lorries in the area which emit harmful greenhouse gases.

6 The annual fundraiser, famous for its sometimes outrageous fashion, saw several outfits advocating social change – in particular addressing inequality experienced by the disadvantaged.

Audio 5.10

A: We need to do something about the number of rough sleepers in the town. It seems to be increasing all the time. I know people give them money and bedding and things, but it doesn't feel like there's a consistent approach to supporting them.

B: You mean that the council aren't doing anything.

A: Exactly. How can we pressure them into doing something?

C: I think their funding was cut a few years back so they're struggling to afford temporary shelters and there's been a long-term housing issue for a while. A couple of other non-profit organisations are doing what they can, but they're limited by funds, too.

A: So we need to raise money then.

C: Yeah, I think so.

A: And to do that, we need to raise people's awareness of the increase in homelessness, although I suspect a lot of people are already aware.

C: Probably. It's hard not to notice the issue when you walk around town, but then again people have their own things to worry about so they may notice, but not necessarily think too much about it.

B: We could have a 'Big Sleep Out'.

C: What's that?

B: In a nutshell, it's where you get a load of people together to sleep rough for the night in the town centre. There was one worldwide a few years back. Tens of thousands of people slept rough for a night.

C: Why?

B: It got attention – press coverage in the paper and online and so on. It raised people's awareness of the situation **and** raised money. I think it's a really good way to build empathy, too – when you sleep out, you get a better idea of the challenges that homeless people face. We could work with a local homeless charity to organise this.

A: Do you think it'll have that much of an impact though? I wonder if a march to the town square would be better. It'd force people to stop and listen. We could end it with a speech on the steps of the Town Hall.

B: Hmm, well it would get more attention if we could get enough people to attend, but it'd also be more difficult to organise and it would probably annoy some people rather than get them on side, what with redirecting traffic and the crowds and so on. I don't suppose local businesses would like it either.

C: So you're saying we shouldn't do anything to upset anyone? Shouldn't we be upsetting everyone? Get their attention?

B: Not really. We want to engage people and draw them in, not push them away.

A: I can see what you're both saying. Basically, it's a choice between getting lots of attention but annoying people and risking little attention but upsetting no one.

B: We can get more attention with the Big Sleep Out if we invite some local celebrities – you know, there's that actor that lives here, the one in that drama about nurses in the 1950s, and his wife. She writes and directs it, plus there's a certain celebrity chef here, too. Get them involved and it'll get lots of attention. Maybe in the national press, too.

A: Oh, well that changes everything.

C: I agree. That sounds more promising. So how do we go about this then?

B: Well, I guess the first thing is to contact both the council and some other charities, those that have direct experience of supporting …

Audio 5.11

1

A: We need to do something about the number of rough sleepers in the town. It seems to be increasing all the time. I know people give them money and bedding and things, but it doesn't feel like there's a consistent approach to supporting them.

B: You mean that the council aren't doing anything.

A: Exactly.

2

B: We could have a 'Big Sleep Out'.

C: What's that?

B: In a nutshell, it's where you get a load of people together to sleep rough for the night in the town centre.

3

B: Hmm, well it would get more attention if we could get enough people to attend, but it'd also be more difficult to organise and it would probably annoy some people rather than get them on-side, what with redirecting traffic and the crowds and so on. I don't suppose local businesses would like it either.

C: So you're saying we shouldn't do anything to upset anyone? Shouldn't we be upsetting everyone? Get their attention?

4

A: I can see what you're both saying. Basically, it's a choice between getting lots of attention but annoying people and risking little attention but upsetting no one.

Audio 5.12

So, in a nutshell, to get people to change their habits you first need to raise their awareness of the problem. To do this, you can organise a petition, a debate, a concert or a social media campaign.

Audio 5.13

We tried a petition last year to get a company to become more sustainable and managed to get over 10,000 signatures online, which was just brilliant, but there were issues with people having signed twice and whether or not it was completely reliable. Plus of course, people had signed it without really understanding what they were signing – they just did it because someone told them to – so although we were able to present it to the company, they made out it wasn't reliable. They made some promises about changing their ways, but they were pretty empty promises so in the end not much came of it.

Audio 5.14

A: If you think about it, routines are something we can use to get all the boring bits of life out of the way – cleaning your teeth, washing your clothes, keeping your home clean. If you have strong routines, you get these things done as efficiently as possible, so you can focus on the more important things, like building your career. That's why I think strict routines are necessary if you want to do well in life.

B: That's not the way I see it at all. For me, routines get in the way of being successful because they take you away from the things you need to do if you want to really get to the top – like, working long hours if you have to. How can you put that extra effort in and work late if you have a strict bedtime every day?

A: That's true. But you have to admit that there are lots of mundane things that need to be done on a daily basis, even if you're really ambitious. You can't just ignore them. You still have to make sure you have clean clothes to wear to work, for a start. If you have strict routines, you don't actually have to think about them too much – you just get them done in the most efficient way.

B: Hmm, maybe.

UNIT 5 REVIEW

Audio R5.01

Social factors drive human development

In the natural world, animals have always evolved and changed in response to their environment. We know that animals are continuing to evolve in response to events such as deforestation and climate change. But what about humans? If we hadn't evolved in the past, we would still look more like our ape-like ancestors. But are we still evolving now, and how will we evolve in the future? Scientists believe that social factors may be driving evolution now. Compared to the past, when there were huge differences between rich and poor, there is generally more equality now, and fewer people are employed in jobs requiring a large amount of physical strength. As a result, there is some evidence that human bones are slowly becoming weaker. Also, in the past, twins were at a disadvantage because they were generally smaller and weaker than single babies. However, with modern healthcare and welfare schemes, fewer families suffer physical and financial hardship and there is evidence that the number of twins in the population is increasing. It is, however, unclear how humans may evolve in the future.

Audio MB5.01 and MB5.02

1

A: Hello! If you can spare a minute of your time, I'd like to talk to you about shopping local and the environment.

B: Er … OK.

A: I bet you shop online. It's not a bad thing, we all do it, and it can often seem pretty energy efficient. I mean, we don't go out in the car, someone comes to us, on their way to lots of other places in your area, and so of course the carbon emissions can be lower. This is especially true if your goods have travelled from the factory via slow boat. If they've come by plane, they'll be sixty-five times higher, but this might still be lower than the emissions produced by a car trip from out of town to a town centre. It really depends on how you travel, how far you travel and how many items you buy during your trip. Generally, if you walk or cycle, then carbon emissions related to your purchase will be almost nothing – it'll just be the emissions related to producing the product and getting it to the shop. If you live in the town and you drive to the centre and buy twenty-four items, then it can be more environmentally friendly than purchasing one item online.

B: Hmm.

A: But the main issues with shopping online are non-delivery and returns. It's predicted that up to sixty percent of deliveries have to be made a second time because no one is available to receive them the first time round. This increases carbon emissions related to shopping online significantly. It's estimated that one in seven online purchases are returned to online shops globally, increasing carbon emissions significantly. So, in the end, shopping local is much better, right? So, that's what I wanted to say. Shop local.

2

A: Hello! We're talking to people today about why shopping local is much better for us than shopping online. The fact is that our High Street is dying. Did you know that a quarter of the shops in our town are empty due to the large decrease in shoppers?

B: No, I didn't, but I'm not surprised.

A: No, and this has the potential to negatively affect our sense of community and our mental health. The reason is that when we shop in store, we connect to people locally. We bump into old friends and have a chat, we make small talk with people in queues and we have the opportunity to get personal customer service when we need support or we need to return something. These personal connections are important for us and we don't have them when we shop online. Research shows that these connections can help us to keep our anxiety low, our moods in check and even, unbelievably, they help to keep our immune systems strong.

B: Wow.

A: Yes. And then there's the positive impact on the community as a whole. When our sense of community is strong, we are more connected to each other, we feel safer and more secure. We help each other more and this is also positive for our mental health. It gives us a sense of pride. I know that shopping online can be cheaper and more convenient, but we don't benefit from this kind of connection to people online, so if our local High Street dies and we only have online shopping, we'll lose our connection to our community. And that is why we're asking people to think twice about shopping online and consider shopping local instead. To benefit not just local businesses, but to benefit you, your health and the community.

3

A: Good afternoon, do you have a minute?

B: Sure.

A: It's great that you're here in the town centre and I can see you've been shopping and spent some money here.

B: Er, yes.

A: That's great. We need to do more of that. You see, it's not easy for local shops. They have to pay high rents here in the town centre whereas online stores usually have their distribution centres in low-rent areas. There are also high business taxes for high-street stores, or rates as we call them. I don't know if you know this, but small businesses typically pay 755 percent more in rates than large online stores. Can you believe that? Independent bookshops in 2017 were found to be paying eleven times more corporate tax than a certain large online bookseller. It's hard enough for independent stores to compete against large online stores without having rent and taxation make it harder for them.

B: Right.

A: There's often talk of an online delivery tax which would of course level things out a bit and make things easier for local shops but nothing has actually happened with that as far as I know. The fact is we need these local shops for local employment and for the local economy. In 2020, over 170,000 high-street jobs were lost as shops closed and chains went bankrupt. Some were lost here in the town and it may get worse, but without those job opportunities, unemployment will rise and people will be unable to feed themselves and their families. They'll move away to cheaper areas, fewer people will visit and the town will become a ghost town with a tiny economy. We can't afford this to happen to us and we can't rely on an online delivery tax, so we have to stop it happening ourselves.

UNIT 6

Audio 6.01

1 In no way do I think that algorithms are perfect.

2 Under no circumstances should a computer be making such important decisions.

3 Never before have computers had so much power over our lives.

Audio 6.02 and 6.03

L = Liam   A = Anita

L: Anita, you'll never guess what I've gone and done. Something really stupid and now I've got a meeting with Diane first thing on Monday and someone from HR will be there and I think … , well, I'm worried they might fire me. And even if they don't, I'll get a huge telling off … I'm so stupid!

Audio 6.02 and 6.04

A = Anita   L = Liam

A: Why? What on earth happened?

L: Well, I … I … I mean … in some ways it's quite funny. … OK … so it was a really quiet morning for me today. I'd ended up with some time on my hands after handing over a big project. So, I decided, you know, for a laugh, to draw some of the managers as fruit and vegetables, and I gave them silly names like Mike the Mighty Melon and Kevin the Cool Cucumber. Look, here.

A: Er … Oh, wow. Those are brilliant! You're so talented. I wish I could draw like that. That one looks exactly like Mike in melon form!

L: I know, it's funny, right?

A: Yeah.

L: Anyway, I did them here on my tablet and after I'd finished them, I sent them to Parveen for a laugh, but I … uh … they might have accidentally been sent to the whole team.

A: They might have been sent? Or they **were** sent?

L: They were sent. I completely messed up and sent it on the team chat and not Parveen's. It went to ten people including three of the managers in the pictures.

A: Oh no! That's not good. I mean, hilarious, but not good.

L: I know. I can't believe I did it. What was I thinking? You know me. I'm a hard worker. I produce good stuff. I don't usually do stupid stuff like this. I'm an idiot. And after they'd promised me a promotion soon, too. I keep replaying that moment I tapped the send button over and over in my head. Why didn't I just check which chat group I was in first? I'm such an idiot!

A: Look … don't be too hard on yourself. If you think about it, the pictures aren't that bad. I mean, they're just funny, not insulting. In fact, the names are quite complimentary really. And Mike's got a great sense of humour. You might get a warning about wasting time, but I don't think they'll fire you. Everyone here knows what a good designer you are.

L: Yeah. Yeah, you're right. The drawings aren't really rude or anything and it's … it's not like I've done anything like this before. It was just a one-off and so … so yeah, maybe it won't be as bad as I think. Maybe I'll get a telling off and no more.

A: Exactly. You never know – maybe they were so impressed with your designs that they want you to create something similar for one of the new advertising campaigns!

L: Hmm, I think that's too much wishful thinking! I doubt Diane will be happy about this. I don't suppose she enjoys the senior managers calling her on a Friday afternoon. I just wish she'd been in the office to meet today. No one wants to be fired just before the weekend, but at least I'd have got it out of the way. Now I've got a ruined weekend to survive before the meeting on Monday. And I've got tickets to a gig I was really looking forward to tomorrow night. There's no enjoying that now.

A: Well, there's not much you can do about it until Monday when you can own up and say sorry. Until then, try not to think too much about it. Keep yourself active to take your mind off it all. Now, show me them again!

Audio 6.05 and 6.06

1 I uploaded the wrong photo and now I can't delete it.
2 We learn more from mistakes than from getting things right.
3 I should have paid more attention to what I was doing.
4 You've got to help me clear up this mess.
5 It's not what I expected.
6 You've made a huge mistake here.

Audio 6.07

D = Diane   L = Liam

D: So, Liam, needless to say, your cartoons have been doing the rounds since you posted them and certain members of senior management are understandably far from impressed. What on earth were you thinking?

L: Well, so, er, having handed over the supermarket project on Friday morning, and with the garden centre project not starting until today, I found myself with some time that needed to be filled so I ended up sketching some cartoon characters based on members of senior management. Anyway, once I'd completed them, I decided to send them to a colleague to see what he thought, but I mistakenly sent them to the whole team.

D: Right, I see, well that makes it clear how these pictures came to be in circulation.

L: Yes, completely my mistake – it was a poor error of judgement to draw the characters in the first place, and then again to send them to the team chat instead of to a colleague. I apologise profusely for both of these things – you know I don't usually partake in activities such as this. I'm diligent and produce high-quality work.

D: OK, thanks Liam. Well, I'm sure you understand that we can't condone what happened. You're paid to do a job and not to entertain yourself and your colleagues with not particularly flattering drawings of your managers. That said, you're a valuable member of the team, so be advised that this is an official verbal warning, but no further action will be taken.

L: Oh, that's a relief. Thank you. I was worried I might be fired.

D: I don't think it was serious enough for that. If you'd sent the drawings to an important client though, maybe.

L: I'm disappointed in myself, especially after having been promised a promotion. I've definitely learnt my lesson.

D: Good. No one enjoys being called by senior managers on a Friday afternoon, least of all me.

L: Yes, I'm sure, sorry.

D: OK, well let's draw a line under it for now. But one good thing to come out of this is that your work was noticed by Mike, who thinks that he's got a new project for you. You know our latest advertising campaign? Well, it looks like …

Audio 6.08

1 Oh that's a relief. Thank you. I was worried I might be fired.
2 So, er, having handed over the supermarket project on Friday morning, and with the garden centre project not starting until today, I found myself with some time that needed to be filled.

3 Anyway, once I'd completed them, I decided to send them to a colleague to see what he thought, but I mistakenly sent them to the whole team.
4 I'm disappointed in myself, especially after having been promised a promotion. I've definitely learnt my lesson.
5 That said, you're a valuable member of the team, so be advised that this is an official verbal warning, but no further action will be taken.
6 No one enjoys being called by senior managers on a Friday afternoon, least of all me.

Audio 6.09

M = Moussa   A = Alyssa

M: Hi!

A: Oh, hello. I'm Alyssa. I'm your neighbour – I live in flat 6B, next door.

M: Oh, hi. Nice to meet you, I'm Moussa. What can I do for you?

A: Well, I don't want to come across as the annoying neighbour, but I'm really not happy that you play your guitar so late every night. I have to get up really early for work, but you practise until after midnight every night. I mean, this isn't really acceptable. It's really loud in my flat and I just can't get to sleep.

M: Oh, I'm so sorry – I didn't realise anyone could hear me. These flats are quite cosy, but I guess they're not that luxurious, so the walls aren't all that thick. I'm really sorry if I've disturbed you. It's just, I'm a musician and I've got a really important gig coming up in a few weeks and so I've got lots of songs to practise. I work during the day, so evenings are my only time to practise. It's a huge opportunity for me and I've got to get it right.

A: I understand that and I completely get that you want to do well, but I don't think it's fair that I should have to be exhausted just so that you can give a good performance.

M: Yeah, you're absolutely right. I do acknowledge that. Maybe we could come to an arrangement about when I practise. I mean, what about if I stop by ten on weeknights and then maybe continue until eleven on Friday and Saturday nights, when you don't have to get up so early the next day?

A: Hmm, yes. That sounds like a good compromise. I'm usually out with friends on Friday and Saturday evenings anyway, so I'd be happy with that.

M: Cool. And I can offer you two free tickets to the gig if you want. It should be a really good one – some big names are playing, so if you're into rock music, you'll love it.

A: Ah, that'd be really cool, actually. My best friend is really into rock, so I can take her.

M: Good. Well, I'm glad we've sorted that out. I'll drop the tickets round to you next week and I'll make sure I stop playing in time for you to get to bed.

A: Thanks for that. Let me know about the tickets.

Audio 6.10

1 I'm really not happy that you play your guitar so late every night.
2 I mean, this isn't really acceptable. It's really loud in my flat and I just can't get to sleep.
3 I understand that and I completely get that you want to do well, but I don't

think it's fair that I should have to be exhausted just so that you can give a good performance.

Audio 6.11

A: So, now that everyone's working from home at least two days a week, we're seeing some speed issues.

B: What do you mean?

A: Well, things seem to be taking longer than usual. I'd say that connection speeds are the main issue, but old devices are causing speed issues, too.

B: I'm not surprised. If we ask staff to work from home to save costs on office space, there are bound to be issues. One thing to consider is that top-of-the-range wi-fi is costly and also not readily accessible everywhere, and these slow connections are having an impact on file uploads to the shared system – some staff can't even get into the system.

A: True. Another issue seems to be that meetings are constantly being interrupted by poor connections. Just this morning I was in a meeting where a colleague was so frustrated with her connection that she just asked for an email to summarise what we'd covered. Hardly ideal.

B: I think we need to take this to senior management.

A: What about suggesting the company pays for each staff member's home internet connection? That might help to speed things up.

B: It's a good idea, but it'll add up to a lot of money. Do you think senior management will be willing to pay?

A: Well, they need to take into account the fact that staff just cannot be as productive without the right equipment and they can hardly expect staff to fork out for high-speed broadband themselves if it isn't very accessible. They'll just have to provide some financial support.

B: You're right. Let's suggest it and see what they say. They can only say no!

Audio MB6.01

M = Manager   S = Syed   G = Grace

M: So, you've both explained how you feel about working together and where the issues lie. Syed, you feel that Grace ignores your suggestions and does what she thinks is right. You feel that she's openly criticised some of your decisions in team meetings. Grace, you feel that Syed ignores your views on some of the decisions taken which is why you have to do what you think is right regardless of his view. You think he looks too closely at your work and is very direct in his feedback – feedback you have not asked for. You find this upsetting. Both of you are enjoying the project so you don't want to stop working on it, but you don't feel you can continue working together in the way that you are at the moment. Does that sound like a good summary?

S: Yes.

G: Yes.

M: OK then, let's talk about how we can move forward from here. Is there any chance that, now we've talked, you can find a way to work better together? Grace?

G: I'm not sure if I'm honest. I get the impression that Syed doesn't want to work with me. He feels he should lead the project on his own.

S: Thanks for putting words in my mouth! The thing is, I've been here longer and I have more experience of how things work here. Sometimes your ideas are good, but they just can't work with the systems we have. You don't seem to understand that.

M: OK, OK. Look, from my point of view you have the opportunity to work together brilliantly. I mean, we need fresh ideas, which Grace has, and we need to adapt them to suit how we do things here – that's you, Syed. Syed, I'd like you to be more open to new ideas. Don't just dismiss them immediately but work with Grace to make them work for us – with her creativity and your knowledge and experience of the company, you have the chance to do great things together.

S: OK, I guess I can try to be more open to her ideas.

M: Good. And perhaps you can learn to be a bit less direct with your feedback to Grace.

S: But that's just my way. You know that. I'm direct with everyone.

M: Yes, but communication is about adjusting how you talk to people.

S: Fair enough.

G: I hear what you're saying. I'll try not to take your approach personally. I can be sensitive sometimes.

M: That would be good.

G: And I'll try to be more open to asking for your opinion on what I've done, Syed. It's not that I don't respect the fact that you've been at the company longer, it's just that I'm very confident in my skills and I've brought a lot of experience with me here. Sometimes I feel that this experience is ignored.

M: Can you approach Syed with any issues you have about his ideas and not raise them in meetings in front of others, Grace?

G: Yes, but what if I raise it, Syed doesn't agree and we're back to square one? Can I not raise it in the meetings then?

M: I think you both need to accept that when one raises an issue with something, there is an issue. You can't just ignore it and do what you want. You have to listen to the other person and make some changes.

G: Fine.

S: Fine.

M: Right, so, how will you communicate with each other? Do you feel able to do this face-to-face? Or will email communication provide an opportunity for you to review what you say and how you say it before you press 'Send'?

G: Hmm, good point. Maybe we can use email as a starting point. What do you think?

S: Sure, I'm happy to do it that way. We can then meet face-to-face if we need a longer conversation.

M: OK, good. So, to review, you'll raise issues with each other via email as a starting point, moving to face-to-face if necessary. Grace, you won't raise issues at team meetings but instead you'll approach Syed privately. Syed, you'll be more open to Grace's ideas and you'll

provide any feedback requested in a less direct manner. Grace, you'll take Syed's experience at this company into account and Syed, you'll respect Grace's experience in other companies and the fact she has creative ideas to share. You'll try to work together to make sure both of those things are combined to produce great work. Does that sound right?

G: Yes, I think so.

S: Yes, that sounds right to me.

M: Good. And what happens if one of you breaks this agreement and fails to follow the promises you've made today? It's very likely to happen.

G: Hmm, well I guess we can email each other and politely remind each other about this agreement, and if we feel it's not working, we can speak to our team leader, Naomi.

S: That works for me.

M: OK, great! Let's hope this helps you both to work on the project in a more productive and enjoyable way.

UNIT 7

Audio 7.01

P = Presenter   C = Carl Hendrick

P: Now, I know we're all looking forward to this talk, so, without further ado, I'd like to introduce our speaker for today, Carl Hendrik.

C: Thank you. So, we're all familiar with the idea that there are fashions or trends in clothes and other consumer goods, with things rising to either the height of fashion or becoming completely unfashionable on an almost yearly basis. But it seems that the words we use also rise and fall in popularity, falling in and out of fashion in much the same way as other things, but over slightly longer timescales.

In a fascinating piece of research, Marcelo Montemurro and his team from the University of Manchester used a computer database to track the use of words in a detailed way. They were keen to find out how popular individual words have been in the language at different times in history, going right the way back to 1700 and extending up to the present day. The study focused on over 5,000 common nouns and what the researchers found was that over time, the use of these words rose and fell in a regular pattern, showing on the graph like a wave. Surprisingly, the length of each wave was fairly consistent, with words coming in and out of fashion in a cycle of approximately fourteen years. And it became quite clear to them that the patterns were so regular, and occurring with so many different words, that it was almost inconceivable that this was a random phenomenon. So, what factors might be influencing this cyclical popularity of words?

One possible explanation for the fourteen-year cycle is that it could be related to generations. Words that are popular or fashionable with one generation are often rejected by the next, in much the same way that younger people turn away from the clothes or house décor or food their parents like. This certainly happens with baby names such as George and Florence, which

tend to have periods of great popularity, then fall out of favour for a while, before becoming popular again as a younger age group start to have children of their own and rediscover names that were common at the time of their great-grandparents. Interestingly, the cycle of popularity for words has recently become longer by a few years, which would tie in with the fact that people are living longer and so the time between generations is extending.

But there are other factors to take into consideration. Important historical events can have a big impact on the frequency of words. For example, words such as 'space', 'rocket' and 'lunar' peaked in their use in the 1960s, at the time of the U.S. landings on the Moon. The development of new technologies can also cause words to have a spike in popularity, as people use these new technologies and also discuss them. In the 1920s, cars were first produced and used and the database shows that the words 'car', 'garage' and 'wheel' became much more popular at this time. Social issues also influence language use. For example, words such as 'climate', 'rainforest' and 'tree' have become much more common in recent years, as people talk and write about the issue of climate change.

And finally, old words may bounce back and take on a new meaning and a new life if they become popular brand names. This is certainly true for words such as 'apple', 'window' and 'twitter', which have all shown an increase in use over the last few years as a result of becoming successful product names.

However, the phenomenon of word 'cycles' could also tell us something about the nature of fashion and trends themselves. Take words such as ones meaning 'good', like 'superb', 'brilliant', 'fabulous' and 'amazing', which follow quite regular cycles of popularity. It may be that, as with all fashions, individual words gradually gain momentum and become 'trendy', up to the point where they become so common that they start to become uncool. People then naturally start to avoid them and they become much less common. After a while, they start to look more unusual and attractive again, so people start to choose them again, in much the same way as styles of clothing come back into fashion after a period of being decidedly unfashionable.

Audio 7.02

1 So, we're all familiar with the idea that there are fashions or trends in clothes and other consumer goods, with things rising to either the height of fashion or becoming completely unfashionable on an almost yearly basis.

2 Marcelo Montemurro and his team from the University of Manchester used a computer database to track the use of words in a detailed way.

3 Interestingly, the cycle of popularity for words has recently become longer by a few years.

4 After a while, they start to look more unusual and attractive again.

5 So people start to choose them again, in much the same way as styles of clothing come back into fashion after a period of being decidedly unfashionable.

Audio 7.03

1 Surprisingly, this pattern was fairly regular.
2 They used a computer database to track the use of words in a detailed way.
3 They tend to have periods of great popularity, then fall out of favour for a while.
4 Interestingly, the cycle of popularity for words has recently become longer.
5 After a while, they start to look more unusual and attractive again.

Audio 7.04

A Food fads have existed for a long time. Examples in recent years include TV dinners, chocolate fountains, avocado toast and cronuts. These days, food fads can be heavily influenced by people on social media who want to be seen as eating the latest fashionable food item, but food fads aren't all good. Sometimes they encourage people to adopt imbalanced diets which can cause them health problems.

B Food trends are nothing new. They can result in a loss of much-needed nutrients. Some of them cause our waistlines to grow. The cronut was popular once. There were chocolate fountains which were really common at weddings and other celebratory events for a while. The cronut became very popular in 2013. For a while, anyway.

Audio 7.05

1 As everyone on social media was eating *pho*, we decided to do the same.
2 Since it's fashionable to bake these days, I'm trying my hand at making bread.
3 As a result of increased globalisation, we have a huge choice of food at our disposal.
4 Because of the increase in veganism, fewer people are eating meat.

Audio 7.06

P = Presenter   T = Taruri Gatere

P: 'Vegan' is a term that was originally coined in 1944 bringing together the letters at the beginning and end of the word 'vegetarian', as the next step on. Vegetarians don't eat meat, but vegans don't eat eggs, milk or butter either. They won't wear leather or silk. They won't eat honey. Many won't wear wool. In fact, they won't use or consume anything that originally came from an animal. But the reasons people choose this way of eating, and this lifestyle, are many and varied.

T: It's a really big thing. It's the thing that people eat every single day and everything else just kind of revolves around meat.

P: Taruri Gatere is thirty-two and lives in Nairobi, Kenya.

T: It's like the centre of every single meal.

P: She first experimented with veganism when she was living in Italy.

T: I stumbled upon a challenge just to go vegan for two weeks to see how your body would feel and I was very into healthy living and so I tried it for two weeks and I just loved how my body felt.

P: How does it feel?

T: Much lighter. I didn't realise how heavy meat and dairy were in my body. It's like the sleepiness that you feel when you have a very heavy meal. That left me when I went vegan.

Audio 7.07

M = Maisie   T = Theo

M: Come on, let's go in here. It's the best shop ever.

T: Do we have to? You take forever to find something you want.

M: I don't!

T: You do! My feet are killing me and I'm starving. I just want to have lunch.

M: You'll like it, I promise. There's nothing better than shopping at a vintage store. They've got some great trainers here.

T: Wait? What? Second-hand, you mean?

M: Yeah, but ones from like the 80s and 90s. Trendy retro stuff, classic designs, that kind of thing.

T: I bet they cost a fortune.

M: Not really. Not compared to brand-new ones. Look, here's a great pair.

T: Hmm, yeah, they're quite cool actually. They're about ten sizes too small though.

M: Yeah, finding things that fit can be like finding a needle in a haystack. Shame. They'd look good on you.

T: Yeah.

M: Why don't you go over there and look at the jeans and denim jackets?

T: I've told you a million times before, I don't like denim jackets and I'm not sure how I feel about wearing old jeans. It's like sharing clothes with a stranger. It feels a little too er … intimate.

M: They've been washed! And you can always wash them again.

T: Hmm, still not sure. A leather jacket though. I've been thinking about getting one – one that looks lived in.

M: Like this one here?

T: This scruffy thing? I want one that's been lived in for a few years, not a few centuries! And it's got all these weird zips and badges.

M: It's unique. Remember when Declan wore that vintage jacket and got hundreds of likes on social media?

T: Yeah, but it's odd. And totally recognisable. What if I bump into the previous owner in the street and they say 'Hi'? I'd die of shame.

M: Oh, don't exaggerate. Go on, try something on.

T: Well, I can see some other jackets in the back. I'll go and take a look. What are you going to do?

M: I'm just going to browse and see if I can spot anything I like. I'd love an original band T-shirt.

T: Really? I wouldn't be seen dead in a pop band T-shirt.

M: Well, just you wait until I find the perfect thing. Then you'll be literally green with envy.

T: Hardly!

Audio 7.08

1 Anya's going to kill me when she finds out what I bought.
2 This shirt costs an absolute fortune!
3 I'd never be seen dead in those shoes.
4 A year old? It looks a hundred years old.

Audio 7.09

A: Our past is definitely important because it helps make us who we are today. If you think about your family background, your childhood, your experiences at school – all these things have helped to create the person you are now. So, in that way we do carry the past with us.

B: Yes, it's certainly true that we have experiences when we're young that shape our personality, our way of seeing the world. But that doesn't mean we have to still think about those experiences, keep reliving them. You can take the attitude: 'This is where I am now, and that's all I'm going to think about.' Focusing on the present allows you to deal with things that are happening in your life now, so you can move forwards in the way you want to.

A: Hmm, I'm not sure I go along with that idea because I don't believe you can really forget the important things that happen to you. You might want to forget them, but they're still in your mind, whether you like it or not, and they influence your decisions in the present. Like, if you have happy memories of doing something as a child – like cycling – you're still going to enjoy it as an adult. You can't change that and make yourself prefer something else instead.

B: I don't agree. I think if you keep an open mind and live in the present moment, you can …

Audio R7.01
Tourism trends

The world of travel is changing. We look at four current trends.

Solo travel

Holidays used to be for families, couples or groups of friends, but in recent years, there has been a shift towards travelling alone. Many people are now keen to explore new cultures in a relaxed way, without the distraction of friends or family members.

Eco travel

Influenced by concerns about climate change, a growing number of people are seeking out trips that they consider to be ethical or sustainable. As these travellers are keen to reduce their carbon footprint, they may wish to avoid flying to their destination. Eco holidays also often include some form of volunteering, which signifies a willingness to give back to the communities they are visiting.

Healthy food

Whereas in the past, many tourists were happy to grab a snack in the street, there is now a trend towards trips with healthy food options. A growing number of tourists now specify that they are more likely to stay in hotels serving fresh, organic food.

Automation

The rapid evolution of new technologies is bringing a range of changes in the tourism industry. Customers use chatbots to help them book their trips online, and some top-end hotels are also introducing robot receptionists to greet guests.

Audio 8.01
S = Shabnam Grewal   G = Gregory Claeys

S: What is a dystopia? The word was first used by the philosopher John Stuart Mill to mean an imaginary place or condition in which everything is as bad as possible. The opposite of utopia.

G: If we think of utopia as a society in which people have much stronger engaged social bonds between one another, at the opposite end of the spectrum is precisely the negation or absence of these bonds.

S: This is Gregory Claeys, an academic and a historian of the future, who's written a lot about dystopias and refines the definition to mean …

G: A society which is dominated by fear, so each individual is isolated from every other; every individual is made to feel paranoid about every individual, so the essential juxtaposition here is utopia's oriented towards a maximisation of friendship; dystopia's a maximisation of fear.

Audio 8.02

1 Even though it's said that young people don't read anymore, many of them do.

2 Fiction can be shocking, but at the same time true stories can be more shocking.

3 Admittedly, dystopian stories don't sound positive, but they can be very uplifting.

4 True as that may be, not everyone has the same taste in fiction.

Audio 8.03

P = Presenter   S = Sian

P: Hello and welcome to *The Technology Show*. Now, there are plenty of examples of past inventions that have benefited individuals and societies on a great scale, like electric lights, for example, or satellite navigation. So, this week, we're talking about some possible new inventions that could have similarly huge benefits in the next ten years. With me is Sian Connor, who has written a book called *Inventions that could change the world*. Welcome to the show, Sian.

S: Hi.

P: So, you're interested in the idea that a fairly simple invention can have quite far-reaching advantages.

S: Yes. Technology is a tool that we use to solve problems and the world is facing a lot of very significant issues at the moment, such as the climate crisis, to mention the most obvious. And I'm interested in the fact that the solutions to these problems won't necessarily come from ground-breaking inventions that completely revolutionise our lives, but from fairly small, simple inventions that can make quite a significant difference.

P: OK. So, I know you want to talk to us about three ideas in particular today. You're going to tell us about each one and speculate on how far it could transform our lives. What's up first?

S: The first one is a type of fabric that generates electricity from your body heat when you touch it. Now, we know that finding alternative energy sources to fossil fuels is one of today's real challenges, so anything that can generate clean energy is clearly a great idea.

P: And how could something so simple have such a huge impact?

S: Well, quite simply, it could be used in so many different situations. For example, it could be used on car seats, so when you sit on it, the fabric could generate sufficient electricity to run the car's air-conditioning, or on furniture in the home,

where it could power the lights in the room. Or you could have a jacket made of the fabric, which would then generate electricity to power your phone. These sound like small amounts of energy – and they are – but if the fabric was used widely enough in day-to-day situations, they could add up to substantial amounts.

P: And how likely is it that it will actually be developed?

S: Well, the technology is already there in theory, so it's already possible to produce the fabric, but there are still a couple of technical obstacles and the costs of large-scale production are currently too high. But I'm fairly optimistic that within the next ten years, these technical issues will have been addressed. I'm also hopeful that the costs will have come down by then and we'll be wearing clothes and sitting on furniture that generate power for us.

P: That sounds interesting. And what's your next invention?

S: Well, this is an app that you can use to scan your food and detect and measure its nutritional content. We're all used to reading nutritional information on food packaging we buy in supermarkets, but what about when we eat street food? There's no way of knowing exactly how many calories are in what we're eating or what it contains in terms of protein, vitamins, etc. The idea would be that you would take a photo of the food you're planning to eat and get information on how healthy or unhealthy it is before you buy it. There are so many foods out there that are high in calories but low in nutrition, so an invention like this would be incredibly useful in helping people to make better food choices. In the longer term, this could even translate into much less pressure on health services in many countries.

P: Ooh, no more tasty treats?

S: Well, it might encourage food sellers to improve the nutritional make-up of their dishes, which would benefit all of us.

P: That's true. And how likely is this one?

S: Well, a couple of companies have tried producing and selling apps like this, but they haven't been that reliable and they haven't caught on at all. If I'm honest, I don't think the technology is quite there yet, and I'm not sure it ever will be. It would require some incredibly complicated software to be able to analyse all the different ingredients in a dish. And also, people don't necessarily want to make sensible choices when they're out relaxing and enjoying themselves! So, my guess is we won't be using food-scanner apps any time soon.

P: That's a shame – it's a nice idea!

S: Yes. But the third technology I want to talk about might be more achievable – a shower that recycles its own water. Water is a resource that's under a lot of pressure in some parts of the world already and it's going to become much more of an issue over the next ten years. Daily showers mean that a lot of water is wasted, so how about a shower that collects the waste water, passes it through a cleaning system to purify it and then recycles it back into the system to be used again? The idea is also that as

the water is cleaned, it is heated slightly, which means it's ready for your next shower.

P: That sounds like such a simple idea, impressive. And how likely do you think it is to be developed?

S: Well, some systems are already being developed and it's likely that they'll have made it to the market within the next few years. A shower system like this could save up to ninety percent of the water we use when we shower, and the great news is that a small version of this technology could be used in individual homes or larger versions could be used for whole apartment blocks, so even bigger savings on water could be made.

P: Amazing. So, in ten years' time do you predict this invention will be in use?

S: Yes. I think by then, architects will have been building these kinds of systems into new homes for a while. But it will obviously take a bit longer for them to be installed in existing homes.

P: Well, it's good to end on a hopeful note. Thanks, Sian, for talking us through these three …

Audio 8.04

1 I'm optimistic that scientists will've found a way around this issue.

2 These devices are a great idea and I'm sure they'll've become very popular within a few years.

3 Hopefully, this invention will've been developed soon.

4 It's a serious problem, but experts predict it'll've been solved in the next few years.

Audio 8.05

A = Alina   O = Oscar   B = Beth

A: I was reading something this morning about the FIRE movement – have you heard of it?

O: Oh, yeah. Isn't that when people try to save as much as they can while they're young, so they can retire early?

A: That's right. I'm not sure what to make of it. What do you think, Beth?

B: Well, frankly Alina, I think it's a stupid idea! As I see it, the future is completely unpredictable. I mean, you could spend your twenties and thirties never doing anything fun and just saving all your earnings, then find you aren't fit and well enough to travel or do exciting things when you're older.

O: Point taken, Beth. But the other side of the coin is that it's very easy to waste all the money you earn in your twenties – pricey meals out, holidays, things like that. You could end up at the age of fifty having worked for thirty years, but with nothing to show for it.

B: I guess that's one way of looking at it, but on the other hand, if you focus all your efforts on the future, there's a danger you won't enjoy the present. I'm all for living in the moment and enjoying life while you can!

A: That makes two of us. It's definitely important to enjoy yourself while you're young and I certainly couldn't give up going out and having holidays. But I can see what Oscar's saying, and I dare say most young people could save a small amount each month if they put their minds to it. They wouldn't have to give up fun completely!

O: I'm with Alina here. I reckon most people our age could save a lot of money if they were just a bit more careful about their spending.

B: Well, you'll never convince me that I should give up all the things I enjoy. But it's been great talking to you. I guess we're all different.

Audio 8.06

1 Isn't that when people try to save as much as they can while they're young, so they can retire early?

2 I guess that's one way of looking at it, but on the other hand, if you focus all your efforts on the future, there's a danger you won't enjoy the present. I'm all for living in the moment and enjoying life while you can!

3 Well, you'll never convince me that I should give up all the things I enjoy. But it's been great talking to you. I guess we're all different.

Audioscript 8.07

The story is set in the near future and the plot is fairly straightforward. During a mission to Mars, astronaut Mark Watney is injured by a piece of flying metal during a fierce storm. Believing him to be dead, his crew leave him behind and set off back to Earth. But Watney survives his injuries and awakes to find himself alone on Mars. Watney then has to use all his skills and ingenuity to survive and find a way to signal to Earth that he's still alive and in need of rescue. It's a race against time because he cannot survive forever with limited food supplies and in such hostile conditions. The authorities back on Earth are unwilling to send a mission back to Mars to rescue him, but his own crew decide to go it alone and head back to pick him up. The tension rises as Watney's living conditions deteriorate and he starts to run out of food, while the crew have to overcome many obstacles on their return flight to Mars. As the film builds to its climax, Watney becomes a media sensation back on Earth, with the whole world watching the daring rescue attempt. Of course, it's successful and Watney returns to Earth to a hero's welcome!

UNIT 8 REVIEW

Audio R8.01
Technology utopia

A technology utopia is a utopia where technology is used to solve all of the world's problems. In this utopian world, technology converts the pollutants which factory chimneys emit into gases which are not hazardous to the environment. Technology eliminates hunger and disease. It gets rid of unemployment, and so everyone earning a steady income can then pay for food and energy essentials, and no longer has to be frugal just to survive. Technology creates energy-efficient transportation and communication systems which are available to all, no matter where they live in the world. Basically, technology creates a world of peace and harmony. Admittedly, achieving this kind of utopia is probably near impossible, but if we can invest in technology that will help us to solve global problems rather than help people make money, we might just be able to create a technology paradise.

UNIT 8 MEDIATION BANK

Audio MB8.01

A: So, how are we going to get the money then? It means saving quite a lot over the next year.

B: Well, we could stop going out for a year. That'd save a lot.

A: A whole year? Not sure I could cope with that!

C: I don't think I could stay in for a whole year either but that gives me an idea. We could do more free stuff, you know, activities that don't cost anything. Not everything has to involve food or partying.

A: That's a good idea. Team sports at the park, they don't cost anything. We could go on bike rides, picnics, walks. We could also organise film nights …

B: Film nights would be fun. We could substitute films with games and have games nights, too. We'll have plenty of games between us, we won't have to buy anything.

C: If we made them competitive, that would be even better.

B: But competition means prizes and prizes cost money so I'm not sure that works.

A: It would work if we were creative with the prizes.

C: I know. Rather than monetary prizes, we could offer prizes of time. So, losers have to do something for the winner that involves time – cleaning their car, cooking a meal for them, that kind of thing.

A: Oh, that's genius! One thing I'm worried about, though, is actually putting the money we save aside. I mean, I'm pretty good at spending whatever's in my wallet, so how do I make sure that I don't just spend the money I save on something else?

B: Good point.

C: Er, I heard about this saving scheme where you save money every day. So on the first day, you save a penny. On the second day, two pence. On the third day, three pence, all the way up to day 365 when you save 365 pence – so £3.65.

A: How much does that get you overall?

B: About £670, I think. If we each do that, we'll have more than enough.

C: I guess we won't miss a few pence here and there. It might be difficult to do over the last couple of months, though. We'd have to save two to almost four pounds a day. That's my morning coffee and breakfast. I can't give that up!

B: True!

A: Hmm, how about we change it to a joint challenge for the last three months and not an individual one?

B: What do you mean?

A: Let's save the required amount each day between us in the last three months. So, on the last day, it'll be £3.65 between us rather than each, so not much more than £1.20 each. We wouldn't save as much overall, and I'd need to work it out, but I think we'd still have enough.

C: That works for me. I think I could manage that.

B: Me too. OK, great. Who's setting up the first games night then? And where are we going to save this money to make sure we don't spend it?

UNIT 1

Opener: BBC Vlogs

1 If I think about things which are important to me, probably near the top of the list is my glasses. I have really bad eyesight and last year I, I lost them in the sea and I had a very difficult week.

2 One place that is very important for me is my home country – Greece. I have lived abroad for many years, so every time I get the opportunity to go back home, I really appreciate being connected to my culture, having Greek food, listening to Greek music – it's very special for me.

3 Obviously Sheffield. I went to uni here, studied here for three years and I always wanted to come back and live here. It's a gorgeous city. It's got a tight sense of community for a larger city. It's very green, there's lots of trees, beautiful parks. You've got the Peak District on your doorstep. It's great!

4 An important place to me is the beach. I really like going to the beach because I find it relaxing and calming and I'm lucky enough to live by one where I am now.

5 A place special to me is London, more specifically North London, and it's a place where in the early 70s and 80s I grew up, and as a young family we would enjoy picnics down by the River Thames, trips to London Zoo and playing around in the parks of 'Ally Pally' and the various parks around where we used to live. And even thirty-seven years on, it still holds a special draw for me and it's a place I will always call home. That's why North London's special to me.

1D: BBC Street Interviews
Exs 2A and 2B

Abiha:	I love food so much. I love food from all around the world. Er, my favourite would probably be Italian because I love pasta and all the carbs that come with it.
Meg:	Food is pretty crucial in my life. Er, I get pretty angry if I don't have food when I want it. Er, I get a headache when I don't eat, so food is important for energy and general happiness in my life.
Anugraha:	Well, in being an Indian, food is what we grow up around – a lot. We love our spices, so obviously we are very specific to our tastes and we can't compromise on taste so we love our spices. So yeah, it's really important so we try to bring salt and pepper all the time … and if possible, chillies!
Phoebe:	Food is very important. I love trying different foods and I love going out for meals to different places, so, very important.
Shravash:	I mean I cannot describe in words. I come from a very cultural society, that's Indian, and India is all about food and bonding over food, so I really enjoy having all my Indian meals all the time with family and it's, it's a very integral part of our life and our culture and our society as a whole. So, yeah.

Exs 2A and 2C

Abiha:	Yes, my comfort food is cheese – melted cheese, soft cheese, hard cheese – any cheese. So, yesterday I made a pasta bake, which is my favourite food and it was incredible, it was amazing and it made me feel like the happiest girl in the world.
Meg:	Er, I think my comfort food would be any kind of chocolate, er, when I'm sad I just really want a brownie – it's sweet and rich and delicious.
Anugraha:	So, when I come back after a big, long shift, er, I'm looking for something to calm me down a bit. So, something hot, which is coffee – if it's considered as a food!
Phoebe:	My comfort food is a burger and chips because it's delicious and it's filling and I can eat it with my hands and it's very greasy – and I like that.
Shravash:	So, er, as you know I come from India and a lot, a lot of dishes come to my mind right now, but the one thing which is popping up is *chole bhature*. It's like a traditional Indian food, it's, it's made of chickpea and fried doughballs. It's very spicy, full of … it's very delicious and I just, I just, I'm out of words right now. I cannot describe how amazing it is – and you guys should definitely try some of these Indian restaurants around and see and have the whole experience of your own ones.

UNIT 2

Opener: BBC Vlogs

1 Much as I wouldn't like to admit it, I think I am pretty competitive. You know, if I'm playing a video game or football or something like that, I always want to win and I get pretty annoyed if I don't.

2 So, I would say I'm not generally very competitive with other people, but I am very competitive with myself, so I think I challenge … I like to push myself and challenge myself, for example doing sports. I like to push my body and train better than I did before. Or in board games, I, maybe I am a little bit competitive with people sometimes.

3 I'm a very competitive person, simply because I'm a boxer, and I've been competitive for most of my life. So, I carry that different aspect of my day and of my life in general.

4 My husband and I are very competitive in the kitchen, when we're cooking our family meals.

5 When my kids were young, I really wanted them to do brilliantly at everything they did, whether that's sport, arts, music, whatever. Other parents might tell you otherwise, but secretly you want your kids to be the best.

6 I'm not very competitive about how much I earn or whether I get a promotion at work, but I am competitive about things that don't matter, like video games or quizzes.

7 I think I'm competitive in most things that I do. I don't think anyone enjoys losing, particularly in sports. Having said that, I would rather play well and lose than play badly and win.

2D: BBC Entertainment
Exs 2A and 2B

Mist:	My definition of a petrolhead is going fast, customising cars.
Ryan Thomas:	My relationship with cars started when I was sixteen years old. Anything I could get my hands on with an engine. Right. Come on, guys. Put me out of my misery, what are we doing here?
Luke:	Good luck, mate.
Ryan Thomas:	Your challenge is to go head-to-head in the first ever Gassed Up Gymkhana. You have full control over the car you start with. What you do next is down to you.
Voiceover:	Gymkhana is a serious motorsport, featuring stunts like 360 spins, figure of eights, obstacles, plus the mental challenge of knowing the unmarked course inside and out.
Mist:	So right now, we're in Corby. Get in here!
Ryan Taylor:	I did not expect this. All I can see is a bunch of toy cars. I think he might have gone too far with this one. Mine's going backwards!
Ryan Thomas:	All I really wanna know is, do the lights come up? Yes! This is the car! You've got a lot to take in in one day, but I did have the expertise of Luke.
Luke:	Go, go, go, go, go. Now!
Both:	Yes! That was sick!
Luke:	That was sick!
Ryan Thomas:	Mate! Thanks so much!
Luke:	That was sick!
Andy:	Three, two, one, go! Good, brake, better, better, better, better. Go on! Straighten it up! Very good!
Luke:	Head-to-head racing. Fans having three rounds. So, you go off the starting line, straight up the inside. You do a full 360 rotation, head to the boxes – figure of eight through them. Zigzag through the obstacles at the end. You go back to the start as fast as you can. Best of three wins.
Becky Evans:	You got this. Come on.
Ryan Thomas:	The nerves are kicking in now.
Ryan Taylor:	I think you got this, bro.
Mist:	Yo, buddy.
Luke:	Go! They're neck and neck. It's neck and neck. He's going, he's going. He's going again …
Becky Evans:	Nice, nice, nice.
Ryan Taylor:	Go on!

Becky Evans:	Handbrake!
Luke:	Drivers: three, two, one. Go!
Becky Evans	Get in!
Ryan Taylor:	Let's go, bro.
Becky Evans:	Perfect! Perfect! The competition was actually fierce. They were neck and neck after two laps. Mist had had a bad lap, Ryan had had a bad lap, so it all came down to that one last run.
Luke:	Drivers ready: three, two, one. Go! That's what I'm talking about. The pair of you drove, like, really, really well. The winner of Gassed Up Gymkhana …
Ryan Thomas:	Yes! I won! What an amazing feeling. I love Mist. He took it really well.
Mist:	The best man won, innit. He won on that day. He did his best.
Ryan Thomas:	We were both winners, man.
Mist:	You're a sportsman. You ain't.

UNIT 3

Opener: BBC Vlogs

1 The main way I like to be creative is by writing poetry. I like the way that you can play with words and language to make rhymes or kind of express how you're feeling in a different way from just a normal conversation.

2 I think I get most creative when I'm cooking. I sometimes follow recipes, but most times I don't, and sometimes the result is great, sometimes it's not so great, but at least it's mine.

3 I express my creativity primarily through photography. It's one of my passions. I've been doing photography for many years, and I love capturing moments in my day-to-day life that might be very simple, very everyday moments, but they carry something very special for me. And I love capturing these through an image.

4 I think one way I express my creativity is through the clothes I wear. I really love to buy second-hand clothing off eBay and from charity shops, and I like to curate my outfits. I'm very drawn to colours and prints and natural fibres. And I think it's a more sustainable way of enjoying buying things and spending money.

5 I express creativity in my life through drawing. Mainly doodling, because I find doodling is a lot freer and less restrictive. I think the most creative people on the planet are children, so it's important to stay in touch with your inner child and have lots of fun.

3D: BBC Street Interviews
Exs 2A and 2B

Sarmini:	Erm, I think two people that inspire me are my parents. It sounds really clichéd, but, erm, they make me strive to be better all the time.
Camille:	Erm, my father has really inspired me with how hard he works for our family, and how much love he gives to us.
Tunnvane:	Um, Shackleton, who led the *Endurance* expedition, has inspired me. He inspired me because he taught that changing your goal when your goal can't be achieved is a better idea than carrying on with a goal that will fail.
Gerry:	Erm, the woman that has inspired me in my life is Oprah Winfrey. She is a black female TV presenter who owns her own network. She inspires me because she's come from very humble beginnings and, against all the challenges of being a black woman in America, has managed to own her own company and meet Barack Obama.
Kieran:	Er, I think probably one of my science teachers when I was studying. He was really encouraging and helped me a lot to get into university.
Kwame:	I'd like to say my parents. I know that's a common thing but I think I'll stick with my parents. As I get older, I realise how … how much they helped me, how much they supported me, encouraged me to do things that I maybe didn't want to do, erm, pushed me to my limits, but then also when there was a few obstacles they were there to, you know, kind of help me if I failed, or something like that, you know.

Exs 2A and 2C

Sarmini:	Er, I think a good role model is someone who inspires people through the hidden things that they do.
Camille:	Wow. Erm, kindness and honesty and people who live authentically. Yeah, yeah.
Tunnvane:	Um, you can't expect perfection. I think a good role model is somebody who teaches you things that you can use to make you a better person.
Gerry:	Erm, the characteristics that I believe make a good role model is somebody that can listen, that can support and can give you time.
Kieran:	Erm, being enthusiastic about what you do I think helps. Erm, it's really important because when someone enjoys the things that they do, that rubs off on other people.
Kwame:	Patience – I think patience is a key one. Erm, a good sense of humour – for me personally it was a good sense of humour. Being a leader, knowing when to be a leader, but then also when to, to care for people because not everyone is the same and erm, just, I mean for me, my role model, they were very understanding. I think that's the most important thing, being understanding of the other people, of the individual. I think that's really important.

UNIT 4

Opener: BBC Vlogs

1 Well, I don't spend a lot of money on clothes, but I do try to make an effort when I go out. So, I guess that image is important to me in a way, yeah.

2 I think image is much less important to me now than it once was. When I was much younger, I definitely wanted to project a certain kind of image and I chose my clothes and the way I had my hair cut with that image in mind. I think it was rather artificial. And now I guess if I'm meeting new people, I'm mildly conscious of the kind of image I want to present. But, erm, essentially, I'm now just very much more comfortable being me.

3 Image to me is very important. I like being able to see people that look like me or members of my family in everyday places, such as television, in books or in magazines.

4 Image is important when you're making a first impression, but I feel you should always be yourself.

5 When I was a teenager, image was important to me – the clothes that I wore, the music that I listened to – it all said something about me. People knew who I was. I had that sense of belonging. As time moves on you realise, though, that's very superficial. What somebody looks like tells you nothing about them as a person. It's what's underneath that matters – what they say and what they do. That's the key thing.

6 Image is of relative importance to me. I would like to appear put together and polished, for sure, and maintain good social record. But, it's not as important to me as authenticity. I think it's way more important to stay true to yourself and act on your values in different situations that life throws at you.

4D: BBC Documentary
Exs 2A and 2B

Presenter:	I'm going to put the claims on cosmetics to the test. I want to find out the truth about looking good. The marketing and branding of products clearly play a powerful role in why we buy them. So, to find out more about how these factors influence our shopping decisions, I've invited consumer psychologist Dr Omar Yousef from the University of Bath.
Omar:	So often there's a discrepancy between why we think we buy a product and why we actually buy it. There are other forces at play.
Presenter:	Because there are other factors at play, does that leave us as the consumers very vulnerable to manipulation?
Omar:	Yeah, our vulnerabilities as consumers are not always evident to ourselves so the question is what's driving your decision-making process?

Presenter: To look at what factors affect our shopping decisions, we're setting up a little experiment. We're going to sell our very own face cleanser called Face in two very different ways. We want to see how packaging and the sales assistant's appearance affect what our Beauty Lab customers buy. First up, we've put the cleanser in a no-frills packaging and sales assistant Jo is in casual clothes to welcome our first group of customers through the door.

Jo: Hi.

Customer: Hello.

Jo: Hi. Would you like to take a look at our new cleansing product?

Customer: Yep.

Presenter: If a customer says they would buy the product, it goes in the basket.

Customer: Smells nice.

Jo: Would you buy this product?

Customer: I'm very about packaging, it doesn't really fill me with confidence.

Jo: Would you buy this product?

Customer: Erm no. Probably not.

Customer: I kind of probably wouldn't.

Presenter: After two hours and eighteen customers through the door, just three said they would buy it. Time for stage two of the experiment. The product has been given a makeover and so has sales assistant Jo – both have been made to look more scientific … and more glamorous. So, what will our next group of customers think?

Jo: Hiya!

Customer: Hi!

Jo: Hi, would you like to take a look at our new cleansing product?

Customer: Smells like … minty.

Customer: I like the smell.

Jo: Yes, maybe, no?

Customer: Yes definitely.

Customer: Looking at it, yeah, I would.

Customer: It smells lovely.

Presenter: After the last customers have visited the counter, Omar has the results. So how much effect did the different look of the identical product really have?

Omar: Right, so with the first product we had three people who were actually willing to buy that straightaway. Whereas the other one, we had eight.

Presenter: Same product, just a different bottle.

Omar: That's it.

Presenter: When the face cleanser looked more luxurious and scientific, our customers were more than twice as likely to buy it.

Omar: What we tried to do was to make this product a status product giving it this sense of quality. The other element was we had the seller wear a lab coat. So just gives it this aura of credibility, confidence.

Presenter: The effect of packaging and science on sales is interesting. But it wasn't actually the main thing that Omar was testing.

Jo: Would you be willing to do a survey about this product?

Customer: Yeah.

Presenter: Our beauty lab customers were also asked to complete a questionnaire.

Customer: Yeah, course.

Jo: It would be really helpful, thank you.

Presenter: They thought this was simply market research. But Omar was really looking at how the product affected the way they feel about themselves. He measured each customer's self-esteem at the point of making their purchasing decision.

Omar: What we found was that self-esteem was higher for the cheap product – or the more basic one – compared to the higher one. So, what happens is that when you observe the luxury products, it's likely to drop your self-esteem and as a result you are more likely to then compensate for that by buying the product to elevate the self-esteem.

Presenter: What?
Omar found that our customers actually felt worse about themselves when shopping for the luxury-looking products compared to the ones that looked more basic, and this makes us more likely to buy them.

Omar: A very interesting theory we have in psychology is Self-Discrepancy Theory. It proposes that we have an actual self and we have an ideal self. Sometimes there's a gap between the two and what happens then is we feel a drive to reduce that gap. It creates an ideal, something to be aspiring towards.

Presenter: Because look, here are these gorgeous people and here is an aspirational product.

Omar: That's it.

Presenter: So, it creates the insecurity and then it takes it away.

Omar: Takes it away.

Presenter: In my mind.

Omar: In your mind.

Presenter: So, it seems like the luxury-looking products and the sales tactics can give us lower self-esteem, which is exactly why they can be so tempting to buy.

UNIT 5

Opener: BBC Vlogs

1 A big change in my life recently is that I have moved abroad. I spent four and a half years living in a city in the south-west of England, but I recently quit my job, and I've moved abroad and I'm now currently living in the south of Spain instead.

2 So, a change for me is I've been working from home quite a lot lately. Although it has benefits, like more time with the family, it's sometimes hard to stay focused and motivated to be honest as well.

3 A big change in my life recently is that I've graduated from uni. Now I'm starting work tomorrow and it's a bit daunting. I think it'll be a learning curve.

4 I've had lots of changes in my life recently. I started a new job, I got married and soon I'm going to be moving into a new home. Lots of my friends and family are also having lots of life changes at the moment, too, so it's an exciting time. It's hard to keep up sometimes.

5 Well, I guess one of the biggest change[s] in my life recently has been moving to a different country. I lived in London for many years, but recently I decided to move to Madrid, Spain … and it's been a huge change in terms of language, culture, people, but it was one that I really wanted to try and I'm not regretting it at all.

6 A recent change for me is that I have been travelling a lot less. I used to travel quite a lot and over the last four or five years I've been doing so less and less. I've just become more selective about where I want to go and who I want to see.

5D: BBC Street Interviews
Exs 2A and 2B

David: I'm not really a creature of habit, but I like to do things as they come along and not really plan ahead too much.

Becki: Erm, I don't like change. It makes me, it makes me nervous. So, there's lots of things – the way I work, the programs I use, the TV I watch – it's all very similar, sort of every day really.

Abdullahi: The first one I can think of is that I brush my teeth exactly the same way. Don't know why, but I have some kind of rhythm.

Emma: Uh, I do. It's a little funny, but every time I'm getting dressed I always put my socks on first, then the pants and then the rest of the outfit. I don't know why, but that's my habit every single day.

Loona: Yes, yes there is. So, every morning I make myself a cup of tea and it has to have precisely one and a half teaspoons of Assam tea in it, exactly the same amount of milk.

Exs 2A and 2C

David: I think it can be a good thing, so if you've planned for, to do something, you know what steps you need to take. But on the opposite side, it can be a bad thing. If you've planned for something to happen a certain way and it doesn't, you might not have a back-up plan, so you may not be able to adapt to that situation.

Becki: It depends. For me, I'm trying to be less a creature of habit because [I] get stuck in the same sort of cycles of doing the same thing and if you break out of it, you can learn more things, you can meet more people, you can … you might find something that you've always sort of disregarded that, actually, is something that you really enjoy doing or something that works really well for you. So, I think it can be good because it's a source of comfort, but it also can be a bad thing because it gets you stuck in, in a rut.

Abdullahi: Definitely a good thing 'cos you, it's a little bit of stability in this world, so like, I know no matter what my day looks like, those things that I've done are, d'you know, give me a little bit of control of the day, so definitely a good thing – if they're good habits at least.

Emma: I think so. It gives you a sense of comfort, er, in things where a lot of moments in your life you don't really have very much control, so, being a creature of habit does allow [you] to kind of feel like you're doing something right, even if the rest of your day goes totally awry.

Loona: I think the formation of good habits is a good thing. Um, but it's also good to break up your habits, 'cos I think breaking up habits, erm, spurs on creativity and it allows you to go outside your comfort zone, which, which kind of improves you.

UNIT 6

Opener: BBC Vlogs

1 Recently I was visiting some friends in Newcastle, and we were out late and I realised I was going to miss my train. So, I ran to the station, jumped on the first train that I saw and after it had left the platform, I realised it was going north and not south. So, it took me quite a long time to get home.

2 So, recently while I was cooking, I had a bit of a mistake where I put way too much salt into my curry that I was making and completely ruined it.

3 Recently, I actually forgot to take my bin out. Typically, we have our bins collected once a week or once a fortnight and I forgot to take mine out, which meant that I had to wake up really early the next morning and try to beat the binmen in my dressing gown and slippers, which was quite cold. And now I know to remember to put a reminder on my phone and remember next time to take it out the night before.

4 I forgot my sister's birthday recently and I felt awful about that. And she's such a nice person, she was like, 'Oh no, don't worry. I got lots of cards and things,' but I knew in the bottom of her heart she was secretly very angry with me.

5 A recent mistake that I made was a few weeks ago. I called a good friend of mine for her birthday – I don't see her that often – the day after I realised I had got the date wrong, but she had been too polite to say anything, so no harm done.

6 I just recently bought the wrong size of tennis shoes for my son. I bought them online and when I got them, when he tried them on, I realised that I bought them too big.

6D: BBC Comedy
Exs 2A and B

Adam: Welcome to your virtual PA. One unified system that changes the game, integrates your world, syncs you with everything and everyone around you without you doing anything. Syncs you to the BBC itself in real time, wirelessly, continuously and in real time. Eleven years in development, guys, and everyone, I give you Syncopatico.

Ian: I mean obviously anything to do with Syncopatico's always a bit …

Will: Yeah.

Ian: But at some point during the morning I seem to have got all your events in my 'SyncopatiCal'.

Voiceover: Meanwhile, in his new official capacity as Assistant to the Head of Values, Will is already making a big difference to Ian's working life.

Ian: In the meantime, I don't know where my events have gone.

Will: Yeah.

Ian: They've disappeared completely.

Will: Yeah, no, they're all here.

Ian: What?

Will: Yeah, no, it does that.

Voiceover: Keen to learn, he's passed the first half of the crucial 'SyncopatiShare' module of his ongoing BBC 'Syncopatico' induction course with flying colours. But until he's done the second half, he's unable to stop his new 'Syncopatipad' shaking hands automatically with other devices that may stray into its sights.

Ian: I mean I know it's not your fault, Will.

Will: Yeah.

Ian: Although, actually now I think about it I'm not sure I am sure, about that.

Will: Yeah, no, cool, like no worries. Like, why don't you just have mine?

Ian: What?

Will: And I'll have yours – just till, like, something happens.

Ian: Right, but.

Will: Like, I've only just thought of that.

Ian: Yes, I know. I can tell.

Voiceover: But even though he's still new to some of the responsibilities of a personal assistant, Will is not afraid of having big ideas.

Ian: No, I don't think … I mean what if this starts shaking hands with other tablets all over the place?

Will: Yeah.

Ian: Oh no, hang on. You've got some of Simon Harwood's stuff as well.

Will: Yeah.

Ian: Look, no, I'm sorry Will, I can't, I mean this is really …

Will: 'Cos like I had to go into Simon's Harwood's office earlier – I was looking for Izzy – and like it shook hands with him, too.

Ian: Yes.

Will: And then it stopped again when I went.

Ian: Mm.

Will: Yeah, I don't know, yeah.

Ian: No.

Will: Like it's actually really annoying?

Ian: So does this … ? I mean, could I … ? If I wanted to, I mean, would I be able to print this out?

Will: Yeah, no worries, yeah, cool.

Ian: So what, do I just …

Will: Yeah, no, we 'cos we did 'SyncopatiPrint' last week.

Ian: You sure about this, Will?

Will: Yeah no, 'cos like, you can print to any printer anywhere in the building. Like, it doesn't matter where you are.

Ian: 'Cos I wouldn't necessarily want anyone else to …

Will: Yeah, no cool yeah. OK done. Cool.

Ian: Great.

Will: Yeah, no worries.

Ian: So where's it printing?

Will: Yeah, no, co … Say again?

Ian: Which printer's it printing at?

Will: Yeah, no, it doesn't tell you that.

Ian: It doesn't tell you?

Will: Like, it could be literally any printer, anywhere in the building.

Ian: Right.

Will: Yeah, no, it's pretty cool.

Ian: Yes.

UNIT 7

Opener: BBC Vlogs

1 I would say that vegetarianism and veganism have become very popular over the past few years in the UK. I'm vegan myself and I've not … and I've noticed that a lot of people my age are at least reducing their consumption of meats and fish, or if not, going vegetarian or vegan.

2 Wild swimming is really popular at the moment. I've enjoyed swimming in the sea all winter. It's quite cold – my husband doesn't like it very much – but it's really good because he holds my towel.

3 I think a trend that I've noticed over the last few years, definitely in Ireland, where I am at the moment, is that people are becoming a lot more climate conscious. It's not just younger people, it's across the generations. People are making more informed choices about their energy sources, about how, about where they get their food, how their food is packaged and I think it's a really positive trend.

4 A trend that I've noticed recently amongst my friends is extreme sports. Everyone seems to be training for a marathon or a triathlon or some open swim or big cycle trip or something. It seems like just going for a run or going for a cycle is not enough anymore.

5 I think the most prominent trend at the moment in Amsterdam is the rising of house prices. It's er, it's gone up twenty percent in the last year and twenty percent the year before that. So it really is increasing at a dramatic rate.

6 One trend I've noticed is dogs with long ears, particularly cocker spaniels, actually always cocker spaniels, wearing headbands. It's to keep their ears out of the dirt and also out of their food dishes, but I just think that they look really stupid.

D: BBC Street Interviews
2A and 2B

It's often the weather, erm, seeing leaves on the ground a certain colour, around certain trees. Being in the park and the ground is orange rather than green. Erm, yeah it's just scenery really.

Oh – watching old movies or home videos.

Um, seeing friends I hadn't seen in a long time.

...se: Um, smells can make me feel really nostalgic. So, for example, I was playing with my daughter the other day and we were playing with plasticine and that smell just took me back to my childhood and playing with plasticine as a kid as well.

...uel: Erm, 2000s pop music. It reminds me of driving in the car with my mum, in, when I was younger.

Cartoon movies, animation.

Videos from friends from far away and specific types of food and smells. Yeah.

...en: Erm, scents make me feel nostalgic, erm, the smell of coffee in the morning reminds me of growing up and my parents having coffee on. Erm, smells of the beach reminds me of being there and being by the sea and the scent of jasmine reminds me of jasmine bushes outside my home growing up.

and 2C

I grew up in Uganda and I used to love summer holidays because we'd get sent off to the village and we'd just run around in the wildlife, chasing chameleons and running away from goats – all sorts of crazy things that you'd just do in the village in rural Africa.

I would say being able to believe you could do anything. It was, we were always given that opportunity to imagine everything so I would say that, that's probably one of my favourite things from my childhood, yeah.

And for me, it was always doing sport every day, being forced to work as a team and work with your friends, you know, pushing through the, you know, the tension and the, you know the win and the competition – all sort of helps you to be a better person, and keep you fit at the same time.

...e: Erm, I think people were slower and we spent more time doing one thing at a time. Erm, that felt really nice.

Tilly: Erm, so school – erm, I had more routine back then, whereas now I don't really know what to do with my day sometimes.

Samuel: Erm, this is probably really out of the works, but I miss parks. I feel at my age I can't go sit on a swing or a seesaw, 'cos I'm too big. So I really miss just going to the park.

Joy: There was no expectations and no responsibilities. Yeah.

Lauren: Erm, I think the lack of internet meant that we had to, erm, be a bit more adventurous and, erm, to think of different ways to entertain ourselves. You saw your friends more rather than on screens, erm, and it meant that you went out to cinemas and things like that more and had to, yeah, find different ways to entertain yourself.

UNIT 8

Opener: BBC Vlogs

1 I generally feel quite pessimistic about the future, but I think that's because I tend to worry about what things could go wrong. It does also mean though that I tend to be pleasantly surprised when things inevitably do turn out OK.

2 Generally, I'm optimistic about the future. Even though we have serious problems, we have better science and technology than ever to solve them.

3 I generally feel optimistic about the future, so I guess I believe that people are innately good and there are challenges, but we always seem to get over them one way or another. And, and there's lots to enjoy in life and I think that that will continue to be the case.

4 I'm afraid I'm something of a pessimist when it comes to the future. I spent my childhood reading history books about all the terrible things that people did to each other, and I look around me now, and I see all of the same things still happening, so it seems we're not learning and we're not moving on.

5 I would say in general, on balance, I am quite optimistic about the future. I think that technological developments will provide solutions to many of the problems we might be facing now. And I also have a lot of confidence in the younger generations coming through. They're quite creative and I think they will be quite well equipped to deal with any issues we have in the future.

6 Generally, I'm feeling quite optimistic about the future. I'm really excited to see what happens in my career, in my life, all the people I'm gonna meet and all the places I'm going to be able to go. I think it's quite easy to feel pessimistic about the future given the current climate crisis we're experiencing and living in.

8D: BBC Entertainment
Exs 2A and 2B

Ryan: What's that?

Kerblam Man: Delivery for the Doctor.

The Doctor: It's the Kerblam Man.

Yasmin: It's the what?

The Doctor: The Kerblam Man.

Graham: You're just making sounds now.

Kerblam Man: Delivery fulfilled. And remember: if you want it, Kerblam it.

Graham: Space postman! I've seen it all now.

The Doctor: Delivery Bots. Kerblam's the biggest retailer in this galaxy. I don't remember ordering anything. Must've been a while back. Oh! What do you think? Still me?

Graham: Nice!

Ryan: Check it out, they even use bubble-wrap!

Yasmin: Doctor, look at this, the back of the packing slip.

The Doctor: 'Help Me!' … Right, Kerblam here we come.

Graham: Look at the size of it.

Yasmin: There must be thousands of people in there. How are we gonna find out who sent that message?

Ryan: Halfway across the universe and I feel like I'm back at work!

The Doctor:	Ryan! Brilliant! Come on.
Ryan:	What?
The Doctor:	We're going undercover. Chop, chop.
Tannoy:	Good morning, workers. Welcome to another rewarding …
The Doctor:	Can you check again? We just came in from Kandoka. We must be on the list there somewhere.
Judy:	We're not expecting anyone new today. Didn't even know there was a shuttle coming in.
The Doctor:	Do you mind if I take a look? It might just be the spelling. By the way, this is our reference.
Judy:	Oh, no, here you are, got you. Private shuttle landing. Sorry, person error. Me, I mean! Right, well, let's get you on this induction then. Follow me, this way.
Robot:	Good morning, new workers.
Ryan:	Is it me, or are they pretty creepy?
Graham:	It ain't you.
The Doctor:	Oi you two, that's robophobic. Some of my best friends are robots.
Yasmin:	You'll be right at home here then.
Robot:	Kerblam. Fully automated, people-powered.
Judy:	The system allocates work details based on fitness, stamina, dexterity and mental assessments.
The Doctor:	Same model as the Kerblam Man. I love the Kerblam Man.
Judy:	The TeamMates are the friendly face of the system. They're here to assist and to supervise the organic workers.
Graham:	Organic?
Judy:	Sorry! Listen to me! You get so used to the jargon. Gone native.
The Doctor:	So Kerblam is completely automated?
Judy:	No. Ninety percent as per Kandokan guidelines. Proud to be a certified ten percent people-powered company. I know some people are against quotas, but I'm all for that one. Mind you, I would say that, wouldn't I? Head of People. Self-interest. It's funny, I, I don't normally talk this much.
Yasmin:	How's the morale among the workers?
Judy:	I like to think very good. It's my job to make sure that everyone's happy. Not that it's difficult, I mean we're all so grateful to have a job, right? We all know how hard they are to come by. No, I hope that people feel it's a privilege to work at Kerblam! Right, time for the tour: 600 million products; 10,000 employees. The biggest human workforce in this galaxy. Welcome to Kerblam!
Tannoy:	Welcome to another rewarding shift at Kerblam. Fulfilling orders from the human colony of Kandoka.
Ryan:	Ten thousand workers – one little message.
The Doctor:	Might take a while, this.
Judy:	The system instantly relays customer orders to workers in Fulfilments. They scan the product and send it down to the packing stations.
Tannoy:	Product incoming!
Judy:	Once it's packed, the customer's order goes on the conveyor. This is final checks, where parcels are inspected, sealed and go down the hatch to Dispatch. From Dispatch our postmen retrieve the parcels and teleport direct to the customers. Any questions?
The Doctor:	Can I do the packing slips?
Judy:	Sorry, only purple GroupLoops work the packing stations. Leisure breaks in the HomeZone. Right, I'll leave you in the capable hands of the TeamMates.
The Doctor:	Stand still, Graham!
Graham:	What are you doing?
The Doctor:	Switching jobs with you. I need purple. Whoever sent that message had access to the packing stations. That's where I need to be.
Graham:	And where does that leave me?
Robot:	Hello co-workers. We're so thrilled to have you with us. Yasmin Khan, please come with me. Ryan Sinclair and the Doctor (great name!) with my colleague to the left.
Robot 2:	Hello, team!
Yasmin:	Meet at break time in the HomeZone?
Ryan:	Yes, ma'am.
The Doctor:	Roger Wilco. Oh, did I ever tell you about a blo[ke] that I met called Roger Wilco? Never mind …
Graham:	Hey, hold on, what about me? Where am I go[ing]
Robot 3:	Graham O'Brien. A very warm welcome to Premium Maintenance.
Graham:	Not a word.